Understanding Anne Frank's
The Diary of a Young Girl

The Greenwood Press "Literature in Context" Series

Understanding *To Kill a Mockingbird*: A Student Casebook to Issues, Sources, and Historical Documents
Claudia Durst Johnson

Understanding *The Scarlet Letter*: A Student Casebook to Issues, Sources, and Historical Documents
Claudia Durst Johnson

Understanding *Adventures of Huckleberry Finn*: A Student Casebook to Issues, Sources, and Historical Documents
Claudia Durst Johnson

Understanding *Macbeth*: A Student Casebook to Issues, Sources, and Historical Documents
Faith Nostbakken

Understanding *Of Mice and Men, The Red Pony,* and *The Pearl*: A Student Casebook to Issues, Sources, and Historical Documents
Claudia Durst Johnson

UNDERSTANDING
Anne Frank's
The Diary of a Young Girl

A STUDENT CASEBOOK TO ISSUES, SOURCES, AND HISTORICAL DOCUMENTS

Hedda Rosner Kopf

The Greenwood Press
"Literature in Context" Series
Claudia Durst Johnson, Series Editor

GREENWOOD PRESS
Westport, Connecticut • London

Library of Congress Cataloging-in-Publication Data

Kopf, Hedda Rosner, 1946–
    Understanding Anne Frank's The Diary of a young girl : a student
casebook to issues, sources, and historical documents / Hedda Rosner
Kopf.
        p.   cm. — (The Greenwood Press "Literature in context"
series, ISSN 1074–598X)
    Includes bibliographical references and index.
    ISBN 0–313–29607–3 (alk. paper)
    1. Frank, Anne, 1929–1945. Achterhuis.   2. Jewish children in the
Holocaust.   3. Holocaust, Jewish (1939–1945)   I. Title.
II. Series.
DS135.N6F338   1997
940.53'18'092—dc21   96–50294

British Library Cataloguing in Publication Data is available.

Library of Congress Catalog Card Number: 96–50294
ISBN: 0–313–29607–3
ISSN: 1074–598X

First published in 1997

Greenwood Press, 88 Post Road West, Westport, CT 06881
An imprint of Greenwood Publishing Group, Inc.

Printed in the United States of America

∞

The paper used in this book complies with the
Permanent Paper Standard issued by the National
Information Standards Organization (Z39.48–1984).

10 9 8 7 6 5 4 3 2

Contents

Contents

Introduction

On March 25, 1944, a young girl wrote in her diary: "I don't want to have lived for nothing like most people. I want to be useful or give pleasure to the people around me yet who don't really know me, I want to go on living even after my death! And therefore I am grateful to God for giving me this gift, this possibility of developing myself and of writing, of expressing all that is in me!" This entry could have been written by countless adolescents who are filled with the idealism and optimism of youth, who dream of future lives rich with meaning, and who wish to *"go on living even after . . . death."* What makes this heartfelt declaration unbearably poignant is that it was written by Anne Frank, a Jewish Dutch girl whose death in 1945 in Bergen-Belsen, a Nazi concentration camp, ended her possibilities and her dreams. Ironically, it was also her death that transformed her diary from the private expression of a young girl in hiding with her family into a text that has been read, discussed, and taught around the world for more than forty years.

Anne Frank's wish has been fulfilled millions of times in the hearts and minds of her readers, who are both appalled and fascinated by the circumstances under which Anne wrote her "letters" to Kitty. They are moved by her ability to write openly about her feelings, her fears, and her desires; but most of all, readers are inspired by her passion for life despite the inexorable sense that she and her family are trapped in a world where they are targeted for death simply because they are Jews.

The Diary of a Young Girl is a rich and complex text that can be approached from a number of different disciplines. Anne's letters to Kitty are the private outpourings of a young girl in need of a friend who will listen to her innermost self. At the same time, Anne hoped her diary would be a valuable document for future readers interested in what it was like to be alive during World War II, and she prepared it for just such an eventuality. On a more profound level, Anne's letters to Kitty were her refusal to acknowledge her utter isolation from the world outside the secret annex. By expressing herself in the form of letters, Anne insisted on remaining connected to a world where she could correspond with her friends and believe that her letters would be received and answered.

In Chapter 1, "The Diary as Literature," readers can compare early and later diary entries and revisions and trace Anne's development as a writer over her twenty-five months in hiding.

Anne Frank's remarkable spirit is the primary source of her appeal to readers of every age and every nationality. Her courage and optimism are repeatedly mentioned whenever her life and diary are discussed. Chapter 2, "Who Was Anne Frank?" considers how and why Anne maintained her benevolent view of human behavior while at the same time acknowledging the catastrophe occurring beyond her hiding place. These opposing responses will reveal the complex psychological conflict Anne endured.

Many people have become familiar with Anne Frank's story through play and film versions of her diary. Although rich with emotion and suspense, these dramatizations shift the focus away from Anne's thoughtful analysis of her relationship with her family and her struggle to assert her individuality, and transform her experiences into a study of first love. Careful readers of the diary will discover that Anne's relationship with Peter Van Daan, while significant, is only a small part of her emotional, psychological, and sexual development.

The diary is a much more universal text in its descriptions of Anne's struggle to become a separate self. Anne's competition with her older sister Margot, whom she describes as "perfect," is an experience all too common to younger siblings. Honestly, and sometimes brutally, Anne describes her reactions to her mother's attempts to give Anne advice or to teach her how to control herself. In contrast, Anne admires everything about her father and turns to him for comfort and support against her mother.

As Anne matures into a young woman who needs more than her father's love and attention, her interest in Peter Van Daan changes, and she becomes more aware of herself as a sexual being. It is Anne's willingness to confront these feelings and relationships in her diary that makes it a timeless text for adolescents grappling with similar issues and relationships in their own lives.

Although *The Diary of a Young Girl* is a vivid portrait of the psychological development of an adolescent as revealed by her own private writings, it is most often read as a book about the Holocaust. First published in Holland in 1947 and in the United States and Great Britain in 1952, *The Diary of a Young Girl* has now been translated into fifty-five languages. It is more often than not the only text most people, and certainly most young people, read about a period in human history that ultimately defies the kind of analysis and explanation critics and scholars focus on other historical events. Yet, there is a great danger in reading *The Diary of a Young Girl* as a book about the Holocaust if one does not also confront the more graphic and horrible images and events which were Anne Frank's tragic legacy after she and her family were taken from the secret annex. For, as difficult and terrifying as Anne's twenty-five months in hiding were, she herself admits in her diary, *"this is paradise"* compared with the unimaginable horrors that she feared awaited her and her family if they were discovered.

In the more than fifty years since Anne Frank's death, countless descriptions by survivors who were children in hiding during the war, as well as the diaries and letters of those who, like Anne, did not survive, confirm Anne's perceptive understanding of her relatively idyllic existence in hiding.

Ironically, we must acknowledge that during the Holocaust, being able to hide in an attic—although deprived of one's friends and education, lacking fresh air and exercise, and knowing oneself to be in constant danger of being discovered, deported, and sent "East" (to Poland)—was a luxurious alternative to going into hiding all alone in an unfamiliar place at the mercy of strangers, or being taken away on the first transport out of Amsterdam. Thus, *The Diary of a Young Girl* requires a more honest and critical

response than is often brought to it by readers who emphasize
Anne's optimism and courage and who are unwilling to admit that,
although extraordinarily thoughtful and dramatic, Anne Frank's diary is about her experience before Westerbork, before Auschwitz,
before her death in Bergen-Belsen.

In Chapter 3, "The Frank Family History," readers will find out
what happened to Anne and the others before and after August 4,
1944, when they were discovered and removed from the secret
annex. Eyewitness accounts of Anne's final months in Auschwitz
and Bergen-Belsen provide closure to the remarkable narrative she
herself could not complete.

We will also look at texts that reveal other versions of Holocaust
victims' experiences. Of course, none of these other versions is
meant to negate the enormous suffering and terror the occupants
of the secret annex endured during their twenty-five months in
hiding; however, it is critical that other stories be added to Anne
Frank's stunning diary so that students of the Holocaust can begin
to appreciate the endless variations of loss, degradation, and misery that were inflicted on millions of innocent people, among them
more than one and a half million children.

Chapter 4 takes a close look at the circumstances of the Jews
living in Nazi-occupied Holland. Chapter 5, "Children in the Holocaust and Their Rescuers," includes excerpts from a memoir and
diaries of Jewish children whose experiences during the Holocaust
are both similar to and dramatically different from Anne Frank's.
Also represented in this chapter are the Dutch men and women
who risked their lives to save their unfortunate Jewish countrymen.

Throughout Anne's description of "life" in hiding are references
to the larger world beyond the annex. Since the inhabitants of the
annex could get information about the war only through a small
radio and from their Dutch friends who visited every day, the
adults and children could barely imagine the horrors being perpetrated in their own country and in the foreign realms of the East.
Chapter 6, "Anti-Semitism in Modern Germany," and Chapter 7,
"The Holocaust," present extensive background information on
the historical, cultural, and political circumstances that led to the
genocide of 6 million Jews. Included in these chapters are Nazi
legislative decrees, newspaper accounts of Kristallnacht, and maps
of deportation routes to the concentration camps.

Finally, Chapter 8, "Other Holocaust Stories," presents narratives about two young people who survived the Holocaust—a German Jewish boy, born in 1929, who escaped to Cuba in 1941, and a Czechoslovakian Jewish girl who was sent to Auschwitz and Bergen-Belsen. Both subjects now live in the United States.

Each chapter includes an essay that develops a topic related to *The Diary of a Young Girl*, followed by documents that enhance the scope of the subject. Each document is introduced by a brief explanation of its significance to the chapter. Also included in each chapter are Topics for Oral and Written Exploration and Suggested Readings; some chapters include chronologies, and a glossary is provided.

The Bantam edition of *Anne Frank: The Diary of a Young Girl*, translated from the Dutch by B. M. Mooyaart (1993), has been used throughout the text. Diary entry dates are always included so that readers may refer to any of the other available editions.

THE INHABITANTS OF THE SECRET ANNEX, 263 PRINSENGRACHT, AMSTERDAM, HOLLAND

Anne Frank had great hopes for her diary. She believed that it might be published after the war as a document describing what life was like in hiding for the eight Jews in the secret annex. She created pseudonyms for the people she wrote about in her diary, and when her father arranged for the diary's publication after Anne's death, he used the fictitious names for everyone except his own family.

The Frank Family

Otto Frank (Pim), b. May 12, 1889.

Edith Holländer, b. January 16, 1900.

Margot Frank, b. February 16, 1926.

Anneliese Marie (Anne), b. June 12, 1929.

The Van Pels Family (Van Daan in book)

Auguste Van Pels, b. September 9, 1890 (Petronella).

Hermann Van Pels, b. March 31, 1889 (Hermann).

Peter Van Pels, b. November 8, 1926 (Peter).

Fritz Pfeffer

Alfred Dussel, b. April 30, 1889.

1

The Diary as Literature

Unlike memoirs and autobiographies which recollect and report at some later time in the subject's life, a diary records events and feelings as they are happening to the writer or very shortly after they occur. Therefore, the diary is a more immediate and often more accurate account of events and the writer's responses to them. Diary entries, however, do not have the benefit of the writer's understanding of how those events were resolved or what they would come to mean in the writer's life. For the most part, diary entries are made up of the raw material of the self.

Many diaries, especially those written by men before the nineteenth century, were meant to record the public lives of their subjects, and therefore were written with a large audience in mind. Diarists often wrote with the intention of leaving behind a chronicle of their accomplishments for posterity.

Since the nineteenth century, the diary has evolved into a more personal account of the self, and often is written with the expectation that its contents will remain a secret. Many diarists write about subjects they are unwilling to share with others, and so the diary becomes a record of the diarist's most intimate and honest thoughts. At the same time, the diary is always a constructed text, and its author continually makes choices about what to include, leave out, emphasize, and repeat. Most of all, the diary is a work in process. Unlike the writer of the memoir or autobiography, the diarist never knows for sure what the next chapter will be about. Instead, the subject of the diary unfolds with each new day and moves toward an unknown future that the writer observes, records, and responds to within the private pages of the diary.

ANNE FRANK'S DIARY

Anne Frank's diary combines the elements of a public document with those of the outpourings of hidden feelings and thoughts. It is a factual document about the effects of the Holocaust on a young girl and her family, but it is also a chronicle of an adolescent's psychological and spiritual development. Anne began her diary as a private relationship between herself and her imaginary friend Kitty. Yet, as the months in hiding accumulated and she began to recognize the incredible circumstances under which she continued to write, Anne Frank consciously began to shape her diary into a public document as well. She thought about her intended audience, readers after the war, and she paid careful attention to the information she provided about the conditions she and the others endured.

Although her diary tells us about what happens to a real person, it also has many of the elements of the finest works of fiction: fully developed characters, vivid and acutely observed scenes, careful attention to language, and increasing suspense about the fate of the protagonist and the other seven Jews hidden with her in the secret annex. Above all, like all great literature, the diary has a "voice"—a distinct and vivid storyteller who speaks openly about her most private feelings and who endears herself to us as we get to know her fears, her joys, her anger, her dreams.

Anne received a red and white checked diary for her thirteenth birthday on June 12, 1942. In the first entry she listed a number of other birthday presents, but she tells her diary that the first gift *"to greet me was you, possibly the nicest of all."* Her second entry is dated June 20, 1942. During the week that elapsed between the first and second entries, Anne thought about what form her diary should take and what its purpose would be. She decided that she wanted her diary to be a place where she could *"bring out all kinds of things that lie buried deep in my heart."* Although Anne had a loving family and knew many people "*whom one might call friends*," she did not feel that there was anyone in her life to whom she could reveal herself fully.

The diary would be the friend "Kitty" to whom Anne could tell everything. It also became a mirror in which Anne could see her own reflection more objectively. Fortunately for readers of Anne's diary, the "letters" she wrote required her to include information that her friend Kitty did not know. Thus, we learn about daily life in the annex as well as about the private thoughts and feelings Anne wanted to share with Kitty.

Writing to Kitty assumed a sympathetic "reader," a friend for whom Anne had "*waited so long*." Anne felt safe to tell Kitty everything, even the unpleasant truths about herself and her family. She could whine, complain, and have temper tantrums because her friend would accept and forgive her inadequacies in a way that Anne did not believe her family and friends would. Most of all, Kitty was "*patient*" with Anne, in contrast to the grown-ups, who constantly scolded her for her cheekiness and high spirits.

There is a particularly poignant aspect to the letters Anne wrote in her diary, because they did not reach anyone (although eventually, after her death, they reached across the entire world). Also, Anne never got a response to her beautifully written messages. Perhaps in choosing the letter form Anne was unconsciously insisting on keeping herself connected to the world beyond the secret annex, a world where mail was delivered and answered, and where a young girl's life mattered to someone.

PRACTICING HER CRAFT

Anne used her diary as a place where she could practice her writing skills, both because she found it easier to express herself on paper than through speech, and, more important, because she hoped to become "*a journalist someday and later a famous writer*." Her diary was her apprenticeship, or what she refers to over and over again as her "*work*." Deprived of her normal work life—school—Anne created a focus for the countless silent hours, days, weeks, and months during which she was trapped in the annex by writting her letters to Kitty.

Anne's literary ambitions for her diary were fortified when she heard a Dutch News radio broadcast from London in which a

Dutch official said *"they ought to make a collection of diaries and letters after the war"* (March 29, 1944). Inspired by visions of her diary being published, Anne began rewriting and editing it. She went back to earlier letters to Kitty and revised them, adding details, changing words, or rearranging the order of her material. This process validated her image of herself as a writer, as someone who works at her craft. It also gave her a reason to go back and think about what she had written in terms of both its content and its style.

A vivid example of Anne's process of revision is her entry on January 12, 1944. The first version reads:

> *Isn't it odd, Kitty, that sometimes I look at myself through someone else's eyes? I see quite keenly then how things are with Anne Frank.*

Her revised version reads:

> *I have an odd way of sometimes, as it were, being able to see myself through someone else's eyes. Then I view the affairs of a certain Anne Robin at my ease, and browse through the pages of her life as if she were a stranger.*

Although the inherent meaning of the two entries is similar, the changes suggest how thoughtful Anne was about her writing. For example, in the first version she asks Kitty, *"Isn't it odd . . . ?"* as if she needs Kitty's opinion or agreement on the matter. In the second version she simply states how she is *"able to see myself through someone else's eyes."* She takes responsibility for describing herself without depending on Kitty's support. Interestingly, Anne changes her name to Anne Robin, an indication that she was thinking of her writing as material that might be published in the future under a pseudonym. She also made a list of pseudonyms for the other inhabitants of the secret annex for the same reason. The Van Pels family became the Van Daans, and Fritz Pfeffer became Alfred Dussel.

Finally, the second version is much more "literary." Anne uses language that connects her feelings of looking at herself *"through someone else's eyes"* with the idea of being a character in a book. She adds, *"I view the affairs . . . and browse through the pages of her life as if she were a stranger."*[1] In fact, this is just what Anne did as she reread her diary entries and analyzed them objectively both as a young girl who was changing psychologically and as a writer who was improving her skills and nurturing her talent.

PUBLICATION OF *THE DIARY OF A YOUNG GIRL*

After his liberation from Auschwitz in January 1945, Otto Frank made his way back to Switzerland to see his mother and to recuperate from his ordeal in the concentration camp. He returned to Amsterdam in June 1945, hoping to find his daughters alive. He already knew that his wife had perished in Auschwitz, but he tried to be optimistic about the fates of Margot and Anne, who had been young and relatively healthy when they were transferred from Auschwitz to Bergen-Belsen, a labor camp. Otto Frank immediately went to Miep and Henk Gies and lived with them while he tried to find news of his daughters. After many inquiries, he finally received a letter from a nurse who had also been an inmate in Bergen-Belsen. She verified that Margot and Anne had died in the "Schonungsblock no. 19 in Bergen-Belsen prison camp."

Only after Anne's death had been confirmed did Miep give Anne's diary and her other papers to Otto Frank. She herself had never read Anne's private writings, but she had fervently hoped to return them to her young friend when she returned after the war. Instead, Otto Frank now had the enormous pleasure and pain of discovering his daughter's private joys and fears. Over the next several weeks Otto Frank translated sections of Anne's diary into German and sent them to his mother in Switzerland. Later, he transcribed the several versions of Anne's diary, editing out sections he thought might offend living persons or that he found too critical of his wife. Eventually, Otto Frank's manuscript of Anne's diary reached a prominent Dutch historian who was so impressed with the remarkable diary that he wrote an article about it for an Amsterdam newspaper. On April 3, 1946, *Het Parool* printed "A Child's Voice," in which the historian declared:

> To me the fate of this Jewish girl epitomizes the worst crime perpetrated by everlastingly abominable minds. For the worst crime is not the destruction of life and culture as such . . . but the throttling of the sources of culture, the destruction of life and talent for the mere sake of mindless destructiveness.

> If all signs do not deceive me, this girl would have become a talented writer had she remained alive.

With this review, Anne Frank's diary became the subject of much interest. An edition of 1,500 copies was published as *Het Achterhuis* (The Secret Annex) in June 1947, and by 1950 the book was in its sixth printing in Holland. It was soon published in Germany and France, and the English version appeared in the United States in 1952. Although Anne's *Diary* had been turned down by a dozen publishers who did not believe people would be interested in reading about the sufferings of a young girl during World War II, the book was an immediate success. Its popularity continues; more than 25 million copies in fifty-five languages have been sold all over the world.

THE CRITICAL EDITION OF *THE DIARY*

In 1989 the English version of the critical edition of *The Diary of Anne Frank*, prepared by the Netherlands State Institute for War Documentation, was published in the United States. This edition meticulously recreates all of the diary entries and revisions found strewn on the floor of the secret annex on August 4, 1944, the day Anne and the others were discovered by the Gestapo. Readers of the critical edition can compare three versions of many of the diary entries: Anne's original entry (*a* version), her revised entry (*b* version), and the version published as *The Diary of a Young Girl* (*c* version). This third version evolved out of a combination of Anne's *a* and *b* versions as well as her father's editing and the translator's judgment about word selections.

Although many of the differences between Anne's two versions and the published version seem minor, some of the changes reveal important stylistic or psychological subtleties. For example, on May 26, 1944, Anne's diary entry ends: *"for them [their protectors] the suspense is sometimes lifted, even if it is only for a short time, but for us it has never lifted for a moment, not for two years now and how long will it still keep bearing down on us with its almost unbearable, ever more oppressive hand?"* The published version reads: *"For them the suspense is sometimes lifted, even if it is only for a short time, but for us it never lifts for a moment. We've*

been here for two years now; how long have we still to put up
with this almost unbearable, ever increasing pressure?"

Anne's version is one long, nearly breathless sentence. It dupli-
cates the feeling she has of the ongoing suspense, which *"never
lifted for a moment."* In contrast, the published version breaks
her words and feelings into sentences that stop and start again,
conveying a different sensation than the one she describes. More
dramatically, Anne feels that an *"ever more oppressive hand"* is
"bearing down." She means exactly that—human hands create the
misery she and the other victims of the Holocaust suffer. Hands
hold the guns, hands drive the cattle cars to the concentration
camps, hands tear children away from their parents, hands fill the
gas chambers with Zyklon B. The published version pales in comparison.

Some of the changes and omissions suggest that Otto Frank was
not comfortable with his daughter's forthright opinions and ideas.
In order to "protect" some of the people Anne wrote about, and
especially in order to protect the memory of his wife, he changed
some of Anne's harsher words. In addition, on the advice of publishers, Otto Frank entirely omitted several entries, including two
in which Anne writes about sex and describes her genitals in
graphic detail, and a feminist essay which is remarkably contemporary.

AUTHENTICITY OF *THE DIARY*

Only a few years after *The Diary of a Young Girl* was published, articles began to appear in Sweden, Denmark, and Germany that questioned its authenticity. In 1959 criminal charges
for "libel, slander, insult, defamation of the memory of a dead
person and anti-Semitic utterances" were brought against two of
the most outspoken critics. Otto Frank and, later, Bep (Elli) Voskuijl and Miep and Jan (Henk) Gies were called to testify on behalf of the diary. In addition, the diary was analyzed by experts
for consistency of style and the authenticity of the handwriting.
The experts concluded that the diary was definitely written by
Anne Frank.

The controversy over the diary did not end, however. In the
United States, pamphlets, essays, and letters have been published
over the past few decades that not only question the diary's au-

thenticity, but go so far as to claim that it is a forgery. In 1978 *Anne Frank Diary—A Hoax?* appeared in Sweden and used a different tack in denouncing the young author. Anne Frank's character was criticized in such chapters as "Drug Addict at Tender Age" (a reference to her use of valerian pills) and "Teenage Sex."[2]

Finally, in 1985 the Netherlands State Institute for War Documentation requested that the diary be analyzed by the State Forensic Science Laboratory. Additional handwriting samples produced by Anne Frank were scrutinized by experts and found to be absolutely consistent with the diary writings. Every aspect of her handwriting as well as the kinds of paper and ink used were studied. The experts concluded that the diary and all of the additional entries were written by Anne Frank.

THE DEFINITIVE EDITION

In 1995 a new English translation of the diary was published and immediately made its way onto the *New York Times* best-seller list. This "Definitive Edition" expands the old edition familiar to most readers (*c* version) by adding passages from Anne's *a* and *b* versions. The new translation also adds a level of intricacy to reading the diary. Suddenly, Anne's "voice" is more contemporary and colloquial. Instead of telling us, *"All goes well with me on the whole, except that I have no appetite"* (October 29, 1943), the "new" Anne says, *"I'm doing fine, except I've got no appetite."* Many readers will not care how Anne tells her story, which words she uses, or how she constructs her sentences; yet by comparing the translations, just as by comparing Anne's own *a* and *b* versions, readers can gain a much greater appreciation for the way in which particular words written in a particular order affect how we feel about what we are being told.

In the *c* version of the diary (the one we have been referring to throughout) Anne writes of her walk from their home on Merwedeplein to the secret annex:

> *So we walked in the pouring rain, Daddy, Mummy, and I, each with a school satchel and shopping bag filled to the brim with all kinds of things thrown together anyhow.*
> *We got sympathetic looks from people on their way to work. You*

*could see by their faces how sorry they were they couldn't offer us
a lift; the gaudy yellow star spoke for itself.*
(Thursday, July 9, 1942)

The new translation changes the emphasis by rearranging the order in which we get the information:

*So there we were, Father, Mother and I, walking in the pouring
rain, each of us with a schoolbag and a shopping bag filled to the
brim with the most varied assortment of items. The people on their
way to work at that early hour gave us sympathetic looks; you could
tell by their faces that they were sorry they couldn't offer us some
kind of transportation; the conspicuous yellow star spoke for itself.*
(Thursday, July 9, 1942)

Instead of "the pouring rain" and "sympathetic looks" catching our attention at the beginning of each paragraph, we have to search for this extremely important information within one longer description of their flight. The focus has subtly shifted away from the conditions under which they made their escape (pouring rain). We also lose the impact of their Dutch neighbors' unspoken support (sympathetic looks). The new translation diminishes the drama of this extraordinarily painful yet understated scene.

While all of the diary versions tell Anne's story, readers can use the different versions now available as tools for reading Anne Frank's text as literature. The different translations and editions confirm the importance of language and style in Anne's writing and provide readers with vivid examples of the varying effects of word choice and syntax.

At the conclusion of her April 14, 1944 letter to Kitty, Anne writes, " *'The unbosomings of an ugly duckling' will be the title of all this nonsense. My diary really won't be much use to Messrs Bolkenstein or Gerbrandy*" (members of the wartime Dutch Cabinet-in-Exile in London, which planned to publish diaries and letters after the war). The diary is, in fact, a remarkably useful document for students of the Holocaust. Readers of Anne's diary can come to know the absolute depravity and horror of the Nazis' "Final Solution to the Jewish Question" by trying to understand what was lost with each death. Since it is impossible to comprehend the loss of 6 million voices, it is in contemplating the loss of

Anne Frank's voice, only one voice, that we can begin to confront the endless abyss of that event.

Anne's diary does not take the place of history books and documents that explain what happened politically during World War II. Nor does her diary describe the unimaginable atrocities that Anne herself would see and suffer in Auschwitz-Birkenau and Bergen-Belsen. Nevertheless, everything she wrote about happened to her as a direct result of the Nazis' intention to implement the "Final Solution." We must acknowledge that *The Diary of a Young Girl* is about the effects of the Holocaust when we try to imagine how different her diary would have been if Anne Frank had lived in freedom and safety.

The diary entries that follow were written in 1993 by Zlata Filipovic, a thirteen-year-old girl caught in the turmoil of war in Sarajevo, Bosnia. Zlata was inspired by Anne Frank's *Diary of a Young Girl*.

NOTES

1. Anne Frank, *The Diary of Anne Frank: The Critical Edition* prepared by the Netherlands State Institute for War Documentation (New York: Doubleday, 1986), 455.

2. Ibid., 92.

ZLATA'S DIARY

Like Anne Frank, Zlata Filipovic started keeping a diary when she was thirteen. Also like Anne Frank, Zlata found herself caught up in a war that completely disrupted her life and caused her much anguish. The ethnic battles in Bosnia and their effect on her life became the topic of Zlata's diary. Like Anne Frank, Zlata also wrote about her blessed life before the war and her dreams for the future.

Despite these similarities, however, the differences between the two girls' circumstances are significant. First, Zlata had read Anne Frank's diary and consciously modeled her own writings on Anne's remarkable work. Second, because of the fame of Anne Frank's diary, Zlata Filipovic's writing achieved recognition it probably would not have gained otherwise. Described by her publishers as "the Anne Frank of Sarajevo," the young Bosnian girl became an instant celebrity and was able to escape her war-torn country and move to Paris with her family. Ironically, Anne Frank had dreamt of going to Paris after the war.

Anne Frank and Zlata Filipovic have also been connected via a CD-ROM, *Diary Maker*, which includes excerpts from both girls' diaries as well as from the diary of a young Jamaican American, Latoya Hunter. The interactive format of the CD-ROM enables users to explore Anne Frank's life and times and to make their own diaries using the diary-making tool included in the program.

FROM *ZLATA'S DIARY: A CHILD'S LIFE IN SARAJEVO* (1994)

Monday, March 15, 1993

Dear Mimmy,

I'm sick again. My throat hurts, I'm sneezing and coughing. And spring is around the corner. The second spring of the war. I know from the calendar, but I don't see it. I can't see it because I can't feel it. All I can see are the poor people still lugging water, and the even poorer invalids—young people without arms and legs. They're the ones who had the fortune or perhaps the misfortune to survive.

There are no trees to blossom and no birds, because the war has destroyed them as well. There is no sound of birds twittering in springtime. There aren't even any pigeons—the symbol of Sarajevo. No noisy children, no games. Even the children no longer seem like children. They've had their childhood taken away from them, and without that they can't be children. It's as if Sarajevo is slowly dying, disappearing. Life is disappearing. So how can I feel spring, when spring is something that awakens life, and here there is no life, here everything seems to have died.

I'm sad again, Mimmy. But you have to know that I'm getting sadder and sadder. I'm sad whenever I think, and I have to think.
Your Zlata   (132–133)

• • •

Saturday, July 17, 1993

Dear Mimmy,
PROMOTION DAY,
Since I didn't take you with me (just a part of you was there) I have to tell you what it was like.

It was wonderful. The presenter was a girl who looked unbelievably like Linda Evangelista. She read parts of you, Mimmy, and was even accompanied on the piano. Auntie Irena was there. Warm and kind, as always, with warm words for children and adults alike.

It was held in the café Jež, and was packed with wonderful people, family, friends, school friends and, of course, NEIGHBORS. There was electricity (a generator), and the lightbulbs made it all even nicer. You and I, Mimmy, have Gordana Trebinjac of the International Peace Center to thank for the good organization and for having made it as nice as it was.

Naturally, there were film cameras and photographers and a huge bouquet of flowers, roses and daisies, for us, Mimmy.

At the end I read my message. This is what I said:

Suddenly, unexpectedly, someone is using the ugly powers of war, which horrify me, to try to pull and drag me away from the shores of peace, from the happiness of wonderful friendships, playing and love. I feel like a swimmer who was made to enter the cold water, against her will. I feel shocked, sad, unhappy and frightened and I wonder where they are forcing me to go, I wonder why they have taken away my peaceful and lovely shores of my childhood. I used to rejoice at each new day, because each was beautiful in its own way. I used to rejoice at the sun, at playing, at songs. In short, I enjoyed my childhood. I had no need of a better one. I have less and less strength to keep swimming in these cold waters. So take me back to the shores of my childhood, where I was warm, happy and content, like all the children whose childhood and the right to enjoy it are now being destroyed.

The only thing I want to say to everyone is: PEACE!

There was a Spaniard at the promotion—Julio Fuentos. He photographed me standing on some jerrycans (full of water—a precious liquid in Sarajevo), and the woman to whom they belonged almost went crazy. "OOOHHHH, just so long as the jerrycans don't break!" They didn't!

All in all, it was nice. It couldn't have been otherwise, since it was your promotion, Mimmy. I represented you. You know how much I love you. I represented you with all the love I feel for you.

When I got home that afternoon, Auntie Radmila brought me a big flowerpot wrapped in colorful paper and tied up with a bow. Inside the pot was a tomato, a real live tomato. That was the nicest "bouquet" I ever got.
Love,
Zlata

• • •

Friday, July 23, 1993

Dear Mimmy,
Even since July 17, various people have been coming around—journalists, reporters, cameramen. From Spain, France, the US, England . . . and yesterday a crew came from ABC News. They filmed me for American TV as the "person of the week." Hey, imagine, me a personality?

They filmed me in my room, by my piano, in my apartment with my parents. They talked to me. In English, of course. I have to boast and tell you that they told me my English is EXCELLENT.

And tonight the world will be looking at me (and that, you know, is because of you, Mimmy). Meanwhile I'm looking at the candle, and all around me is darkness. I'm looking in the dark.

Can that outside world see the darkness I see? Just as I can't see myself on TV tonight, so the rest of the world probably can't see the darkness I'm looking at. We're at two ends of the world. Our lives are so different. Theirs is a bright light. Ours is darkness.
Your Zlata
P.S. You know that Cici is pregnant? She's going to have kittens. I have to "get" Mommy and Daddy to take one.
Zlata

• • •

Tuesday, July 27, 1993

Dear Mimmy,
Journalists, reporters, TV and radio crews from all over the world (even Japan). They're interested in you, Mimmy, and ask me about you, but also about me. It's exciting. Nice. Unusual for a wartime child.

My days have changed a little. They're more interesting now. It takes my mind off things. When I go to bed at night I think about the day behind me. Nice, as though it weren't wartime, and with such thoughts I happily fall asleep.

But in the morning, when the wheels of the water carts wake me up, I realize that there's a war on, that mine is a wartime life. SHOOTING, NO ELECTRICITY, NO WATER, NO GAS, NO FOOD. Almost no life.
Zlata

• • •

Friday, September 17, 1993

Dear Mimmy,
The "kids" are negotiating something, signing something. Again giving us hope that this madness will end. There's supposed to be a cease-fire tomorrow and on September 21 at Sarajevo airport everybody is supposed to sign FOR PEACE. Will the war stop on the day that marks the change from one season to another???

With all the disappointments I've had with previous truces and signatures, I can't believe it.

I can't believe it because another horrible shell fell today, ending the life of a three-year-old little boy, wounding his sister and mother.

All I know is that the result of their little games is 15,000 dead in Sarajevo, 3,000 of them children, 50,000 permanent invalids, whom I already see in the streets on crutches, in wheelchairs, armless and legless. And I know that there's no room left in the cemeteries and parks to bury the latest victims.

Maybe that's why this madness should stop.
Your Zlata

• • •

Sunday, September 19, 1993

Dear Mimmy,
I keep thinking about Sarajevo, and the more I think about it, the more it seems to me that Sarajevo is slowly ceasing to be what it was. So many dead and wounded. Historical monuments destroyed. Treasure troves of books and paintings gone. Century-old trees felled. So many people have left Sarajevo forever. No birds, just the occasional chirping sparrow. A dead city. And the warlords are still negotiating over something, drawing, crossing out, I just don't know for how long. Until September 29? I don't believe it!
Your Zlata

• • •

Monday, September 20, 1993

Dear Mimmy,

All eyes and ears are on tomorrow's game of War or Peace. Everybody is waiting for that historic meeting at Sarajevo airport. Suddenly, unexpected news. The Serbian, Croatian and Muslim warlords have met on a warship in the Adriatic. For another shipwreck? We'll find out!

Your Zlata

• • •

Tuesday, September 21, 1993

Dear Mimmy,

The historic game of WAR OR PEACE has been postponed. Does that mean PEACE is losing again? I'm really fed up with politics!

Your Zlata

• • •

Wednesday, September 22, 1993

Dear Mimmy,

Although I told you that I didn't think anything good would happen on September 21, 1993, I still had a flicker of hope that it would. But it was no use.

Another D-Day has come and gone. How many have we had? A hundred? A million? How many more will there be?

Politics is making my life miserable!!

Your Zlata

• • •

Saturday, September 25, 1993

Dear Mimmy,

The electricity is back, but it's being rationed. And the rationing, like the life we're living, is stupid. We get four hours of electricity every fifty-six hours. You should see, Mimmy, what a madhouse this is when the electricity comes on! Piles of unwashed laundry waiting to go into the washing machine. Even bigger piles of laundry waiting for the iron. Dust waiting to be vacuumed. Cooking to be done, bread to be baked, and we'd all like to watch a bit of television. There's hair to be washed and dried with a hair dryer. It's incredible. You wouldn't believe it.

Every time Mommy says: "If we're not going to have electricity, then let's not have any at all. That way I don't worry. This is unbearable." Yes, but then again, Mommy . . .

We have water more often now.

There's a problem with bread again, even though the electricity is back. We get 300 grams per person every three days. Ridiculous!

I had to laugh at lunch today when Daddy said: "This 'German' lunch is good." You must be wondering, Mimmy, why we would be eating a "German lunch." The potato salad was made of potatoes and onions bought for Deutsche Marks at our "rich" market. With it we had German fish from the humanitarian aid package. So that's "German," isn't it?
Your Zlata

· · ·

Wednesday, September 29, 1993
We waited for September 27 and 28. The 27th was the Assembly of Bosnian Intellectuals, and the 28th was the session of the B-H Parliament. And the result is "conditional acceptance of the Geneva agreement." CONDITIONAL. What does that mean? To me, it means non-acceptance of the agreement, because there's no peace. To me it means the continuation of the war and everything that goes with it.

Once more the circle closes. The circle is closing, Mimmy, and it's strangling us.

Sometimes I wish I had wings so I could fly away from this hell.

Like Icarus.

There's no other way.

But to do that I'd need wings for Mommy, wings for Daddy, for Grandma and Granddad and . . . for you, Mimmy.

And that's impossible, because humans are not birds.

That's why I have to try to get through all this, with your support, Mimmy, and to hope that it will pass and that I will not suffer the fate of Anne Frank. That I will be a child again, living my childhood in peace.
Love,
Zlata

New York: Viking Penguin, 1994, 189–193.

TOPICS FOR WRITTEN OR ORAL EXPLORATION

1. What impression do you get of Anne from her first diary entry? What details do you find most revealing?

2. What do her birthday gifts suggest about her interests?

3. What other forms can a diary take? Does it have to be in written form?

4. Imagine that you have been given a blank diary. Write an entry in which you introduce yourself and describe the purpose of your diary.

5. Which passages help you to get a vivid idea of what life was like in the annex? What details does Anne give that help you "see" where she was in hiding?

6. How does Anne describe the other people in hiding with her? What examples does she give of their behavior that help you understand what they are like?

7. Write diary entries in which you describe someone you know well; someone you have just met. What kinds of details do you include?

8. Imagine that you are Kitty, and respond to one of Anne's "letters."

9. Write a letter from yourself in response to one of Anne's letters to Kitty.

10. Compare three of Anne's entries: one written at the beginning, in the middle, and at the end of her time in the annex. Are there differences in subject? in style? Are there similarities?

11. Anne's diary does more than tell what happened in the secret annex. Find passages that prove that she was a "writer."

12. Anne Frank "escaped" from the secret annex by writing fables and tales about the world outside her covered window. By imagining elves, fairies, guardian angels, and even a "girl next door" named Kitty, Anne expressed her anxieties and wishes by projecting them onto her characters. Anne was forced to turn inside herself and create "friends" to help her cope with the abnormal circumstances of hiding. Read Anne Frank's tale, "Cady's Life," in *Tales from the Secret Annex*, and note all of the similarities between Cady and Anne. Why does Anne not make Cady Jewish? What kinds of feelings and ideas can Anne explore by making Cady a gentile girl?

13. Write your own tale or fable in which you project some of the issues and experiences in your own life onto another or several other characters. Have you learned anything about yourself or your situation by writing the tale?

14. Zlata Filipovic has been called "the Anne Frank of Sarajevo." How

has reading Anne's diary influenced Zlata? Is her diary similar to Anne's stylistically? In what ways is Zlata's life like Anne's? How is it different? Find book reviews of Zlata's diary and compare them to your own analysis of her book. Try to find out what Zlata is doing now.

15. Read diary excerpts by other people included in Chapter 5 of this book and compare them to Anne's diary in style and content.

16. Find a recent news article that describes a difficult situation in some part of the world, for example, Liberia, South Africa, or an inner-city neighborhood. Imagine that you are a teen living in that situation and write several diary entries describing what you see around you and how you feel about it.

17. Anne Frank's *Diary of a Young Girl* was transformed by Frances Goodrich and Albert Hackett into a play, *The Diary of Anne Frank*. Read their play and compare a scene they have created with the way that event is described in the diary. How are they similar? Different? Write your own dramatic version of that entry. What do you need to change or exclude in order to make it work as a play?

18. Compare the way several of the people in the annex are characterized by Anne and by playwrights Goodrich and Hackett. What has been changed or accentuated?

19. Watch the film version of *The Diary of Anne Frank* and write about how it is similar to and different from the diary.

20. Imagine that you are Anne Frank watching the play or film version of *The Diary of Anne Frank*. Write a diary entry describing your reaction.

21. Why do writers reimagine Anne Frank? What are they trying to achieve? Are there other examples of "famous" people who became characters in literature, film, art? Choose one and write about the way that person is portrayed by artists.

22. Yevgeny Yevtushenko's poem "Babii Yar" includes a lyrical section about Anne Frank. Read the poem and explain why he includes the Dutch girl in his poem about the 33,000 Soviet Jews slaughtered in the woods of Kiev.

23. Opera and musical pieces have also been written in response to *The Diary of a Young Girl*. Write your own music or song based on any aspect of Anne Frank's story.

SUGGESTED READINGS

Anne Frank's Diary and Tales

Frank, Anne. *Anne Frank's Tales from the Secret Annex.* Translated by Michel Mok and Ralph Manheim. New York: Doubleday, 1983.

———. *The Diary of Anne Frank: The Critical Edition.* Prepared by the Netherlands State Institute for War Documentation. New York: Doubleday, 1986.

———. *The Diary of a Young Girl.* New York: Doubleday, 1967.

———. *The Diary of a Young Girl: The Definitive Edition.* Edited by Otto H. Frank and Mirjam Pressler. New York: Doubleday, 1995.

Diaries and Memoirs

Appleman-Jurman, Alicia. *Alicia: My Story.* New York: Bantam Books, 1988.

Auerbacher, Inge. *I Am a Star: Child of the Holocaust.* New York: Prentice-Hall, 1987.

Filipovic, Zlata. *Zlata's Diary: A Child's Life in Sarajevo.* New York: Viking, Penguin Books, 1994.

Heller, Fanya Gottesfield. *Strange and Unexpected Love: A Teenage Girl's Holocaust Memoirs.* Hoboken, N.J.: KTAV, 1993.

Isaacman, Clara, and Joan A. Grossman. *Clara's Story.* Philadelphia: Jewish Publication Society, 1984.

Kopelnitsky, Raimonda, and Kelli Pryor. *No Words to Say Goodbye: A Young Jewish Woman's Journey from the Soviet Union into America. The Extraordinary Diaries of Raimonda Kopelnitsky.* New York: Hyperion, 1995.

Leesha, Rose. *The Tulips Are Red.* Cranbury, N.J.: A. S. Barnes, 1978.

Schloss, Evan, and Evelyn Julia Kent. *Eva's Story: A Survivor's Tale by the Step-Sister of Anne Frank.* New York: St. Martin's Press, 1988.

Segal, Lore. *Other People's Houses.* New York: Harcourt Brace, 1964.

Sender, Ruth M. *The Cage.* New York: Macmillan, 1986.

Sommer, Jay. *The Golden Door: A Survivor's Tale.* New York: Shengold, 1994.

Tec, Nechama. *Dry Tears: The Story of a Lost Childhood.* New York: Oxford University Press, 1984.

Anne Frank as a Character

Goldman, Derek with Peter Barrett. *Right as Rain.* Chicago: StreetSigns Production, n.d.

Goodrich, Frances, and Albert Hackett. *The Diary of Anne Frank*. New York: Random House, 1956.

Graver, Lawrence. *An Obsession with Anne Frank: Meyer Levin and the Diary*. Ewing: University of California Press, 1995.

Levin, Meyer. *The Obsession*. New York: Simon and Schuster, 1973.

Margulies, Donald. *The Model Apartment*. New York: Dramatists Play Service, 1990.

Roth, Philip. *The Ghost Writer*. New York: Farrar, Straus and Giroux, 1979.

Related Works

Rosenberg, David, ed. *Testimonies: Contemporary Writers Make the Holocaust Personal*. New York: Times Books, 1989.

Schiff, Hilda, ed. *Holocaust Poetry*. New York: St. Martin's Press, 1995.

2

Who Was Anne Frank?

The year 1995 marked the fiftieth anniversary of the end of World War II. It was also the anniversary of the deaths of millions of victims of Nazi aggression and racism. Of all of those countless people who lost their lives, one young girl, Anne Frank, was remembered and memorialized throughout the world. Prime-time television programs, news broadcasts, documentaries, plays, readings, and memorial services all honored this Jewish adolescent whose diary has sold more copies than any other text except the Bible.

The enormous impact of Anne Frank's diary cannot be explained solely by the fact that she writes about the Holocaust. Many other diaries, memoirs, and narratives describe the Holocaust experience more fully and graphically. Nor can the diary's success be attributed to Anne having been a celebrity about whom readers were curious. When her diary was first published in the Netherlands, Germany, Great Britain, and the United States, Anne Frank was simply an unknown Jewish girl who had kept a diary during her two years in hiding from the Nazis and had perished in a concentration camp shortly before the end of the war.

The diary has been hugely successful because it gives readers insight into the ordeal Anne endured with her family and friends. More important, it reveals with honesty and, for the most part, good humor Anne's interior life, the life of her longings and needs, conflicts and dreams. Readers succumb to her charm and spirit and read her diary to get close to Anne Frank. It is the juxtaposition of the horrors Anne faces with the beauty of her adolescent nature that has captured the imaginations and hearts of her readers. Also, in honoring Anne Frank's vivid existence and premature death, readers acknowledge the loss of the millions of other lives destroyed by the Holocaust.

Anne Frank's diary was written under extraordinary circumstances. At a time in her life when her friends and social life were most important to her developing sense of identity and independence, Anne was forced to hide in a small annex for more than two years with her parents and older sister, another family, including their adolescent son, and a middle-aged man who was separated from his Christian wife. All of Anne's everyday activities and encounters suddenly came to an abrupt end, and she had to cope with the loss of her "normal" life and at the same time adjust to an abnormal existence filled with constant danger.

Her earliest diary entries, written before she went into hiding, reveal her interest in boys and her concerns about her progress in school. Although Anne's life and mind are filled with typical adolescent issues—her popularity, her grades, her relationship with her parents and sister—another element, the persecution of the Jews, is also developed in the first few entries. Everything about her life in Amsterdam was affected by anti-Jewish decrees that limited her freedom and often made her feel ostracized in her city. Yet despite these limitations, Anne was able to enjoy herself with her girlfriends and to explore her emerging interest in boys.

In *The Last Seven Months of Anne Frank*, Lies Goosen, Anne's best friend, described Anne as

very good-looking. Everyone generally liked her, and she was always the center of attention at our parties. She was also the center of attention at school. She liked being important—that isn't a bad quality. I remember that my mother, who liked her very much, used to say, "God knows everything, but Anne knows everything better."[1]

Anne's diary is an important document precisely because she paid close attention to the details in her surroundings. She ana-

Photograph of Anne Frank and her friends on Anne's tenth birthday, June 12, 1939. Anne is the second from the left. Hanneli Goslar (Lies), one of Anne's best friends, is the fourth girl from the left. (ANNE FRANK—Fonds, Basel, Switzerland.)

lyzed the people in her life, trying to figure out why they behaved the way they did. Her friend Jopie's mother said that Anne "saw everything exactly as it was, and sometimes she would make a remark—sharp as a needle. Only it did not hurt, because she always hit exactly to the point."[2] Most of all, she was extremely thoughtful about her own feelings and opinions, critically evaluating herself and her behavior and striving to correct her faults as often as possible.

The years between thirteen and fifteen are an important time when young adolescents begin to break away physically as well as psychologically from their parents. One's peer group increasingly becomes the most important source of identity and relationship as the adolescent works toward becoming independent and establishing his or her own values, interests, and goals. As a necessary step toward achieving this goal, teens turn to their friends and turn away from their families. During these crucial years of individuation and maturation, the young adolescent often actively rejects and rebels against his or her family's values. This process is normal, necessary, and difficult under the best of circumstances. For Anne Frank it was a process to be struggled with under nearly impossible conditions.

Anne felt that everything she did and said was constantly being judged. The only way she could be by herself and express herself freely was by writing in her diary. "Kitty" not only replaced the outside world for Anne Frank, she also fulfilled Anne's need to find a private space, an interior world that could not be invaded by anyone else, but one Anne could *choose* to share when she read excerpts from her diary to the others.

Like a toddler taking her first tentative steps, the young adolescent needs to break away from the comfort and safety of her family's protection and control. A teen must take risks, make mistakes, challenge authority, and question her elders in order to develop a strong sense of her own abilities. At the same time, adolescents remain very dependent on their family for physical and emotional support and need to be able to move back and forth between dependence and independence during the early teen years. This psychologically trying period (for both parents and teens) was made even more complicated for Anne Frank because of the conditions under which she needed to accomplish this very necessary process.

On the one hand, Anne knew that her life depended on the physical protection from the Nazis her father had arranged and provided for her and the others. She turned to her father constantly to assuage her enormous fears and anxieties as unexplained noises threatened their safety or bombs dropped around them. Night after night, she went to her father for comfort, unable to bear the terror of knowing that at any moment they might be discovered and killed. On the other hand, Anne needed to prove to herself and her family that she was no longer a child. She did not want to be criticized and scolded like a child. She wanted her opinions respected and her feelings considered. She often wrote of her painful encounters with the others:

I'm boiling with rage, and yet I mustn't show it. I'd like to stamp my feet, scream, give Mummy a good shaking, cry, . . . because of the horrible words, mocking looks, and accusations which are leveled at me repeatedly every day, and find their mark, like shafts

*from a tightly strung bow, and which are just as hard to draw
from my body. . . .*
  *. . . The whole day long I hear nothing else but that I am an
insufferable baby, and although I laugh about it and pretend not
to take notice, I do mind.* (Saturday, January 30, 1943)

Under other circumstances Anne could have gotten away from it
all, at least for a few hours, by turning to her classmates, friends,
or other adults. Instead, she was hermetically sealed into both the
horrible pressures of having to hide in order to save her life and
having to cope with the personality clashes that occur whenever
teens and their families struggle to change.

FAMILY RELATIONSHIPS

Margot

If Margot Frank had not had a younger sister who had kept a
diary, she would have been one of the 6 million anonymous Jews
who perished in the Holocaust without having left behind her
story. Ironically, the story of the secret annex begins with Margot
Frank, because it was to protect Margot from being deported to a
German labor camp that the Frank family went into hiding so suddenly in July 1942. Like her younger sister, Margot was a young
woman who also had to cope with enormous fears, dangers, losses,
and deprivations. Two years older than Anne, Margot was forced
to leave behind a world that offered her opportunities for an education, romance, and the experiences most young people take for
granted.

We can only imagine Margot's loneliness and misery as she hid
in the secret annex for twenty-five months. How did she feel as
she watched her little sister getting so much attention for her
"cheeky" behavior? How did she feel while Anne and Pim spent
hours together working on projects? While Anne and Peter spent
long days together up in the attic? Only a few clues exist to help
us delve into Margot Frank's heart.

The letters between Margot and Anne concerning Peter give
readers an opportunity to hear Margot's voice. On March 20, 1944,
she wrote:

Anne, when I said yesterday I wasn't jealous of you, I was only fifty percent honest. . . . I'm jealous of neither you nor Peter. I only feel a bit sorry that I haven't found anyone yet, and am not likely to for the time being, with whom I can discuss my thoughts and feelings. But I should not grudge it to you for that reason.

. . . I know for certain that I would never have got so far with Peter, . . . because . . . if I wished to discuss a lot with anyone, I should want to be on rather intimate terms with him. . . . it would have to be someone whom I felt was my superior intellectually, and that is not the case with Peter. But I can imagine it being so with you and Peter. . . .

Anne and Margot continued to correspond with each other about Peter for several more days. Like Anne, Margot longed for a friend to talk to and yearned for intimacy and even romance. But instead of encouraging Anne to feel guilty about leaving her out of the relationship with Peter, Margot generously wrote to Anne, "Now that you've found companionship, enjoy it as much as you can."

Almost all of what we know about Margot Frank has been filtered through Anne's sensibilities, interpretations, and moods. According to Anne, Margot was prettier, smarter, and definitely better behaved than her younger sister. But Anne did not wish to be like her sister, whom she described as *"much too soft and passive for my liking, and allows everyone to talk her around and gives in about everything"* (February 5, 1943).

Yet the devotion of the two sisters to each other was confirmed after they were deported to Auschwitz. When Anne was diagnosed with scabies, Margot chose to go with her into quarantine rather than allow her younger sister to go alone. Tragically, while Anne and Margot were in quarantine, other women in the concentration camp were transferred to a labor camp, and many of them survived the war. It is possible that if Margot had not chosen to accompany Anne into the scabies unit, she might have been sent with those other women and lived.

Otto Frank (Pim)

Most of the time, Anne's relationship with Pim, her father, was a source of great joy and comfort to her. Their natures were similar—optimistic, energetic, and creative. It was Anne and her father who worked to organize the secret annex on the day the Franks went into hiding, while Mrs. Frank and Margot were completely overwhelmed by the situation and sat "like lost people."[3] Anne identified with her father and considered him to be far superior to her mother both as a person and as a parent. Anne and Pim studied together and wrote poems and skits together. And it was to Pim that Anne turned when she needed to confide in someone about her sexual feelings for Peter. Yet at times even her father could exasperate Anne (note the entry for January 30 quoted above), because dependence on him was precisely what she did not want to feel. Trapped with her family at a time in her life when she most wanted to be autonomous, Anne had to break the extremely powerful ties that bound her to her father. As the weeks and months in the secret annex continued, Anne withdrew more and more frequently from Pim and the rest of her family and turned to her diary and other writings.

Anne's relationship with Peter Van Daan finally made it possible for her to declare her independence from Pim. Not surprisingly, Anne asserted her position in a letter written to her father on May 5, 1944: *"I'm a separate individual and I don't feel in the least bit responsible to any of you. . . . I don't have to give an account of my deeds to anyone but myself."* Uncomfortable with her father's advice about her escalating relationship with Peter, Anne lashed out at Pim.

To her credit, however, Anne quickly recognized how unfair she had been to her father and was able to take responsibility for the pain she had caused him. She wrote to Kitty: *"Anyone who can cause such unhappiness to someone else, someone he professes to love, and on purpose, too, is low, very low! . . . No, Anne, you still have a tremendous lot to learn . . . "* (May 7, 1944).

Most of the time, the open-hearted quality of Anne's relationship with her father was rich with mutual respect and concern. Anne and Otto Frank continually helped each other endure the terrible deprivations of their two years in hiding.

Edith Frank

Anne's relationship with her mother was far more volatile and difficult than that with anyone else in the secret annex. Mrs. Frank was very different from her outspoken, energetic young daughter. Their personalities continually clashed, and Anne often expressed her frustrations and disappointments in her mother in her diary. Writing about her feelings gave Anne a safety valve. She wanted to be taken seriously by the others and felt humiliated by her mother's criticism and sarcasm. When Otto Frank prepared Anne's diary for publication, he chose to omit or soften some of his daughter's references to her mother. Out of respect for his dead wife and child, he left out several of Anne's angry attacks against her mother. For example, on August 21, 1942, Anne wrote (and Otto Frank omitted):

> *Mama gave me another one of her dreadful sermons this morning. We take the opposite view of everything. Daddy's a sweetheart; he may get mad at me, but it never lasts longer than five minutes.*

Then, on October 3, 1942, Anne wrote (and her father omitted):

> *I simply can't stand Mother, and I have to force myself not to snap at her all the time, and to stay calm, when I'd rather slap her across the face. I don't know why I've taken such a terrible dislike to her. . . . I can imagine Mother dying someday, but Daddy's death seems inconceivable. It's very mean of me, but that's how I feel. I hope that Mother never reads this or anything else I've written.*[4]

Anne Frank's relationship with her mother was complicated by the fact that she was never able to get away from her. Under nearly constant surveillance, Anne broke away in the only way she could, by cutting herself off emotionally and rejecting her mother's love. Without understanding herself fully, Anne knew that in order to establish her own identity she needed to loosen the primary ties she had with her mother. She often blamed her mother for not understanding her, and yet Anne was going through changes that made it nearly impossible to understand herself.

Desperate for freedom, hungry for normality, longing for her old life and a new future, Anne Frank projected her anger and her sense of helplessness onto the person she knew it would be safe to "hate." No matter how cruel Anne could be, her mother always protected her, made sure she got extra food, lit a candle at night when Anne was frightened, and mothered her daughter even when Anne refused to call her "Mummy."

A year and a half after going into hiding, Anne was finally able to confront her complicated feelings about her mother and herself. At the beginning of a new year, 1944, Anne reread her diary and admitted to being "quite shocked" by her own hotheadedness. With scrupulous honesty she analyzed her behavior and motives and was able to empathize with her mother's feelings. By looking back at her diary entries, Anne understood how she was partly to blame for the painful relationship between herself and her mother. She also was willing to take responsibility for her own shortcomings and for the hurt she caused her mother. Most important, Anne revealed her true feelings to herself, admitting that she had "hid myself within myself," unwilling to share her feelings with her mother and unwilling to acknowledge her own behavior.

Anne had made the transition from willful child to thoughtful adolescent, and she had accepted the compromises that were necessary in order to coexist with her mother.

PETER VAN DAAN

In her very next entry, January 5, 1944, Anne turned from analyzing her mother's shortcomings (lack of tact, not a good role model) to writing about her own emerging sexual feelings. The "sweet secret" of her body's awakening was frustrated by Anne's sense of isolation. Without the freedom to browse through libraries or bookstores, and without the opportunity to take health education classes or talk to her girlfriends about their own experiences, Anne had to depend on herself to negotiate the hazards of her sexual development.

She wrote in her diary, *"I never discuss myself or any of these things with anybody"*; yet she was astonishingly open about her feelings on paper. She understood that she was more mature psychologically than the average fourteen-year-old, and she was able to acknowledge and describe the power of her sexual feelings with vivid poignancy in the pages of her diary.

Anne began her very next entry: *"My longing to talk to someone became so intense that somehow or other I took it into my head to choose Peter"* (January 6, 1944). The dull young man Anne had merely considered another inhabitant of the annex suddenly was transformed into a desirable figure with *"deep blue eyes"* and a *"mysterious laugh playing around his lips."* Having made a reasonable peace with her mother and having acknowledged the strength of her own sexual curiosity, Anne was ready to focus her attention and emotional energy on someone outside of herself and her family. She was growing up.

Those who have seen the play *The Diary of Anne Frank* or the film based on the play probably best remember the relationship between Anne and Peter. The playwrights, Frances Goodrich and Albert Hackett, knew that audiences would rather watch young lovers gazing up at the stars of a war-torn city than see the daily misery produced by living in hiding. However, their emphasis on Anne's relationship with Peter distorted the actual duration of that connection. Anne first turned to Peter in January 1944. They quickly became confidants, discussing the problems they had with their mothers, their hopes for the future, and the nature of their friendship.

Yet, by April 4, 1944, Anne had decided that *"now it's all over. I must work, so as not to be a fool. . . . "* Although her romantic relationship with Peter continued for more than another month after that entry, and her sexual longings continued to grow, Anne quickly realized that Peter was not able to give her the emotional intimacy she craved. His deep blue eyes did not express the profound feelings she hoped would match her own.

Nevertheless, in the midst of incredible tension and chaos, Anne and Peter did share the exhilaration and joy of first love. Anne's lyrical account of their increasing attraction and dependence on one another is both typical of first love and uniquely magical for the two young lovers involved. She wrote: *"This is the first Saturday for months that hasn't been boring, dreary, and dull. And Peter is the cause"* (March 4, 1944). Two days later, she added a postscript to her entry: *"You know that I'm always honest with you, so I must tell you that I actually live from one meeting to the next"* (March 6, 1944).

By the following week, Anne was obsessively thinking about Peter and longing to be with him. Lost in the turmoil of these new feelings, she admitted to her diary (and her father omitted from publication):

> *The hardest thing of all is to keep looking normal, when I feel so dismal and sad. I have to talk, to help, sit with the others and*

above all to be cheerful! Most of all I miss Nature, and a little corner where I can be alone as long as I like! I think I'm getting everything mixed up, Kitty, but then I'm completely confused: on the one hand I am mad with desire for him, can hardly be in the same room, without looking at him and on the other hand I ask myself why he should matter to me so much, why I am not sufficient to myself, why I can't be calm again![5]

All of the confusion and intensity of adolescent development are encapsulated in this passage. In addition, because of the pressures of war, Anne was doubly in hiding. She could not reveal her feelings to the others, and she was trapped in the secret annex when she longed to get away from everyone. When Anne wrote that she missed nature, she meant that she also missed all of the "natural" activities associated with being outside in the world—bicycling, swimming, walking through a park. She missed *herself* in nature, and she missed the Anne who would have been free to turn her attention to a world larger than the one she was forced to survive in with Peter and the others.

Although Anne admitted to being *"mad with desire"* for Peter, she was astute enough to question her own feelings. She understood that her longings, while for the moment attached to Peter, were actually an expression of her own ability to feel deeply rather than a reflection of her love for Peter. He was the object of her passion rather than its source.

Anne Frank never had the chance to grow up and discover the wonders of her own body. She never made love with the person she would choose to spend her life with. She was never pregnant, never gave birth, never nursed her babies. It was only in her diary, and tentatively with Peter Van Daan, that Anne Frank created and expressed her emerging sexual identity. By writing about her sexual feelings she made them real, insisted that they were real. In the cramped confines of the third story attic, Anne Frank got to live out the sexual part of herself prematurely and incompletely, but she wrote about it with a wholeheartedness that touches everyone who reads her diary.

"TWO ANNES"

A recurring theme in Anne Frank's diary is the presence of two Annes. The "outside" Anne was often too talkative, was disrespectful of her elders, and seemed not to care what the others thought of her. The "inside" Anne observed and analyzed herself and others carefully, and felt deeply hurt by the criticism leveled against her by her family. Afraid to show her vulnerability, Anne revealed herself only to Kitty.

On one occasion, Anne wrote about the two Annes existing while she was with Peter, "*sitting on the divan, our arms around each other's waists. Then suddenly the ordinary Anne slipped away and a second Anne took her place, a second Anne who is not reckless and jocular, but one who just wants to love and be gentle*" (April 28, 1944). On another occasion, shortly after her fifteenth birthday, Anne again mentioned her sense of internal division when she wrote about her frustrations with Mrs. Van Daan and her own mother, neither of whom Anne admired or turned to for advice. Anne wrote that she longed for someone to "*draw out some of my real self.*" Because Anne was so sensitive to the opinions of the others, she often found herself hiding her true feelings but also desperately wanting to reveal them.

In the very last diary entry Anne Frank ever wrote, she focused on explaining her "dual personality." It was as if Anne knew that this would be her final opportunity to explain herself to the world. She contrasted her "*exuberant*" cheerfulness with the side of herself which was "*much better, deeper and purer*" but which she was afraid to show to others because "*I'm afraid they'll laugh at me, think me ridiculous and sentimental, not take me seriously.*" Anne's ability to write about her complex personality helped her release the frustration she felt in not being understood or known by others.

ANNE'S SENSE OF HUMOR

Anne also was able to see the humor in the most trying situation. Right from the beginning of her confinement, she chose to see her ordeal as something unusual instead of something intolerable. She described staying in the secret annex as "*being on vacation in a very peculiar boardinghouse*" (July 11, 1942). In honor of the arrival of the eighth Jewish inhabitant, Mr. Dussel (Fritz Pfeffer), Anne prepared a humorous "PROSPECTUS AND GUIDE TO THE 'SECRET ANNEXE' " (November 17, 1942). Yet her sense of humor and playfulness did not always console her. At times, Anne felt overwhelmed by their situation and wanted only to escape into sleep.

As the months in hiding continued, Anne sometimes felt crushed by a *"restlessness"* to know what their fate would be: *"Let the end come, even if it is hard; then at least we shall know whether we are finally going to win through or go under"* (May 25, 1944). Moving from optimism to depression, from lethargy to restlessness and back to humor again, Anne responded to each day in hiding with whatever emotional resources she had available to her. She did not pretend to be more courageous or cheerful than she actually was. The wonder is that she managed to be cheerful and courageous at all.

ANNE FRANK AND JUDAISM

If Anne Frank had not been born a Jew, her family would not have had to leave Germany in 1933 to escape from ever-increasing Nazi persecution. If Anne Frank had not been born a Jew, she would not have had to go into hiding in Amsterdam, nor would she have suffered from disease and starvation, and finally died in a German concentration camp. The fact that her parents were Jewish defined her fate according to the Nazi policy that called for the annihilation of all Jews.

It was never a question of a Jewish person's innocence or guilt. Because of virulent anti-Semitism, 6 million Jews were killed regardless of their positions in the community, their skills and talents, or their contributions to others. Even Jews who were completely assimilated into their societies and who did not observe Jewish practices and traditions were targeted for extermination because they carried the "taint" of Jewish blood in their veins.

Although the Frank family identified themselves as Jews and lived in a Jewish section of Amsterdam, they did not hold religious observances in their own home. Instead, the Franks visited Anne's friend Lies Goslar's family every Friday evening to celebrate the Sabbath; they also observed the Jewish holidays of Passover and Sukkoth with the Goslars. As an observant Orthodox Jew, Lies did not go to school on Saturday, the Jewish Sabbath, but Anne did. In addition, while Lies and Margot Frank went to Hebrew school twice a week to get a religious education, Anne did not.

Yet, despite her lack of a religious education, Anne Frank wholeheartedly identified herself as a Jew. Unlike Peter Van Daan, who *"would have found it much easier if he'd been a Christian and if he could be one after the war,"* Anne was proud of her heritage and felt that Peter's position was dishonest. While Anne understood that she was in hiding from the Nazis only because she was a Jew, she never expressed in her diary any wish to be other than who she was. She wrote about "us Jews" and never denied her Jewish ancestry.

Even though Anne Frank did not go to synagogue regularly, she did express a deep belief in God. When she felt most alone and alienated from the others in the annex, she wrote about what did sustain her, her ability to appreciate what she had, and above all, the beauty of nature, which connected her to God. In a passionate (and ironic, given her circumstances) entry she wrote about how she coped with melancholy:

> *My advice is: "Go outside, to the fields, enjoy nature and the sunshine, go out and try to recapture happiness in yourself and in God. . . .*
> *. . . I've found that there is always some beauty left—in nature, sunshine, freedom, in yourself; these can all help you. Look at these things, then you find yourself again, and God, and then you regain your balance.* (March 7, 1944)

Of course, *"Go outside, to the fields"* was an impossible solution for a young girl who lived in constant fear of being discovered and taken away to her death, and yet Anne Frank's vivid spirit made it possible for her to replenish herself with thoughts of the beauty of nature. Like the love she projected onto Peter, her intense longings for the physical wonders of the natural world were an expression of her ability to feel deeply. Anne attributed these feelings and their source to God, and she was grateful for the gifts he bestowed upon her and the world.

Anne Frank's diary reveals her varying moods—from despair to delight, from anger to reconciliation. It also shows us how she was able to sustain a brave and mostly cheerful attitude throughout her ordeal in the secret annex. It is this spiritual generosity that has made a lasting impression on her countless readers, including Nelson Mandela, the black South African leader who spent twenty-eight years in prison for his efforts to end apartheid. Mandela credited Anne Frank's *Diary of a Young Girl* with giving him the inspiration and courage to continue his battle against the oppressive forces of discrimination in his own country.

Anne's ardent, forthright spirit is what has made her diary one of the most beloved texts of the twentieth century. Yet, while readers are enormously moved by her vibrant personality, it would be a terrible mistake to be seduced by Anne's seemingly endless supply of renewable hope and optimism. We must not forget for one instant what ultimately happened to Anne Frank and the millions of others who perished because they were Jews or Gypsies or handicapped or homosexual or any "other" whom the Nazi perpetrators and their accomplices decided did not deserve to live.

NOTES

1. Willy Lindwer, *The Last Seven Months of Anne Frank* (New York: Random House, 1991), 16–17.

2. Ernst Schnabel, *Anne Frank: A Portrait in Courage*, translated by Richard and Clara Winston (New York: Harcourt, Brace and World, 1958), 48.

3. Miep Gies, with Alison Leslie Gold, *Anne Frank Remembered: The Story of the Woman Who Helped Hide the Frank Family* (New York: Simon and Schuster, 1988), 98.

4. Anne Frank, *The Diary of a Young Girl: The Definitive Edition*, edited by Otto H. Frank and Mirjam Pressler (New York: Doubleday, 1995), 51.

5. Anne Frank, *The Diary of Anne Frank: The Critical Edition*, prepared by the Netherlands State Institute for War Documentation (New York: Doubleday, 1986), 524.

TOPICS FOR WRITTEN OR ORAL EXPLORATION

1. Imagine that Anne Frank was able to leave the annex and go outdoors once again. Write a diary entry describing her feelings. Where does she go? What makes her happiest?

2. What do the books Anne reads while in hiding tell you about her? Be specific.

3. What are some of the interests Anne shares with her father? What do they reveal about Anne and Otto Frank? How do Anne and her father differ from the others in the annex?

4. Why does Anne have so much difficulty getting along with her mother? What kind of mother would she have liked to have had?

5. Find examples of Mrs. Frank's "good mothering." Does Anne acknowledge it?

6. Write a letter from Anne to her mother in which Anne explains the kind of relationship she would like to have with her. Write a response from her mother.

7. Imagine that you are Peter. How does it feel to be the only young male in the annex? What do you miss most? Write about it in a letter to a friend who is not in hiding.

8. Why is the relationship with Peter so important to Anne? Would she be so "ardent" if they were not in hiding? Would Peter have been interested in Anne?

9. Imagine that you are Anne Frank and write a letter about Peter to a friend. Imagine that you are Peter and write about Anne.

10. Imagine that you are Margot Frank. Write a diary entry about Anne and Peter's relationship. Write about the kind of relationship you would like to have with a young man.

11. What are some of the changes Anne describes in herself? Peter? Pim?

12. Find examples of times when Anne was misunderstood. Why is she unwilling to reveal the "inner" Anne to the others? Do you have an inner self? Write a diary entry in which you describe the two "yous."

13. Choose one episode Anne describes in her diary and rewrite it from the point of view of another member of the annex; from the point of view of one of the helpers.

14. Is there a difference between being religious and being spiritual? Explain. Are there experiences in your life that help you to feel connected to God?

15. Anne turned to her diary and to her love of nature whenever she needed emotional support. What do you turn to for comfort? How would you feel if it were unavailable to you? Write a diary entry describing your feelings about being deprived of this "comfort" and compare them to entries in which Anne describes her feelings.

16. What other forms of creative expression could be used to convey Anne's spirit? the anxieties of hiding in the secret annex? the terrors of Auschwitz and Bergen-Belsen? Create an artistic "piece" which expresses those feelings.

SUGGESTED READINGS

Amdur, Richard. *Anne Frank*. New York: Chelsea House, 1993.

Anne Frank in the World, 1929–1945. Amsterdam: Uitgeverij Bert Bakker, 1985.

Bull, Angela. *Anne Frank*. London: Hamish Hamilton, 1986.

Hurwitz, Johanna. *Anne Frank: Life in Hiding*. Philadelphia: Jewish Publication Society, 1988.

Kennet, John. *Anne Frank: A Story Based on Her Diary*. London: Blackie, 1974.

Prince, Eileen. *The Story of Anne Frank*. New York: Maxwell Macmillan, 1991.

Schnabel, Ernst. *Anne Frank: A Portrait in Courage*. Translated by Richard and Clara Winston. New York: Harcourt, Brace and World, 1958.

Steenmeijer, Anna G., ed., in collaboration with Otto Frank and Henri van Praag. *A Tribute to Anne Frank*. Garden City, N.Y.: Doubleday, 1971.

Tyler, Laura. *Anne Frank*. Englewood Cliffs, N.J.: Silver Burdett, 1990.

van der Rol, Ruud, and Rian Verhoeven, for the Anne Frank House. *Anne Frank Beyond the Diary: A Photographic Remembrance*. New York: Viking by the Penguin Group, 1993.

Wilson, Cara. *Love, Otto: The Legacy of Anne Frank*. Kansas City: Andrews and McMeel, 1995.

3

The Frank Family History

CHRONOLOGY: ANNE FRANK AND HER FAMILY

May 12, 1889	Otto Frank is born in Frankfurt am Main, Germany.
January 16, 1900	Edith Holländer is born in Aachen, Germany.
May 12, 1925	Otto Frank and Edith Holländer are married.
February 16, 1926	Margot Frank is born in Frankfurt am Main.
June 12, 1929	Anneliese Marie Frank is born in Frankfurt am Main.
1933	The Franks move to Holland after Adolf Hitler becomes Führer and begins implementation of anti-Semitic decrees.
May 1940	Germany invades Holland; anti-Semitic actions begin.
December 1, 1940	Otto Frank's Opekta-Works Company moves to 263 Prinsengracht.
June 12, 1942	Anne Frank's thirteenth birthday. She receives a diary and writes her first entry two days later.

July 6, 1942	The Frank family goes into hiding one day after Margot Frank receives a call-up notice to report for deportation to a laborcamp in the East.
July 13, 1942	The Van Pels (Van Daan) family joins the Franks in hiding.
November 16, 1942	Fritz Pfeffer (Alfred Dussel) becomes the eighth inhabitant of the secret annex. Anne Frank must share her tiny room with the middle-aged dentist.
March 29, 1944	Anne Frank hears a radio broadcast from London about collecting "diaries and letters" to be published after the war. She begins revising her diary in hopes of future publication.
August 1, 1944	Anne Frank writes her last diary entry.
August 4, 1944	The secret annex is raided by Nazi officers and Dutch police. The eight inhabitants are arrested and sent to Westerbork to await deportation.
September 3, 1944	Anne Frank and the seven others are sent to Auschwitz-Birkenau concentration camp on the very last transport from Westerbork.
September 5, 1944	Allied armies liberate southern Holland.
October 1944	Anne and Margot Frank are separated from their mother and sent to Bergen-Belsen concentration camp in Germany.
January 6, 1945	Edith Frank dies at Auschwitz-Birkenau.
January 27, 1945	Otto Frank is liberated from Auschwitz by the Russian army.
March 1945	Margot Frank dies of typhus in Bergen-Belsen. Anne Frank dies a few days later.
April 15, 1945	British troops liberate Bergen-Belsen.
June 3, 1945	Otto Frank returns to Amsterdam and moves in with Miep and Jan Gies.
April 3, 1946	*Het Parool* publishes an article about Anne Frank's diary.
Summer 1947	Anne's diary is published in Amsterdam.

| 1952 | *The Diary of a Young Girl* is published in the United States. |
| August 19, 1980 | Otto Frank dies in Switzerland at the age of ninety-one. |

The Diary of a Young Girl gives readers who have little or no knowledge of what happened during the Holocaust a relatively gentle introduction to the subject. Those unfamiliar with the documents and testimonies that describe the horrors of the ghettos and concentration camps, or with other stories of hiding from the Nazis, may incorrectly assume that the story Anne tells in her diary is representative of what happened in the Holocaust.

Anne Frank's story is only one unique account of one particular way of trying to outwit the Nazis' Final Solution. For twenty-five months, Anne and her family managed, with the help and sacrifice of non-Jews, to elude the forces that were determined to destroy them. The diary provides readers with a vivid picture of "life" under these unnatural circumstances, but it does not describe the shockingly brutal circumstances and events that were to occur after the Franks were taken from the annex. The Frank family's Holocaust happened after Anne stopped writing.

FAMILY HISTORY IN GERMANY

Although Anne Frank thought of herself as a Dutch girl, she and the other members of her family were all born in Germany. Her father's family had lived in Frankfurt, Germany, since the seventeenth century. Her mother, Edith Holländer, came from Aachen, Germany, where her father had been a successful manufacturer. Both Otto Frank and Edith Holländer belonged to the liberal Jewish middle class, but they had many friends who were not Jewish, and they were active participants in Frankfurt's vibrant social and cultural life.

Otto Frank and Edith Holländer married in 1925. By that time the Frank family's banking business had suffered from a number of serious difficulties, and by 1929 the worldwide economic depression and fluctuations in the Frankfurt Stock Exchange had created an extremely unstable economic situation. Industrial activity in Frankfurt decreased dramatically, and unemployment steadily increased. These economic problems also affected the family's banking business. Financial problems and setbacks made it impossible to sustain the bank, and it was closed in the spring of 1933.

By 1933 severe economic problems and ever increasing poverty and dissatisfaction in Germany created an environment in which Adolf Hitler, leader of the National Socialist German Workers' (Nazi) Party, came to power with promises of reform and prosperity.

Very quickly everything changed for the Jews in Germany. They were not permitted to participate in the political, economic, and social life of their community. In Frankfurt, the Jewish mayor was forced to resign, and all Jewish employees of the city were dismissed. Jewish businesses were boycotted beginning April 1, 1933. Otto Frank was particularly concerned about the drastic actions in his city when Jewish children were forced to use separate benches at school so that they could be distinguished from their "Aryan" classmates. Before long, separate schools taught by Jewish faculty were set up for Jewish children.

THE FRANKS MOVE TO HOLLAND

Otto Frank decided to move his family to Amsterdam, Holland. He believed that in the Netherlands his family would be safe from the harsh and frightening laws being implemented against the Jews in Germany. In 1933 he went to Amsterdam and established the Dutch Opekta Company, a branch of his brother's business, which made pectin, an ingredient used in making jam. His family soon joined him in their new homeland, and by 1938 the company was so successful that it was expanded to include the production of spices. Hermann Van Pels (Hermann Van Daan in Anne's diary), also a German Jewish refugee, joined the business.

Only seven years after immigrating to the Netherlands, the Frank family was comfortably settled in a neighborhood that included many other German Jewish families. Anne and Margot attended a Montessori school (which is now named the Anne Frank School) and later a Jewish lyceum, a school set up for Jewish children after they were expelled from their Dutch schools. For those several years, the young sisters flourished in the security of a loving family and a prosperous life. It seemed as if the Franks had escaped the terrible persecution inflicted on the Jews of Germany.

GERMAN INVASION OF THE NETHERLANDS

Unfortunately, their freedom was temporary and their sense of safety an illusion. German forces invaded the Netherlands in May 1940. Queen Wilhelmina and her government went into exile in Great Britain, leaving the Dutch army to fight against the Germans. After four days of fighting, the Dutch army surrendered. Quickly, many Dutch citizens found themselves becoming accomplices of the brutal Nazi regime which would lead to the deaths of well over 100,000 of the 140,000 Jews living in the Netherlands.

Soon, ever increasing restrictions made life more and more difficult and frightening for Dutch Jews. The Nazis, both German and Dutch, limited the kinds of information Dutch citizens had available to them. The official newspapers printed only German news; many books were removed from libraries; the official Dutch radio was allowed to play only German music, and it was illegal to listen to Radio Orange, the Dutch Government in Exile radio station broadcast from London. By censoring and limiting free speech, the Nazis prevented the Dutch people from communicating openly with each other, and the Nazis were able to spread propaganda which the Dutch people could not publicly contradict or challenge.

ANTI-SEMITIC REGULATIONS

Life continued to become more difficult for the Jews living in Holland. Those in public positions or with civil service jobs were forced to resign, and Jewish businesses had to be registered with the Nazi police. Restrictions on Jewish businesses continued to increase. On October 23, 1940, Otto Frank created a new company that was "officially" owned and run by "Aryans," Victor Kugler and Henk Gies; in reality Frank still owned the company. By December 1940, the company moved to new quarters at 263 Prinsengracht— the site of the hiding place that would come to be known as the secret annex.

As German Jews living in Holland, the Franks were particularly vulnerable to Nazi persecution. Fourteen thousand five hundred Jews of German nationality had been required to register with the

Nazi police, and increased raids in the Netherlands during 1941 and 1942 primarily targeted non-Dutch Jews. The first transport from Holland to "Germany," on July 15, 1942, was composed of mostly German Jews who had moved to Holland after January 1933. The Franks would very likely have been among those rounded up in the first large deportation if they had not already gone into hiding on July 6.

The marginalization of the Jews was now occurring rapidly. In her memoir, *Anne Frank Remembered*, Miep Gies describes how the Jewish population in Holland was relentlessly driven toward poverty, isolation, and desperation. An anti-Jewish edict

> ordered that a large "J" was to be added to the identity cards of all persons who had registered during the census as having two or more Jewish grandparents. . . . Now, as though we had been tricked, the Germans knew exactly who and where all the Jews of Holland were. When the "J's" were ordered, a penalty was established: any Jews who failed to register would be imprisoned for five years and also would have all their property confiscated. The lesson taught by those who had been sent to Mauthausen and either vanished or died was vividly in everyone's mind.[1]

In the spring of 1942, all Jews were required to wear yellow six-pointed stars with the word "Jood" (Jew) printed on them. Now Jews could be immediately recognized by German and Dutch Nazis and police, and they became even more vulnerable as they tried to go about their increasingly limited lives. Miep Gies writes: "On the day that the order was to begin, many Dutch Christians, deeply rankled by this humiliation of our Jews, also wore yellow stars on their coats. Many wore yellow flowers, as emblems of solidarity." Unfortunately, this expression of support "swelled briefly until the Germans started cracking heads and making arrests. A threat was delivered to the population at large: anyone assisting Jews in any way would be sent to prison and possibly executed."[2]

Although Anne and Margot did not know it, their parents were making plans for the family to go into hiding. For over a year, while pretending to be sending furniture and household items out to be cleaned or repaired, Otto Frank had actually been moving them, as well as large stocks of food and valuables, into the rooms above his pectin factory. According to a decree issued on September 15,

1941, Jews could not remove furniture from their homes without written permission. Otto Frank knew he was risking his life, and perhaps that of his family, as he secretly prepared the annex, but as the decrees against the Jews multiplied, and as round-ups occurred more often, he had to find a way to elude the Nazis. He asked Miep Gies, the young woman who was his personal secretary, if she would be willing to take care of them while they were in hiding, even though the punishment for hiding Jews could be death. Miep agreed immediately.

By the time Anne started her diary in June 1942, the secret annex was nearly ready for the family's arrival. It is painful to read Anne's first diary entries, which describe her friends and social life, and to realize that they would be the very last relatively carefree experiences Anne would ever have. Although her life had already been greatly restricted after May 1940, Anne still was able to enjoy some ordinary, but very soon to be extraordinary, pleasures.

On July 5, 1942, Margot Frank was ordered to report for deportation to a forced-labor camp in Germany. Otto and Edith Frank decided that they could wait no longer. They asked Miep Gies to help them escape into hiding.

Both Margot and Miep were in great danger as they rode their bicycles through the streets of Amsterdam. Margot had not turned in her bicycle as ordered, nor was she wearing the star that identified her as a Jew. Miep was helping a Jew escape from Nazi orders. As a result, both young women were now "criminals." Although Margot and Miep understood that they were breaking Nazi rules, the alternative, reporting for labor camp, would probably have been a death sentence for Margot. Fortunately, in Miep Gies the Frank family had found a friend who was determined to help fight "against the might of the German beast among us,"[3] even if it meant risking her own life.

HIDING

The twenty-five months Anne Frank spent in hiding with her family were full of psychological, intellectual, physical, and emotional changes. The most obvious change was the actual confinement, which required Anne and the others to be silent and still during the hours that workers were below them in the factory. Stifling sneezes, controlling bladders, being careful not to drop anything or cause a floorboard to creak—all required the kind of self-discipline an active thirteen-year-old would find particularly difficult to achieve.

Yet the inhabitants of the secret annex considered themselves fortunate to have a hiding place that provided more than the minimum conditions for sanitation and physical comfort. The annex was actually a second "house" connected to the back of 263 Prinsengracht. It could not be seen from the street, and its unusual floor plan made it an unlikely residence. It had been used as a laboratory and to store supplies until Otto Frank began preparing it for his family's eventual use. He also had a swinging bookcase built in front of the door that led to the entrance of the secret annex. Anyone approaching the secret annex would have to walk through the front office and down a long hallway past storerooms, and would come to a bookcase that seemed to be standing against a solid wall. There was no way of guessing that behind that bookcase was a door and a stairway up to the annex, where eight Jews struggled to keep up their spirits and anxiously endured the knowledge that they could be discovered at any moment and forced to suffer a terrifying fate.

WHY HIDE IN AMSTERDAM?

Over the years, many people have wondered why Otto Frank decided to hide himself and his family right in the heart of Amsterdam instead of trying to escape to the countryside, or better still, to another country. Others have questioned his decision to keep the family together instead of arranging for separate hiding places for each member, so that the odds of one or more of them surviving would be increased. Still other readers of the diary have been surprised and frustrated by how utterly unprepared the inhabitants of the secret annex were to defend themselves if they were discovered. All of these questions, although valid, are dependent on hindsight, and one can only guess at possible explanations for Otto Frank's decision. Perhaps he was an optimist (as a number of his responses in the diary indicate) and did not think the war would last very long; or perhaps he could not imagine or believe the depravity of the Nazis' plans to exterminate all Jews. Perhaps Otto Frank could not bear to have the family separated, or felt that he could protect his family better if he kept them all together. Whatever his reasons, the Franks went into hiding precisely where no one would expect them to be—within easy striking distance of the round-ups, which began to occur more and more frequently.

"LIFE" IN THE ANNEX

As the months accumulated, Anne became more and more desperate for the life she had known before she went into hiding. Yet, despite her longing for the simplest pleasures, Anne also recognized that she was far more fortunate than many other Jews who had already been deported to the East or who were in hiding without their families. This double awareness—her intense wish to be released from confinement and anxiety, coupled with her knowledge of *"how lucky we are compared with other Jewish children"*—is an ongoing motif in her diary. Often, after she describes the uncomfortable conditions in the annex, she ends her entry with a confirmation of how luxurious their situation is when compared to the alternatives.

Going into hiding forced the Franks to admit that their lives were drastically and irrevocably altered. If Otto Frank had hoped that the war would not last very long and that he and his family could return to their comfortable life in Amsterdam, the relentless and horrifying news about the situation outside of the annex must have changed his expectations. Yet, despite the disruptions created by going into hiding, the Franks managed to save many basic elements of their lives. They stayed together as a family. Anne continued to do her "work"—that is, to study, read, and write. Most important, the eight inhabitants of the annex and their protectors formed a community which gave them the psychological and physical support they needed to survive while in hiding.

Family, work, and community provided Anne with a sense of connection to her past life and her past self. Studying with her father and Margot, tutoring Peter, writing her diary and stories, even fighting with her mother—all took place in an environment that allowed her to continue to develop intellectually and emotionally. Occasionally, Anne would peek out of the annex window and observe the way other Jews, and especially other Jewish children, were being treated, and she could appreciate the differences between them and herself.

Anne often described the effects of the war on young people. After a heavy bombing, she wrote, *"You hear of children lost in the smoldering ruins, looking for their parents"* (July 19, 1943). Nearly a year later, she reported, *"The police are continually on the go, tracing girls of fifteen, sixteen, seventeen and older, who are reported missing every day"* (May 6, 1944). Clearly, Anne identified with the misery of the young, innocent victims of the Nazi persecution. Her dependence on her own parents (even if she would not admit it) was reflected in her concerns about lost children and missing girls, and her greatest fear seemed to be the possibility of being separated from her family.

The psychological complexity of Anne's experience in hiding constantly needs to be acknowledged. Despite her comparative good fortune in being hidden and aided by a small group of Dutch women and men, Anne Frank did endure painful hardships. She lacked physical privacy and had to share a tiny room with Fritz Pfeffer, a man she barely knew. She often had very little to eat, or too much of only one thing to eat. Anne missed her friends, and, more important, she missed her life at school. As the months in hiding continued she became increasingly concerned about being too far behind in her classes when she finally returned to school after the war. Yet all these limitations and losses were usually tolerable. It was the relentless fear of being discovered and being deported to their deaths that was the most difficult aspect of her ordeal.

THEIR RESCUERS

The Diary of a Young Girl provides readers with a teenager's view of World War II. Although Anne mentions world leaders like Churchill, Roosevelt, and Ghandi, and refers to "invasions" and "capitulations," she herself admits that she is not interested in "politics." Instead, what she gives us are small episodes in the annex that reveal glimpses of the world beyond. On July 26, 1943, Anne wrote about the sirens and bombs that began in the afternoon:

I clasped my "escape bag" close to me, more because I wanted to have something to hold than with an idea of escaping, because

*there's nowhere we can go. . . . the street would be just as danger-
ous as an air raid.*

Later in the entry she wrote about their elation upon hearing that
Mussolini, the fascist dictator of Italy, had resigned. Although they
"jump for joy," the wonderful news is simply information. Nothing
really changes inside the annex, nor does the future suddenly become transformed. The news they get from the outside often gives
them hope that their ordeal will end soon; yet, they have absolutely no control over their own fate.

In fact, they are completely dependent upon the willingness of
strangers to help them survive. When their vegetable man is
"picked up for having two Jews in his house," Anne understands
that the repercussions in their own lives will be drastic but not
fatal (as they may be for the two Jews). She writes that they are
" . . . *going to be hungry, but anything is better than being discovered"* (May 25, 1944).

Miep Gies writes about the vegetable man in her memoir as well:

The man had a kind way about him. I would buy whatever I could,
depending on what he had that day. After several weeks, the man
noticed that I always bought large amounts of vegetables. Without
words passing between us, he began to put vegetables aside for me.
When I came, he would bring them to me from another part of his
shop.[4]

The silent understanding between Miep and the vegetable man
also was reenacted with other shopkeepers. A butcher, baker, and
milkman all provided larger quantities of their foods when they
could, without asking for explanations. Of course, their motives
were not always altruistic. Miep managed to pay for the supplies
either with ration cards or with cash. Still, there was real risk involved in aiding Jews in hiding, and there were some Dutch merchants willing to take the risk.

Anne Frank wrote about the risks that Miep and other Dutch
citizens took in order to hide "their Jews." She described the work
of " '*The Free Netherlands,*' " and praised their own "helpers,"
who *"put on the brightest possible faces, . . . are always ready to
help and do all they can . . . ; although others may show heroism
in the war or against the Germans, our helpers display heroism*

in their cheerfulness and affection" (January 28, 1944). At times, however, the pressures of their situation were overwhelming. She was often anxious about the safety of the men and women who helped them remain hidden in the annex. She knew that without them, she and the others in hiding would be doomed. Anne cared deeply about these good Dutch people who were risking their own lives for her and her family.

BETRAYAL AND DISCOVERY

On August 4, 1944, what they had all dreaded for more than two years happened. Miep Gies was confronted by Karl Silberbauer, a Nazi SD (Security Service), and several Dutch collaborators. As if they knew exactly where Jews were hiding, the men went directly to the door that led to the secret annex.

In addition to the eight Jews who were discovered in the annex, the Gestapo also arrested Kraler and Koophuis. After they were taken away, Henk described to Miep how he watched the round-up from across the canal:

> Suddenly the door opened, and I saw our friends in a bunch, each carrying a little something, going right from the door into the truck. Because I was across the canal I could hardly see their faces. I could see that Koophuis and Kraler were with them. There were two men not in uniform escorting the group. They put the prisoners into the back of the truck and went around to the front and got in.[5]

After their Jewish friends were taken away, Miep went up to the annex with Bep Voskuijl (Elli in the diary). They found everything "in utter confusion." Strewn all over the floor were many loose sheets of paper with Anne's handwriting on them, an account book Anne had been using for her writing, and Anne's beloved diary. Miep collected all of Anne's work and put it away in an unlocked desk drawer. She did not read the diary, because "I realized that if I would actually see the names she wrote, then yes, of course, I would burn everything."[6] As a resistance worker, Miep knew that the diary could contain names of people whose lives would be jeopardized if the information fell into Nazi hands.

Miep's motives for keeping the diary were simple and humane. Fifty years after Anne's death, at a memorial service in New York

City, Miep Gies said she kept the diary because "I was hoping she would still come back and that I would be able to give it to her. I wanted to see her smile at me."

Like thousands of other Jews in hiding, the Franks and their friends were probably betrayed by a Dutch citizen. The Nazis offered rewards for information leading to the capture of Jews, and as conditions in the Netherlands worsened economically, Dutch collaborators helped locate and round up Jews in hiding for payment. A warehouseman who had come to work at 263 Prinsengracht in 1943 was suspected of the betrayal. From the beginning, Miep Gies and her helpers were uncomfortable with his behavior. He asked too many questions and seemed to be suspicious about what went on in the building. In addition, food supplies were sometimes missing from the warehouse, and when the SD raided the annex, they seemed to know exactly where to go and what to look for, as if they had been told in advance about the floor plan of the building.

Immediately after the war, Karl Silberbauer admitted to having served as a Gestapo in Holland. After a brief time in jail, he was allowed to resume his work on the police force in Vienna. In 1963 he was identified as the Gestapo sergeant who had been in charge of the raid at 263 Prinsengracht. A year later, as a result of the enormous popularity of Anne Frank's diary, an investigation into Silberbauer's role in her arrest was initiated by the Viennese and Dutch authorities. The former Gestapo member claimed that he had only acted on orders from his superiors and was therefore not guilty of committing any war crimes. Astonishingly, Otto Frank testified that Karl Silberbauer had "behaved correctly" during the arrests; Frank's testimony helped exonerate Silberbauer.

Other Nazi perpetrators who were indicted for their roles in the deaths of more than 100,000 Dutch Jews stood trial and were given varying prison sentences. At one trial, a defendant explained that informers received a payment of the equivalent of $1.40 for each Jew they reported to the Gestapo.

We will never know the actual motives of the person who betrayed the inhabitants of the secret annex, nor is it possible to understand how one behaves "correctly" by sending innocent people to their deaths. The full horror of what the Holocaust did to people is illustrated not only by the overwhelming numbers of

Jewish victims, but also by the institutionalization of a system that made it possible for one human being to profit (receiving $11.20 for the eight inhabitants of the secret annex) from the deaths of others.

AFTER THE SECRET ANNEX

Westerbork

The day after her Jewish friends were taken from the secret annex, Miep Gies tried to buy their freedom. With money collected from people who knew Otto Frank, Miep visited Gestapo headquarters, but she was unsuccessful in negotiating the release. The Franks, the Van Pels family, and Fritz Pfeffer were held in a prison for several days and then transferred to Westerbork, the transit camp from which Jews were sent to German extermination camps.

Some people who saw Anne Frank at Westerbork described her as "happy" there. It is hard to believe that this is possible, and yet if we consider that she had just spent more than two years confined inside a small hidden annex without fresh air, exercise, or the company of young people other than Margot and Peter, it is reasonable to imagine that Anne could have experienced those first days in Westerbork as another "adventure." She could finally walk around in the out-of-doors, look up at the entire sky, and talk to a variety of people. Also, although it was clearly a detention center, Westerbork was in Holland. It was still *home*.

One valuable source of information about life in Westerbork comes from another young Dutch Jewish woman, Etty Hillesum, who provided a detailed picture of the misery endured in Westerbork in her *Letters from Westerbork*. Because Hillesum worked for the Jewish Council in Amsterdam, she was entitled to exemption from deportation (at least for a while). Yet, she volunteered to go to Westerbork to help the inmates in any way that she could.

Despite Anne Frank's relief at being out of hiding, and despite Etty Hillesum's decision to go to the deportation camp rather than remain in Amsterdam, Westerbork was not a pleasant or comfortable facility. Although it was not a labor or concentration camp, the sanitation facilities at Westerbork were minimal, food was increasingly poor and limited, and most of all, the inmates knew that each and every Tuesday morning a transport would carry off a thousand or more Jews (sometimes extras were put on the train, since some people died along the way) to the East. However, in contrast to labor or concentration camps, families in Westerbork could stay together; mail could be sent and received; and some people, including Etty Hillesum, were able to request and receive packages of food and other necessities from friends outside the camp. Compared to what would come after they left Westerbork, this detention camp was a safe haven.

Etty Hillesum stayed in Westerbork from November 1942 until September 1943. During that time she worked in the camp hospital, trying to provide comfort and aid to other inmates and writing about the people she met there. Excerpts from a letter she wrote on August 24, 1943, describe what she saw as people were taken away for transport to the concentration camps:

> There was a moment when I felt in all seriousness that after this night, it would be a sin to ever laugh again. . . .
> When I think of the faces of that squad of armed, green-uniformed guards—my God, those faces! I looked at them, each in turn, from behind the safety of a window, and I have never been so frightened of anything in my life. . . .
> . . . But the babies, those tiny piercing screams of the babies, dragged from their cots in the middle of the night . . . I have to put it all down quickly, in a muddle, because if I leave it until later I probably won't be able to go on believing that it really happened.[7]

In September 1943 Etty Hillesum, her parents, and her brother, a brilliant pianist, were also put on a transport to Auschwitz from Westerbork. None of them survived.

Auschwitz

On September 3, 1944, Anne Frank and the other seven inhabitants of the secret annex were among the very last thousand Jews from Holland to be packed into a freight train from Westerbork and taken to Auschwitz-Birkenau death camp in Poland. Only two days later, Allied armies liberated southern Holland. If Anne Frank and the others could have remained in hiding just a few weeks longer, they probably would have survived the Holocaust.

Instead, upon their arrival in Auschwitz, men and women were immediately separated, and Anne saw her beloved father for the very last time on September 5, 1944.

Each new group of arrivals was required to pass in front of an SS officer, often the infamous Dr. Josef Mengele. He decided who would remain alive to serve as "slaves" to do forced labor and who would be put to death in the gas chambers. Mothers and their children under the age of fifteen, as well as anyone who appeared to be ill, frail, or elderly, were selected for immediate death. None of the inhabitants of the secret annex were among those selected when they arrived, but the very next day, 549 people, including all of the children who had arrived on that last transport from Westerbork, were sent to the gas chambers. They were among nearly 2 million people, the majority of whom were Jews, who had already been gassed in Auschwitz.

All the information we have about Anne Frank in Westerbork, Auschwitz-Birkenau, and Bergen-Belsen comes from other people who saw her there. We do not have any of her own words to reveal how she felt and what she thought as she was separated from her father. We can only imagine how Anne felt when the beautiful dark hair she was so proud of was completely shaved from her head, and we do not know if she was one of the unfortunate many whose identity was transformed into a series of tattooed numbers on the inside of her forearm. In Auschwitz, the young girl who had signed her name after every diary entry became another anonymous victim of Nazi cruelty.

EYEWITNESS ACCOUNTS

Because Anne Frank did not record her feelings and observations during the last seven months of her life, we must rely on firsthand accounts of survivors who saw Anne, Margot, and Edith Frank in the camps. One survivor who went from Westerbork to Auschwitz with the Franks explains how she herself felt as she realized that their train of cattle cars was headed for the concentration camp:

> We didn't understand what it would be really like, and we didn't want to believe it. . . . It would be severe we thought, and the work would be hard. Now for that we were all prepared. But beyond that,

that people would be murdered—I didn't expect that. Later, I was looking right at it, and even then, I doubted that it was true.[8]

This recurring theme of disbelief and being unable to imagine their fate runs through the testimonies of many survivors of the Holocaust. They could not begin to understand how it was possible that so many people, including doctors, engineers, train conductors, manufacturers, and vast numbers of other anonymous accomplices and bystanders could allow and even be instrumental in the destruction of innocent men, women, and children. Victims tried to convince themselves that what they feared might happen couldn't possibly come to pass because "we were living in the middle of the twentieth century."

Spared the gas chamber when she first arrived, Anne Frank existed in the midst of starvation, disease, and threats of imminent extermination. As a forced laborer she was under the control of *Kapos*, criminals who served as labor overseers and who were notorious for their sadistic behavior. Every morning and night Anne and the other frozen and starved victims would stand for hours in formation while the *Kapos* read the roll call and tortured them with physical brutality or threats of immediate death.

In October 1944, Anne and Margot Frank and Auguste Van Pels were among the women considered strong enough to be transferred to Bergen-Belsen, a labor camp in Germany. Since she was too weak to be of further use to the Nazis, Edith Frank was not selected go with her daughters. She died in Auschwitz-Birkenau on January 6, 1945.

Bergen-Belsen

Although Bergen-Belsen was a concentration camp that did not have gas chambers, its inmates continually died of starvation and disease, especially typhus. One survivor of the camps explained the difference between Auschwitz-Birkenau and Bergen-Belsen this way:

Dying was the order of the day in Bergen-Belsen. Probably fewer people died there than in Birkenau, but it was more visible. In Birkenau, entire groups would simply disappear—the entire gypsy camp disappeared. There wasn't even any mourning. Whether you were skinny or not skinny, sick or not sick, you vanished. In Birkenau, if your name was listed, you were gone. As far as that goes, it was efficient and neat. In Bergen-Belsen, you didn't say good-bye, you died slowly, from illness, exhaustion, cold, most of them from hunger. Most of the people were apathetic. Typhus makes you apathetic. It affects your brain.[9]

In Bergen-Belsen, Anne made contact once again with Hannah Elisabeth Pick-Goslar, the "Lies Goosens" Anne writes about in her diary. Lies's poignant remembrances about Anne Frank appear in a collection of interviews with Holocaust survivors, *The Last Seven Months of Anne Frank* by Willy Lindwer. Lies describes what her life was like in Amsterdam during the time her friend Anne was already in hiding. She explains that she and her family could not go into hiding with the Franks because her mother was pregnant and Lies had a two-year-old sister. It would have been too risky to have a small child and an infant in the annex. Lies's family remained in Amsterdam until June 1943. During that time, people were constantly being stopped on the street and asked for their identification cards. "If you were Jewish, you were taken away and you never returned home."[10]

While Anne Frank remained hidden in the annex and worried about the fate of her friends, Lies continued to go through the motions of her "normal" life in Amsterdam. Although Lies was able to remain at her Jewish school, something Anne desperately missed and longed for, the constant fear and danger were unwelcome distractions:

> It became more dangerous every day. And day by day our classroom became emptier. We arrived in the morning and this boy would no longer be there and that girl wouldn't be there. I shall never forget how Mr. Presser, our history teacher . . . began to read to us about the meeting of Dante and Beatrice in paradise. Suddenly, in the middle of the lesson, he began to cry and ran out of the class.
> "What's the matter?"
> "Last night they took my wife away."[11]

After Lies's mother and the newborn infant died, Lies, her little sister, and their father were sent to Westerbork and then to Bergen-Belsen, where Lies saw Anne Frank once again.

In Bergen-Belsen, Lies and Anne met with a barbed-wire fence between them. Lies described their meeting: "There wasn't much light. Maybe I saw her shadow. It wasn't the same Anne. She was a broken girl. . . . She immediately began to cry, and she told me, 'I don't have any parents anymore.' "[12] Since men of her father's age were routinely sent to the gas chamber upon arrival, Anne believed he had been killed in Auschwitz. She knew that her mother had been close to death when she and Margot were taken to Bergen-Belsen. With Margot dying from typhus, Anne seemed to lose her will to live.

THE FATE OF THE INHABITANTS OF THE SECRET ANNEX

All of the inhabitants of the secret annex also endured the terrors and miseries of "special actions" in Auschwitz. Hermann Van Pels died in the gas chamber of that concentration camp. Edith Frank died in Auschwitz-Birkenau. Otto Frank survived Auschwitz by spending his final weeks there in the camp infirmary. When most of the other inmates were forced to go on a death march in an attempt by the Germans to elude the approaching Russian army, Frank remained behind and was liberated by the Russians.

Peter Van Pels was not so lucky. He survived the death march, but died on May 5, 1945, in Mauthausen, just a few days before the camp was liberated. His mother, Auguste Van Pels, was moved to Bergen-Belsen with Margot and Anne Frank, and then moved to Buchenwald and Theresienstadt, where she died in the spring of 1945. Fritz Pfeffer was transferred from Auschwitz to a concentration camp in Germany, where he died on December 20, 1944.

Margot and Anne Frank died of starvation and typhus in Bergen-Belsen in March 1945. Of the 1,019 people who had left Westerbork for Auschwitz on September 3, 1944, only 127 survived.

THE LAST DAYS

In the description that follows it is nearly impossible to recognize the vibrant Anne Frank whose energetic mind and vivid spirit inhabit her diary. It is the Anne Frank we *do not see* in *The Diary of a Young Girl*.

The Frank girls were so emaciated. They looked terrible. They had little squabbles, caused by their illness, because it was clear that they had typhus. . . . Typhus was the hallmark of Bergen-Belsen. They had those hollowed-out faces, skin over bones. They were terribly cold. They had the least desirable places in the barracks, below, near the door, which was constantly opened and closed. You heard them constantly screaming, "Close the door, close the door," and the voices became weaker and weaker every day. . . .

. . . I don't know which one was carried out earlier, Anne or Margot. Suddenly, I didn't see them anymore, so I had to assume that they had died. Look, I didn't pay any special attention to them because there were so many others who also died. When I didn't see them again, I assumed that they had died there, down there on that bunk. One fine day, they weren't there any longer—actually, a bad day.

The dead were always carried outside, laid down in front of the barracks, and when you were let out in the morning to go to the latrine, you had to walk past them. . . . Possibly it was on one of those trips to the latrine that I walked past the bodies of the Frank sisters, one or both—I don't know. At the time, I assumed that the bodies of the Frank girls had also been put down in front of the barracks. And then the heaps would be cleared away. A huge hole would be dug and they were thrown into it.[13]

Sometime in March 1945, just a few weeks before Bergen-Belsen was liberated by the British, Anne Frank died all alone in the concentration camp. She was not yet sixteen years old. Her impact on millions of people all over the world is a mixed blessing. Anne's honesty about her own emotional and spiritual turmoil and her ability to describe the people and situations around her are gifts to her readers, who get a glimpse of Anne's world through her vivid prose. However, her diary has often been appropriated by those who wish to turn her thoughtful adolescent musings into truths for all of us to live by.

For example, one publication prepared for students claims:

Anne Frank also symbolizes the ultimate goodness in people and the hope that good will triumph over evil in the end. Her belief that "everything will turn out right" has been proven by her very example. Nothing, not even the evil Nazis and their cruelty, destroyed her faith in people. Nor did Hitler's men destroy her, for it is she, not they and their powerful weapons, who has survived.[14]

It is difficult to imagine that Anne's "faith in people" remained intact as she suffered and died in Bergen-Belsen. One can only marvel at the assertion that "everything will turn out right" when Anne, Margot, Peter, and a million and a half other Jewish children perished in the Holocaust. Most of all, although the memory and words of Anne Frank have survived for the past fifty years, the flesh-and-blood Anne Frank, the Anne who would have continued to write, to travel, to perhaps marry and have a family, and above all, the Anne Frank who would have had a *life*, has not survived. It is easy to write "it is she, not they and their powerful weapons, who has survived," but they are merely words that distort the truth. Anne Frank died because she was a Jew, an innocent victim of Nazi genocide.

THE DOCUMENTS

The documents that follow provide us with additional points of view from which to understand Anne Frank's experiences in hiding and in the concentration camps. Miep Gies's memories of Anne and her family, as well as of Miep's experiences outside of the secret annex, help us more fully imagine life in Amsterdam under Nazi occupation. So too, Etty Hillesum's letters from the detention camp, Westerbork, are the kinds of narratives Anne might have written had she still had connections to the larger world. The eye-witness accounts of concentration camp survivors who were with Anne and her family in Auschwitz and Bergen-Belsen complete the compelling story of Anne Frank's tragic fate.

NOTES

1. Miep Gies, with Alison Leslie Gold, *Anne Frank Remembered: The Story of the Woman Who Helped to Hide the Frank Family* (New York: Simon and Schuster, 1988), 79.

2. Ibid., 87.

3. Ibid., 96.

4. Gies, *Anne Frank Remembered*, 121.

5. Ibid., 200.

6. Ibid., 246.

7. Etty Hillesum, *Letters from Westerbork*, translated by Arno Pomerans (New York: Pantheon Books, 1986), 124–125.

8. Willy Lindwer, *The Last Seven Months of Anne Frank* (New York: Random House, 1991), 177–178.

9. Ibid., 106.

10. Ibid., 21.

11. Ibid., 21.

12. Ibid., 27.

13. Ibid., 104–105.

14. Betty Merti, *The World of Anne Frank: Readings, Activities, and Resources* (Portland, Me.: J. Weston Walch, 1984), 53.

DEPORTATIONS OF JULY 1942

The map (on the following page) showing deportations from the Netherlands in July 1942 indicates that nearly 6,000 Jews deported from Holland at that time eventually died in Auschwitz. A huge round-up of Jews on July 14 was followed by a steady procession of trains to what was then still an "unknown destination."

The additional information provided on the map concerns the fate of Jewish orphans and of women used for medical experiments. The other concentration camp indicated on the map, Theresienstadt, was located outside of Prague, Czechoslovakia. It was created to serve as a "model" Jewish ghetto to be displayed to visiting officials who were interested in seeing what was being done with the Jews. Propaganda films claimed that Theresienstadt was "a gift the Führer has given the Jews."

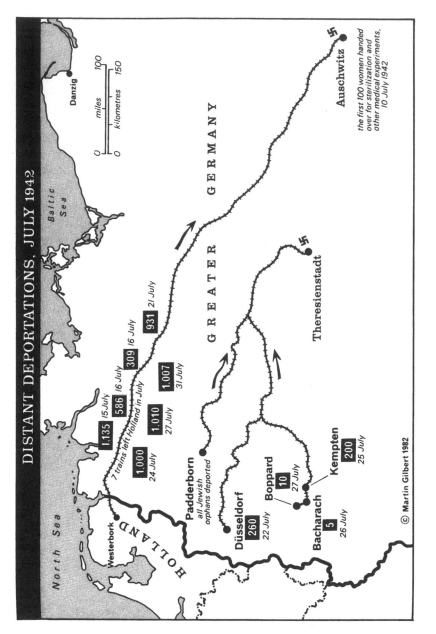

DISTANT DEPORTATIONS, JULY 1942

Danzig

Baltic Sea

North Sea

HOLLAND

Westerbork

1,135 *15 July*
586 *16 July*
309 *16 July*
931 *21 July*
1,007 *31 July*
1,010 *27 July*
1,000 *24 July*

7 trains left Holland in July

Paddderborn
all Jewish orphans deported

Düsseldorf **260** *22 July*

Boppard **10** *27 July*

Bacharach **5** *26 July*

Kempten **200** *25 July*

G R E A T E R   G E R M A N Y

Theresienstadt

Auschwitz

the first 100 women handed over for sterilization and other medical experiments, 10 July 1942

0   miles   100
0   kilometres   150

© Martin Gilbert 1982

Martin Gilbert, *Atlas of the Holocaust* (New York: William Morrow and Co., Inc., 1988, 1993), p. 107.

THE MEMOIRS OF MIEP GIES

Miep Gies, Otto Frank's secretary at the Opekta Company, opens her memoir with the words, "I am not a hero." Despite the many risks she took to help protect her Jewish friends, Miep considered herself just one of many "good Dutch people" who simply did what needed to be done to help save others. Miep and her husband, Henk, helped hide or relocate Jews who were being deported to concentration camps in the East. They also hid a non-Jewish university student who refused to sign a loyalty oath to the German Reich and the German army. Such students could be arrested and imprisoned for their refusal to support the Nazi regime.

Miep Gies never seemed to consider the danger to herself as she shopped for large quantities of food or bribed shopkeepers with extra ration cards or money. Any one of the merchants could have become suspicious about her behavior and reported her to Nazi officials. However, Miep believed that the shopkeepers silently collaborated with her to protect the Jews.

Miep Gies was not originally from the Netherlands. She was born in Vienna, Austria, in 1909 and sent to Holland "to be fed and revitalized" after World War I had devastated the Austrian economy. Malnourished and sickly, the eleven-year-old girl traveled by train with a group of other needy children to a distant country where people spoke a language she did not understand and no one looked familiar. Dropped off at a train station waiting room with other children like herself, the little girl from Vienna sat waiting for someone to claim her. Finally, a man she had never seen before took her hand and led her away to a new life. The family that rescued the ailing Miep fed her frothy milk and thick bread flecked with bits of chocolate. But it was "the kindness" of this Dutch family that healed the young Miep, and years later she would return the compassion and care to others who desperately needed aid.

Reading Miep Gies's memoir gives us an opportunity to see Anne Frank through someone else's eyes. The Anne Miep describes is every bit as lively and appealing as the young diarist we come to know through Anne's own words. We also have an opportunity to compare Anne's descriptions of the other inhabitants of the secret annex with Miep's versions. The "characters" Anne creates are consistent with the older woman's portrayal of the same people, helping us further appreciate the mature insights Anne had while still a young teen.

The first excerpt describes the events on July 6, 1942, the day the Franks went into hiding. The second excerpt describes a round-up (*razia*) that occurred shortly after the Franks "disappeared" from their apartment. Mrs. Samson was a Jewish neighbor of Miep and Henk Gies.

FROM MIEP GIES, WITH ALISON LESLIE GOLD, *ANNE FRANK REMEMBERED: THE STORY OF THE WOMAN WHO HELPED TO HIDE THE FRANK FAMILY* (1988)

Walking to the Franks', I suddenly felt a great sense of urgency for my friends. Conscripting a sixteen-year-old girl for forced labor was a new abomination the Germans were inflicting on the Jews. Yes, I thought, the sooner our friends got safely out of sight, the better. And how many more young girls like Margot have they conscripted? Girls with no father like Mr. Frank and no hiding plan? Girls who must be horribly frightened tonight. With these thoughts, I had to force myself not to run the rest of the way to the Merwedeplein.

When we arrived at the Frank apartment, few words were exchanged. I could feel their urgency, an undercurrent of near panic. But I could see that much needed to be organized and prepared. It was all too terrible. Mrs. Frank handed us piles of what felt like children's clothes and shoes.

I was in such a state myself that I didn't look. I just took and took as much as I could, hiding the bunches of things the best way I could under my coat, in my pockets, under Henk's coat, in his pockets. The plan was that I'd bring these things to the hiding place at some later date when our friends were safely inside.

With our coats bursting, Henk and I made our way back to our rooms and quickly unloaded what we'd had under our coats. We put it all under our bed. Then, our coats empty again, we hurried back to the Merwedeplein to get another load.

Because of the Franks' lodger, the atmosphere at the Frank apartment was muted and disguised. Everyone was making an effort to seem normal, not to run, not to raise a voice. More things were handed to us. Mrs. Frank bundled, and sorted quickly, and gave to us as we again took and took. Her hair was escaping from her tight bun into her eyes. Anne came in, bringing too many things; Mrs. Frank told her to take them back. Anne's eyes were like saucers, a mixture of excitement and terrible fright.

Henk and I took as much as we could, and quickly left.

Early the next day, Monday, I woke to the sound of rain.

Before seven thirty, as we had arranged the night before, I had ridden my bicycle to the Merwedeplein. No sooner had I reached the front stoop than the door of the Franks' apartment opened and Margot emerged. Her bike was standing outside. Margot had not handed her bicycle in as ordered. Mr. and Mrs. Frank were inside, and Anne, wide-eyed in a nightgown, hung back inside the doorway.

I could tell that Margot was wearing layers of clothing. Mr. and Mrs. Frank looked at me. Their eyes pierced mine.

I made an effort to be assuring. "Don't worry. The rain is very heavy. Even the Green Police won't want to go out in it. The rain will provide a shelter."

"Go," Mr. Frank instructed us, taking a look up and down the square. "Anne and Edith and I will come later in the morning. Go now."

Without a backward glance, Margot and I pushed our bicycles onto the street. Quickly, we pedaled away from the Merwedeplein, going north at the first turning. We pedaled evenly, not too fast, in order to appear like two everyday working girls on their way to work on a Monday morning.

Not one Green Policeman was out in the downpour. I took the big crowded streets, from the Merwedeplein to Waalstraat, then to the left to Noorder Amstellaan to Ferdinand Bolstraat, Vijzelstraat to Rokin, Dam Square, Raadhuisstraat, finally turning onto the Prinsengracht, never so glad before to see our cobbled street and murky canal.

All the way we had not said one word. We both knew that from the moment we'd mounted our bicycles we'd become criminals. There we were, a Christian and a Jew without the yellow star, riding on an illegal bicycle. And at a time when the Jew was ordered to report for a forced-labor brigade about to leave for parts unknown in Hitler's Germany. Margot's face showed no intimidation. She betrayed nothing of what she was feeling inside. Suddenly we'd become two allies against the might of the German beast among us.

Not a soul was about on the Prinsengracht. After opening the door, we carried our bicycles into the storeroom, then we left the room and shut the door. I opened the next door to the office and shut the door against the rain. We were soaked through to the skin. I could see that Margot was suddenly on the verge of crumbling.

I took her arm and led her past Mr. Frank's office and up the stairway to the landing that led to the hiding place. It was approaching the time that the others would be coming to work. I was now afraid that someone would come, but I kept silent.

Margot was now like someone stunned, in shock. I could feel her shock now that we were inside. As she opened the door, I gripped her arm to give her courage. Still, we said nothing. She disappeared behind the door and I took my place in the front office.

My heart too was thumping. I sat at my desk wondering how I could get my mind onto my work. The pouring summer rain had been our shelter. Now one person was safe inside the hiding place. Three more had to be protected by the rain.

Mr. Koophuis arrived at work and took Margot's bicycle somewhere that I didn't know. Soon after he left I could hear the warehouseman arriving, stamping the water off his shoes.

Late in the morning I heard Mr. and Mrs. Frank and Anne coming through the front office door. I had been waiting for that moment and quickly joined them and hurried them along past Mr. Kraler's office up the stairway to the door of the hiding place. All three of them were quite wet. They were carrying a few things, and all had yellow stars sewn onto their clothes. I opened the door for them and shut it when they had vanished inside.   (94–97)

• • •

As the *razias* continued, Jews searched frantically for places to hide. Some made desperate, sometimes foolhardy attempts to cross the border to Belgium. Everyone was looking for a "safe address." A safe address, a hiding place, had suddenly become the most blessed acquisition. It was better than a job in the diamond trade, more valuable than a pot of gold. People scrambled in every possible way for information that might lead to a safe address.

Mrs. Samson's daughter and son-in-law, Mr. and Mrs. Coenen, had been desperately searching for a hiding place. They were in a panic for themselves and their two small children as the *razias* in early July continued and spread into many parts of Amsterdam. They managed at last to find one.

When they found their hiding place, they wanted to tell us, but Henk and I had quickly learned that the less one knew about others, the better. None of us knew what the Germans might do with you when they captured you, except that every kind of torture was acceptable to these barbarous people.

Noticing their preparations around the apartment, we realized that their departure was imminent. Knowing that they were in such a panic to get away, Henk warned them to stay away from the Centraal Railway Station. "The Green Police are patrolling the Centraal Station day and night. It's foolish to go near there."

Other than that, we said nothing to these frightened people, with their children understanding nothing that was going on around them. We asked them no questions, and they told us nothing.

One evening, we came home from work and they had vanished.

That day there had been a particular rash of *razias* around town. When Henk and I returned home from work, Mrs. Samson told us that her son-in-law and daughter and their children were so nervous and frightened that they had decided to go immediately to the safe-hiding address. Mrs. Samson was still very shaky from their departure. Henk and I thought she might be better in a safe place until the *razias* had ended, so we suggested that she go and stay with my adoptive parents. She agreed, and I quickly made the arrangements for her.

Just after midnight that night the doorbell rang. Henk and I were in bed and froze at the sound of the bell. Telling me to stay, Henk went to the door. I was too apprehensive to stay, and followed him to the door. There was a woman at the door. With her—one at her side, and one in her arms—were the tiny sleepy children of Mrs. Samson's daughter, Mrs. Coenen.

The woman explained that the children's parents had been captured by the Green Police at the Central Station.

She held out the little girl in her arms. I came forward and took her. She nudged the little boy toward us as well, and Henk took him into his arms. "I have orders to bring these children to this address." That was all she said; then she turned and left and, walking quickly, disappeared into the darkness. We were speechless. Our thoughts were the same: Who was she? Was she Jewish or Christian? Why had the Green Police let her take away two Jewish children?

We brought the children into the kitchen, made warm milk and buttered bread, and put them to sleep.

The next day Mrs. Samson returned, and found her grandchildren. She tried to learn from them what had happened, but neither of the children was old enough to tell her anything about their parents. Nothing could be learned. Their parents had simply disappeared into the hands of the Germans.

Now more than ever, we realized that it was very important to find a place for these children to go into hiding. Discreet inquiries were made. We discovered an organization of students in Amsterdam that had addresses where children could be brought. Very quickly, in barely a week, the little granddaughter was brought, through this organization, to a hiding place in Utrecht. Then the grandson was taken to hide in Eemnes.

Now the search began for a "safe address" for Mrs. Samson. With each day that passed, life was becoming more and more difficult for Jewish people all over Amsterdam. The sooner she could go, the better, to avoid a *razia*.

We were encouraged to learn that ten Christian churches in Holland had banded together and issued a public protest in the form of a telegram sent to the highest German authorities. Together, these Christian churches expressed profound "outrage" at the German deportations of Jewish people. They called the measures "illegal" and accused the Germans of going blatantly against all Dutch morality and against God's "Divine Commandments of justice and charity."

These telegrams were totally ignored by the Germans.   (105–107)

• • •

Jews who had so far avoided arrest were now afraid to go outdoors. Each day was filled with unbearable anxiety. Each sound heard was a possible arrival of the Green Police; each doorbell, tap on the door, footstep, squeak of a car, a *razia*. Many stayed in their homes and just sat. Waiting.

Mrs. Samson announced that she would be going into hiding, that she had found a "safe address." We were very glad. She wanted to tell us more, but we reminded her that the less we knew, the safer it would be for her, and for us as well. Henk made a request: "Could you wait a few days until Miep and I go on vacation? Wait until September; that way we can't know anything about your disappearance, and in case we're picked up and they beat us, we can say that we don't know where you went, that we were on vacation then."

Mrs. Samson said she would wait. We knew that this was a lot to ask of her, to wait even a few days, but we now had seven in hiding on the Prinsengracht to think about—that is, more than ourselves to consider. If something happened to us, it would create grave problems for them.

(118)

• • •

The Germans described the Jewish deportations as "resettlement" and claimed that those taken were being treated decently, given proper food and shelter, that families were being kept together. But at the same time, the BBC claimed that Polish Jews in German prison camps were being gassed, that Dutch Jews were being used for slave labor, and that the Dutch Jews had been taken to camps very far from Holland, in Germany and Poland.

While we didn't know what was true, we did know that the Germans made those Dutch Jews taken for labor send postcards back to their families. The cards always said positive things about life in the camps: that the food was good, that there were showers, and so on. This was what the Nazi captors had ordered their prisoners to write.

Somehow, the Jews managed to transmit other information. For example, at the end of a card sent from one of the camps, a Dutchman

would say, "Give my regards to Ellen de Groot." This was a common
Dutch name and the Germans did not censor it. What the Germans didn't
know was that in Dutch *ellende* meant "misery" and *groot* meant "terrible." So the message managed to tell of "terrible misery."

My head churned with the contradictory bits of information. I dreaded
to think about the unpleasant rumors that were circulating, rumors of
harsh treatment being doled out by the Germans to their helpless prisoners in these remote camps. For the sake of morale, I had taken to
believing only the good news. I passed along all the good news to the
hiding place and let the bad go in one ear and out the other. To go on,
I had to believe totally that this war would come to a good end for us.

Because times were not normal, Henk and I couldn't take much of a
vacation. We desperately needed a holiday, and managed to go for ten
days to a little town outside Amsterdam. There, in the country, we walked
and rested, but I couldn't keep my mind from wandering back to our
friends in hiding.

When we returned to Hunzestraat, Mrs. Samson had gone without leaving a trace.

The Frank family and the Van Daan family managed to keep healthy
throughout the summer. This was of the utmost importance, as the worst
fear of all of us was that someone would get sick and we could not go
to a doctor. This anxiety wore on all of us, especially Mrs. Frank. She was
particularly careful always for the health of the children, always watching
what they ate and wore, whether they were cold, whether there were any
signs of illness.

Mr. Van Daan's butcher friend was not the only merchant to help us
provide the essential staples for our friends. Mr. Koophuis had a friend
who owned a chain of bakeries in Amsterdam. When our friends went
into hiding, Koophuis made an agreement with his friend to deliver a
quantity of bread to the office two or three times a week. We paid for as
much bread as we had coupons for. The extra bread would be paid for
in cash after the war. As about the same number of people worked at the
Prinsengracht as were in hiding upstairs, there was no cause for suspi-
cion.

I had started to go to the same vegetable man in his little shop on the
Leliegracht. The man had a kind way about him. I would buy whatever I
could, depending on what he had that day. After several weeks, the man
noticed that I always bought large amounts of vegetables. Without words
passing between us, he began to put vegetables aside for me. When I
came, he would bring them to me from another part of his shop.

I would put the food into my bag, take it quickly back to the office on
the Prinsengracht, and put it between my desk and the window so that

it could not be seen by anybody who did not belong to our group of insiders.

Later on in the day when it was safe, I'd take the groceries upstairs. Except for the heavy potatoes. These were brought by the kind greengrocer during lunchtime. I was always waiting for him in the kitchen, so that everything would work smoothly while no one else was about. He'd put the heavy load into a small closet I had shown him, and during the night Peter would go down and get the potatoes and bring them up. No words were ever exchanged about this between the greengrocer and me. Nothing needed to be said.

I was shopping for seven people in hiding as well as for Henk and myself. Often I had to go to several shops to get the quantities I needed, but I wasn't particularly conspicuous. These were not normal times. People were all trying to get as much as they could. There was nothing unusual about buying in bulk. Many shopkeepers were not so strict about coupons, either. Often if I had a coupon for, say, two pounds of potatoes and I wanted three pounds, I'd give the coupons and a little bit of money and they'd gladly give me the extra pound.   (119–121)

. . .

Mr. Frank was the supervisor of the children's studies up in the hiding place. Rigorous studying was expected; assignments were corrected by Mr. Frank. Because Peter Van Daan was not much of a student, Mr. Frank made a point of taking extra time and care with him. Otto Frank would have made a wonderful teacher. He was kind and firm, and always included a little bit of humor with his lessons.

The children's studies took great chunks of time each day. For Margot, it was easy. For Anne, although she didn't concentrate as hard as Margot, it was easy too. Anne was often writing in a little red-orange checkered cloth-bound diary that her father had given her for her thirteenth birthday on June 12, several weeks before the Franks had come into hiding. She wrote in her diary in two places, her own room or her parents' room. Although everyone knew that she was writing, she never wrote when other people were present. Obviously, Mr. Frank had spoken about this matter and given instructions for no one to disturb her.

As I heard from Mr. Frank, the diary was a constant companion for Anne, and also a source of teasing by the others. How was she finding so much to write about? Anne's cheeks went pink when she was teased. She would tease right back, always quick with a reply, but to be safe, she kept her diary in her father's old leather briefcase.

Anne thought her best feature was her thick, shining dark brown hair. She liked to comb it several times a day to keep it healthy and to bring out its sheen. When she combed her hair, she always covered her shoulders with a triangular shawl of fine cotton, beige with pink, light green, and blue roses and other small figures on it. This combing shawl, tied under her chin, caught the hair that broke off from her vigorous combing and brushing. She set her hair nightly in pin curls to turn up the ends. Margot curled her hair as well.

Both girls helped with the cooking and pot-scrubbing and potato-peeling and tidying-up. Both girls were learning or reading always. Sometimes Anne would spread out her movie-star photo collection to look at and admire the glamorous faces. She'd talk about movies and movie stars with anyone who would listen.

Each time I silently walked into the hiding place, I'd see each person engaged in activity. They looked like living cameos: a head lowered intently over a book; hands poised over a pile of potato peelings; a dreamy look on a face whose hands were mindlessly knitting; a tender hand poised over Mouschi's silky back, stroking and touching; a pen scratching across blank paper, pausing as its owner chewed over a thought, then scratching again. All of them silent.

And when my face appeared above the landing, all eyes would light on me. A flash of enthusiasm would widen all eyes. I would be sponged up by all the eyes with a voracious thirst. Then Anne, always Anne, would be upon me with a rapid-fire barrage of questions. "What's going on?" "What's in the bag?" "Have you heard the latest?" (122–123)

• • •

All summer roundups of Jews continued in Amsterdam. During a Sunday, I think, at the very end of summer, on one of the most beautiful days we'd had all season, the Germans staged a huge roundup in our River Quarter, South Amsterdam. All the streets were blocked off. Truck after truck of German police went driving by. Before my eyes I could see the men wearing green uniforms sitting side by side in two rows in the trucks. The soldiers would pull up the bridges and stand guard at intersections so no one could get away.

All through the neighborhood could be heard the shrill, piercing whistles and then the sound of boots on steps, rifle butts pounding on doors, insistent ringing of doorbells, and the coarse, frightful voice demanding in German, "Open up! Be quick. Be quick!"

Henk and I were home that entire day. All day sorry-looking groups of Jews wearing the yellow Star of David, carrying knapsacks and suitcases, were pushed and marched in loose groups surrounded by Green Police past our street, right past our window. The sight was so anguish-making, so terrible, that we turned away and didn't look.

Late in the day there came a timid knock at our door. I went to the door and opened it. There stood an upstairs neighbor, a woman whom

I knew just slightly. She was about forty, was always very chic, and worked in one of the finest, most expensive ladies' clothing shops on the Leidseplein, a shop called Hirsch. I'd very many times admired the clothes in the windows, but had never been able to afford their prices.

She lived with her old mother in the apartment above ours. They were Jews.

In her arms she carried a fluffy cat and a cat box. With a pleading look in her eyes she said, "Please, would you take my cat and give him to the animal shelter, or . . ."—her eyes were dry and full of fear—". . . if you want, you can keep him."

Immediately, I took in the situation. I realized that she was being taken away by the Germans and had been given a very short time to get ready. I reached out my hands for the cat. "Give."

She put him in my arms. I thought, I'll never, never give this cat away to the animal shelter. Never. I told her, "I'll take care of him until you come back."

"His name is Berry," she told me, and quickly, she was gone.

I looked at the cat's face. He was almost all white, with some black on his back. He looked at me too. I held him in my arms and brought him into our apartment.

He made himself right at home. What a sweet cat! I thought. I loved him right away.

From that day on, Berry was like our child. Every day Berry would wait in the hallway for Henk to come home from work. And every day, when Henk came home, Berry would spring up and nip him very softly on his chin.

New York: Simon and Schuster, 162–163.

ETTY HILLESUM'S LETTERS FROM WESTERBORK

Like Anne Frank, Etty Hillesum, a young Dutch woman, wrote about her experiences during the grim period that later came to be known as the Holocaust. In her diaries and letters she left behind a chronicle of the suffering endured by innocent men, women, and children during their internment at Westerbork.

The detention camp had been built in 1939 to house about fifteen hundred German Jews who were fleeing Germany. Eventually, the facility was used to house more than thirty thousand Jews at a time, as Dutch Jews were rounded up from all over the Netherlands and held in Westerbork before deportation to concentration camps in the East. The "Catholic Jews" Hillesum refers to were priests and nuns of Jewish parentage who were captured and brought to Westerbrook for deportation.

In her letters to her gentile friends, Hillesum described in dramatic detail the unusual circumstances and conditions in Westerbork. "Life" went on in this detention camp, which included a synagogue and prison! Yet, at the same time, everyone there knew that every Tuesday a train would arrive to take many of them "away to unknown parts and unknown destinies deep within Europe."

Hillesum wrote about her own imminent death, and about how much more painful it was to watch her parents suffer. Nevertheless, she ended one letter by reassuring her friend not to worry. "What tens and tens of thousands before us have borne, we can also bear. For us, I think, it is no longer a question of living, but of how one is equipped for one's extinction."

FROM ETTY HILLESUM, *LETTERS FROM WESTERBORK* (1986)

If I understand it correctly, this place, now a focus of Jewish suffering, lay deserted and empty just four years ago. And the spirit of the Department of Justice hovered over the heath.

"There wasn't a butterfly to be seen here, not a flower, not even a worm," the very first German inmates told me emphatically. And now? Let me give you a rough idea from the inventory. We have an orphanage, a synagogue, a small mortuary, and a shoe-repair factory under construction. I have heard talk of a madhouse being built, and my latest information is that the expanding hospital barracks complex already has a thousand beds.

The two-person jail that stands like something out of an operetta in one corner of the camp is apparently no longer large enough, for they plan to build a bigger one. It must sound strange to you: a prison within a prison.

There are minor "cabinet crises," what with all the people who like to have a finger in every pie.

We have a Dutch commandant and a German one. The first is taller, but the second has more of a say. We are told, moreover, that he likes music and that he is a gentleman. I'm no judge, although I must say that for a gentleman he certainly has a somewhat peculiar job.

There is a hall with a stage where, in the glorious past when the word "transport" had not yet been heard, a rather faltering Shakespeare production was once put on. At the moment people sit at typewriters on the same stage.

There is mud, so much mud that somewhere between your ribs you need to have a great deal of inner sunshine if you don't want to become the psychological victim of it all. The physical effects, such as broken shoes and wet feet, you will certainly understand.

Although the camp buildings are all one story, you can hear as many accents as if the Tower of Babel had been erected in our midst: Bavaria and Groningen, Saxony and Limburg, the Hague and East Friesland; you can hear German with a Polish accent and German with a Russian accent; you find all sorts of dialects from Holland and Berlin—all in an area of half a kilometer square.

The barbed wire is more a question of attitude.

"*Us* behind barbed wire?" an indestructible old gentleman once said with a melancholy wave of his hand. "*They* are the ones who live behind barbed wire"—and he pointed to the tall villas that stand like sentries on the other side of the fence.

If the barbed wire just encircled the camp, then at least you would know where you were. But these twentieth-century wires meander about inside the camp too, around the barracks and in between, in a labyrinthine and unfathomable network. Now and then you come across people with scratches on their faces or hands.

There are watchtowers at the four corners of our wooden village, each a windswept platform on four tall posts. A man with a helmet and a gun stands outlined against the changing skies. In the evening one sometimes hears a shot echo across the heath, as it did once when the blind man stumbled too close to the barbed wire.

Finding something to say about Westerbork is also difficult because of its ambiguous character. On the one hand it is a stable community in the making, a forced one to be sure, yet with all the characteristics of a human society. And on the other hand, it is a camp for a people in transit, great waves of human beings constantly washed in from the cities and provinces, from rest homes, prisons, and other prison camps, from all the nooks and crannies of the Netherlands—only to be deported a few days later to meet their unknown destiny.

You can imagine how dreadfully crowded it is in half a square kilometer. Naturally, few follow the example of the man who packed his rucksack and went on transport of his own accord. When asked why, he said that he wanted the freedom to decide to go when *he* wanted to go. It reminds me of the Roman judge who said to a martyr, "Do you know that I have the power to have you killed?" And the martyr answered, "Yes, but I have the power of letting myself be killed."

Anyway, it is terribly crowded in Westerbork, as when too many drowning people cling to the last bit of flotsam after a ship has sunk. People would rather spend the winter behind barbed wire in Holland's poorest province than be dragged away to unknown parts and unknown destinies deep within Europe, from where only a few indistinct sounds have come back to the rest of us. But the quota must be filled; so must the train, which comes to fetch its load with mathematical regularity. You cannot keep everyone back as being indispensable to the camp, or too sick for transport, although you try it with a great many. You sometimes think it would be simpler to put yourself on transport than have to witness the fear and despair of the thousands upon thousands of men, women, children, infants, invalids, the feebleminded, the sick, and the aged, who pass through our helping hands in an almost uninterrupted flow.

My fountain pen cannot form words strong enough to convey even the remotest picture of these transports. From the outside the impression is of bleak monotony, yet every transport is different and has its own atmosphere.

When the first transport passed through our hands, there was a moment when I thought I would never again laugh and be happy, that I had changed suddenly into another, older person cut off from all former friends. But on walking through the crowded camp, I realized again that where there are people, there is life. Life in all its thousands of nuances—"with a smile and a tear," to put it in popular terms.

It made a great difference whether people arrived prepared, with well-filled rucksacks, or had been suddenly dragged out of their houses or swept up from the streets. In the end we saw only the last.

After the first of the police roundups, when people arrived in slippers and underclothes, the whole of Westerbork, in a single horrified and heroic gesture, stripped to the skin. And we have tried, with the close cooperation of people on the outside, to make sure that those who leave are equipped as well as possible. But if we remember all those who went to face the winter in eastern Europe without any clothes, if we remember the single thin blanket that was sometimes all we were able to dole out in the night, a few hours before departure . . .

The slum-dwellers arrived from the cities, displaying their poverty and neglect in the bare barracks. Aghast, many of us asked ourselves: what sort of democracy did we really have?

The people from Rotterdam were in a class by themselves, hardened by the bombing raids. "We don't frighten easily anymore," you often heard them say. "If we survived all that, we'll survive this too." And a few days later they marched singing to the train. But it was midsummer then, and there were no old people yet, or invalids on stretchers bringing up the rear . . .

The Jews from Heerlen and Maastricht and thereabouts came telling stories that reverberated with the great sendoff the province of Limburg had given them. One felt that morally they could live on it for a long time. "The Catholics have promised to pray for us, and they're better at that than we are!" said one of them.

People came with all their rivalries. The Jews from Haarlem said somewhat loftily and acidly: "Those Amsterdammers have a grim sense of humor."

There were children who would not accept a sandwich before their parents had had one. There was a remarkable day when the Jewish Catholics or Catholic Jews—whichever you want to call them—arrived, nuns and priests wearing the yellow star on their habits. I remember two young novices, twins, with identical beautiful, dark ghetto faces and serene, childish eyes peering out from under their skullcaps. They said with mild surprise that they had been fetched at half-past four from morning mass, and that they had eaten red cabbage in Amersfoort.

There was a priest, still fairly young, who had not left his monastery for fifteen years. He was out in the "world" for the first time, and I stood next to him for a while, following his eyes as they wandered peacefully around the barracks where the newcomers were being received.

The others—shaven, beaten, maltreated—who poured in along with the Catholics that day stumbled about the wooden hut with movements that were still unsteady and stretched out their hands toward the bread, of which there was not enough.

A young Jew stood very still next to us. His jacket was much too loose, but a grin broke through his stubbly black beard when he said, "They tried to smash the wall of the prison with my head, but my head was harder than the wall!"

Among all the shaved heads, it was strange to see the white-turbaned women who had just been treated in the delousing barracks, and who went about now looking distressed and humiliated.

Children dozed off on the dusty plank floor; others played tag among the adults. Two little ones floundered helplessly around the heavy body of a woman lying unconscious in a corner. They didn't understand why their mother just lay there without answering them. A gray-haired old gentleman, straight as an arrow and with a clear-cut, aristocratic profile, stared at the whole infernal canvas and repeated over and over to himself: "A terrible day! A terrible day!"

And among all this, the unremitting clatter of a battery of typewriters: the machine-gun fire of bureaucracy.

Translated by Arno Pomerans. New York: Pantheon Books, 1986, pp. 24–29.

ANNE FRANK'S FINAL DAYS

In preparation for a film he was making about the last seven months of Anne Frank's life, Willy Lindwer, a German gentile, interviewed six women who knew Anne during that brief period. Excerpts from two interviews follow. These interviews are the closest we can get to knowing what it was like for Anne Frank as she endured Westerbork, suffered in Auschwitz, and then finally succumbed in Bergen-Belsen.

Lenie de Jong–van Naarden was in hiding with her husband for more than a year and a half, moving from one site to another and even hiding in a "beautifully camouflaged" hole in the ground. In August 1944, a Dutch SS found Lenie, her husband, and their protector in their underground shelter. Although the SS had threatened to kill the wife of the man who was hiding them, she did not reveal where the three were hiding. Instead, the Dutch Nazi tore the house apart and finally discovered the secret hiding place.

Lenie met the Frank family in Westerbork and then saw them again in Auschwitz. Her heartbreaking description of Edith Frank and her daughters is particularly touching when we remember Anne's earlier exasperation with her mother during the months they were confined in the secret annex.

Janny Brandes met Anne Frank on the day they were transported to Westerbork. Janny had been arrested for working in the resistance against the Nazis. While her husband (a non-Jew who also fought against the Nazis) and their two children were able to escape arrest and deportation, Janny was taken to Westerbork, and like Anne and Margot was sent on to Auschwitz-Birkenau and Bergen-Belsen. It was Janny Brandes who wrote to Otto Frank in 1946 to tell him about his daughters' deaths.

In the excerpts from Lindwer's interview, she describes seeing the sisters on the transport from Westerbork to Auschwitz and again in Bergen-Belsen, the final destination of Margot and Anne Frank.

FROM WILLY LINDWER, *THE LAST SEVEN MONTHS OF ANNE FRANK* (1991)

The train rumbled along at a terrible speed. Sometimes it stopped for several hours, and once in a while the doors would be opened. Most of the time, however, they stayed shut. The young man at the little window kept on saying, "Now we are at so and so," and he would name one place or another. "Everything's been shot to pieces, I can tell you; there's been some bombardment here." That gave us a great deal of satisfaction.

Afterward, we heard that the train had stopped because people in another car had sawed a hole through the floor of the car. While they were still in the Netherlands, they had dropped through that hole and let the train ride over them. A few people were successful. One woman lost her hands and one man lost an arm. In one way or another, they were given help in the neighborhood which they had crawled to. They got out of it alive.

But no one else escaped—it was impossible. I know that people jumped out of the transports, but they must have been on some kind of regular train. It wasn't possible to escape from a cattle car since it was bolted from the outside. (146–147)

. . .

. . . we had to line up in alphabetical order, and then we landed in front of a woman, an anti-Semitic Pole. She grabbed my left arm in a hard grip, twisted it around, and started stabbing it with a needle. That stabbing was painful. We still had our clothes on then.

Once the number had been tattooed, we were pushed along, to the outside. My watch and my wedding ring had been returned in the prison. I took the watch apart and stomped it into the ground (along with my wedding ring) because I had found out in the meantime that it would all end up with the Nazis. Maybe they did, but in any case the watch was broken.

When we were all standing together again with tattooed numbers, we were directed to a large hall. "Take everything off." And all our clothes were thrown together in a pile. The women who had their periods kept something on, and when we were grouped together again, but naked now, they removed the hair from our heads with a pair of clippers. I had very long, pinned-up hair. All of the hairpins had to come out. I had them in my hand; the hair was on the floor. A bit farther on, stood other women and they had their body hair shaved off. They saw that I was still wearing something; they took that off and I had to figure out how to manage.

Afterward, we went to a large room. They announced that the only thing that we could keep was our shoes. We had to put them into a disinfectant at the entrance and leave them there. Then we had to go to the middle of the room.

Now I had very good shoes, sports shoes, and I was actually very concerned that nothing should happen to them, so I watched them very carefully. They were taken and a pair of pumps was put in their place. Because it was a life-and-death struggle, and since I thought that I wouldn't stand a chance of survival without my shoes, I went to an SS man, period and all, completely naked. They were walking around with whips and whenever one of those naked women—who were helpless— didn't please them, she got whipped. I said to that SS man, "*Befehl ist Befehl* (An order is an order)." You said that we could keep our shoes. My shoes were stolen." And he pushed me backward with his whip and looked me over from top to bottom.

He said, "Who did that?"

"That woman there," I said.

She was wearing my shoes. It was someone who wasn't in our group. She had some kind of function—I don't know what. He had her come up to him. She had to take those shoes off and set them down. The SS man struck her so severely with the whip that I don't think she survived. Look, there were so many things that you saw happen; one incident didn't stand out. They were busy with our extermination. She, too, was a Jewish woman, who was, it seems, allowed to sweep the floor.

Afterward, we went under the showers, where, of all things, there was still a little water. Still wet, we were sent outdoors. We didn't have a towel or anything. There, they threw us a bundle of clothes. I had a torn pajama top, some kind of skirt, and nothing underneath, absolutely nothing.   (149–151)

• • •

Older girls who could still be expected to be productive as workers, could stay with their mothers. That is why Margot and Anne Frank stayed with their mother. But most of the mothers had to surrender their daughters. They were always asking, "Do you know where my child is? Do you know?" And I always said, "No, I don't know, but we can't let it get to us; we have to try to get through it. Just hope for the best." I knew that mothers with children were the worst off. Women who were pregnant didn't have any chance at all. Many women threw themselves against the electrified wire fence.

As an individual, I think, one didn't have a glimmer of a chance. Maybe there are people who say now, "I am glad that I was alone; that is how I got through it." But for me, that didn't apply, and it didn't apply to our little club either.

In the period that we were in Auschwitz—about two months—Mrs. Frank tried very hard to keep her children alive, to keep them with her, to protect them. Naturally, we spoke to each other. But you could do absolutely nothing, only give advice like, "If they go to the latrine, go with them." Because even on the way from the barracks to the latrine, something could happen. You might walk in front of an SS man by accident, and your life would be over. They simply beat people to death. It didn't make any difference to them. A human being was nothing.

The work that we did consisted of dragging stones from one end of the camp to the other end. Why that was necessary, heaven knows. There was another group who brought the stones back. We had to work. But we didn't hurry. We did obediently bring the stones to the men who needed the stones, but we still always tried, even without words, to delay it a little. We said to each other, "Let him drop dead." And, "Don't go so fast." We kept up a very slow tempo. Later, too, when we worked in the factory in Libau, making tire chains, we always did something or other so that the machines would break down. Nothing was said; it happened spontaneously.

We were always together in Auschwitz. All in our little club did the same work, dragging stones. We were always more or less together. We didn't walk close together, of course, but we kept our eyes on each other, and when we could go back into the barracks, then we snuggled together again.   (153–154)

· · ·

The hygiene in Auschwitz was abominable. There was water, if you could get to it. In the mornings, the Nazis expected us to stand in neat rows of five, with our hair combed, washed and clean, but we didn't have anything. Water did come out of the faucets, but there were signs with skulls and crossbones everywhere. Maybe it was indeed poisoned, but I know for certain that I drank the water. We were dying of thirst. Each day our food was a piece of bread, sourdough bread; sometimes we got a small dab of butter as well, sometimes also a teaspoon of honey in your hand. Annie and I always shared our portions in the mornings and evenings. At most, it was a slice and a half of bread. It was very minimal, and later there was even less.

I remember that Anne Frank had a rash and ended up in the *Krätzeblock*. She had scabies. Margot voluntarily went to stay with her. Those two sisters stayed with each other, and the mother was in total despair. She didn't even eat the piece of bread that she got. Together with her I dug up a hole under the wooden wall of the barracks where the children were. The ground was rather soft and so you could dig a hole if you had strength, and I did. Mrs. Frank stood next to me and just asked, "Is it working?"

"Yes," I answered.

I dug close in under the wood, and through the hole we could speak with the girls. Margot took that piece of bread that I pushed through underneath, and they shared that.

Shortly thereafter, we went on the transport and they stayed behind. Later they were sent, sick, to Bergen-Belsen. At least, Anne was sick. We knew that already. Mrs. Frank didn't go with us on the transport, nor did she go with the children. She stayed behind in Auschwitz.

In the barracks where they were, women went crazy, completely crazy. There were people who threw themselves against the electric fence. Not that we endured it easily, but perhaps we could let off steam in one way or another by talking to each other. To work it out completely alone— that didn't work; even very strong women broke down.

Auschwitz was really the end of everything.   (154–155)

Interview with Janny Brandes-Brilleslijper

During the trip, we stood—or tried to sit. Some people had brought stools with them. Everyone had brought things in a bag or a backpack. Also, some money. Ironically, later we used the money that we were able to bring to the camp to wipe our bottoms. We simply didn't have any other paper. We tore ten-guilder notes into quarters and then we could use them four times. That was just fine, because it's not pleasant to have a dirty behind.

But in the train, of course, it was much different. We stood pressed close against each other. There were large cracks in the cars, and there were two grids of heavily rusted wire netting that let in some light. If by chance you landed next to such an air hole, you had some relief from the stench, but you could catch cold because it was so drafty.

The Frank family was with us in the car, but I only had contact with my sister. We protected each other against the shoving and the aggressiveness. The longer the trip lasted, the more belligerant people became. That's just the way it was. You couldn't get upset about that, because the kindest, gentlest people become aggressive when they've stood for a long time. And you get tired—so terribly tired—that you just want to lean against something, or if possible, even if only for a minute, to sit down on the straw. Then you sit on the straw and they step on you from all sides because you are sitting so low. All those feet and all that noise around you makes you aggressive—that goes without saying. And then you, too, push and hit. That's unavoidable, but Lientje tried to hold a small place clear for me and I tried to do the same for her. Near the bolts on the door, there was a hole through which you could look to see the landscape. If you were lucky enough to get a glimpse outside without being pushed away, you could breathe a little and put your thoughts in order.

By putting your thoughts in order, what I mean is that all the time you are busy thinking: How can I keep my feet on the ground? Can I sit down now for just a minute? How am I going to get past these legs? Watch out that Lientje doesn't push against that man, or he'll punch her. We weren't the only people who had these thoughts. Through that hole, you could see the marvelous landscape; we rode through magnificent cornfields. Everything was so peaceful and the weather was so wonderful that you forgot for a moment that you were sitting in a cattle car and that a war was going on. (54–55)

• • •

. . . "Oh, we're going to Bergen-Belsen, now that's a good camp!" But disillusionment followed immediately. In the streaming rain and cold—oh, it was so cold—we had to walk. We stayed close together, two horse blankets over two thin girls. I can still see us walking those few kilometers from the Celle station to the Bergen-Belsen camp. We walked through the woods and breathed deeply . . . hmmm, woods, delightful. . . . We were surrounded by guards, and we passed the little town—the people saw us, us poor outcasts. No one lifted a finger to help us. And it rained and stormed and hailed.

Finally, we arrived at the camp on a moor with a bush here and there, and we sat down on a small hill, two girls pressed close together. But then another gray shape appeared and we threw the blankets off and called, "Oh, you're here too." It was Anne and Margot.

I have always assumed that they arrived on the same transport. There was a long, endless line entering the camp, and we sat on a little sand hill, as close together as possible, the blankets up to our noses, and then we suddenly saw those two girls also wrapped in blankets, and we thought, Well, they've gone through the same things we have. And then you are completely happy because you see that they've made it.

At that moment there was only happiness. Only the happiness of seeing each other. And we stayed together until we went into the tents. We also found the Daniëls girls whom we knew from Westerbork.

Maybe it was a "sister complex" that attracted our attention to the Frank girls and also to the Daniëls sisters. Sisters or mothers and daughters always tried to stay together. At that very moment, that feeling of togetherness, of having made it, was theirs as well. We had sort of motherly feelings for them because they were ten years younger than we were. On that same transport, we also found Sonja Lopes Cardozo and the daughter of Greetje van Amstel. We were reunited with quite a few of the young people, but that one moment, sitting on that little hill, we felt real joy because the children were still there. Now we felt at home. We took care, somehow, to see that the children stayed near us.

Large tents were put up hastily because, as we heard later, Bergen-Belsen had not counted on these transports at all. Beds were shoved into those army tents, one, two, three on top of each other. We were soaked and cold, and as soon as the tents were up, everyone ran to them. There was terrible elbowing and pushing to get inside the tents as quickly as possible. But we held back; at one point, the Frank girls were bickering about whether they should go in, and then they did.

We really weren't always nice to each other. Sometimes it almost came to blows. But the Frank girls decided to go on ahead of us. We waited a bit longer in the rain, and finally we were the very last ones to go into the tents. That was our usual strategy, and had been our salvation often. We had to scramble all the way to the top.

During the night there was a terrible storm, with thunder and lightning and hail and you name it—everything that the weather gods could produce came down on us and shook and tore at the tents. Two or three tents, including ours, collapsed.

In each tent, there were a couple of hundred people. A lot of people were injured and, I think, even a few died. We were fortunate. Because we had crept up high and the canvas was torn, we were able to get out. But there was terrible devastation. And in the morning, it was as if there had been a shipwreck. People and piles of wreckage everywhere—moaning and pain. (66–67)

• • •

There was no gas chamber in Bergen-Belsen, at least not within our range. But there was an enormous pit and we dragged our dead there. I always have a little trouble with the word "corpse." I never think of a corpse as a dead human being.

Young girls who were still strong, such as Roosje and Carrie, and whoever else could, also carried dead people wrapped in blankets, to the pit. But we wanted to keep those blankets and, in a manner of speaking, they were shaken empty into that large, stinking pit. The smell was indescribable. And then the birds that flew down into it . . .

Anne had typhus. I had typhus myself, but right up to the end, I was able to stay on my feet. I took only aspirin since I had a raging fever. There was too much to do. Lientje was sick. Water had to be fetched. I always tried to first make sure that Lientje had water; that wasn't egotistical, that was normal; I thought that I had the right to favor my sister. And in fact, I wouldn't have wanted to come back to Holland if my sister hadn't survived. Only on the day of liberation did I finally collapse. But up to then I kept myself on my feet, in spite of being sick.

Anne was sick, too, but she stayed on her feet until Margot died; only then did she give in to her illness. Like so many others, as soon as you lose your courage and your self-control . . .

We did what we could, but there was no question of real nursing. The nursing only consisted of giving the sick some water to drink and, if you had the chance, washing them off a little. In the first place, the most we could do for people with open, gaping wounds was to use a paper bandage. There wasn't anything else, no nursing supplies. An awful lot of people had frostbite. When you stood, for hours, at the *Zählappell* [roll call], then there were black toes, noses, and ears—jet black.

The women who were ill, including the Frank sisters, were in the regular barracks, not in the infirmary barracks. They were once in the infirmary barracks, but then one got another of them out, just as we had done. Our help wasn't enough, but we couldn't do more than we did.

At a certain moment in the final days, Anne stood in front of me, wrapped in a blanket. She didn't have any more tears. Oh, we hadn't had tears for a long time. And she told me that she had such a horror of the lice and fleas in her clothes and that she had thrown all of her clothes away. It was the middle of winter and she was wrapped in one blanket. I gathered up everything I could find to give her so that she was dressed again. We didn't have much to eat, and Lientje was terribly sick but I gave Anne some of our bread ration.

Terrible things happened. Two days later, I went to look for the girls. Both of them were dead!

First, Margot had fallen out of bed onto the stone floor. She couldn't get up anymore. Anne died a day later. We had lost all sense of time. It is possible that Anne lived a day longer. Three days before her death from typhus was when she had thrown away all of her clothes during dreadful hallucinations. I have already told about that. That happened just before the liberation.   (73–74)

New York: Random House, 1991, pp. 73–74.

JEWISH VICTIMS, SEPTEMBER 1944

The numbers inside the black rectangles in Martin Gilbert's map indicate the men, women, and children who were killed or deported to their deaths in September 1944. Included in the 1,019 figure for September 3 are the eight inhabitants of the secret annex. The map traces their horrific journey from Westerbork to Auschwitz, as well as the histories of many thousands of other Holocaust victims who were massacred, evacuated (moved to other camps), or liberated by Soviet or Allied forces.

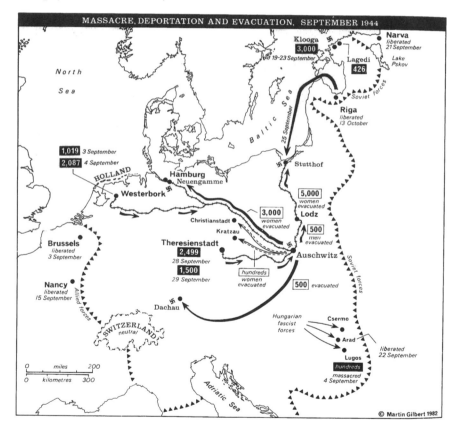

Martin Gilbert, *Atlas of the Holocaust* (New York: William Morrow and Co., Inc., 1988, 1993), p. 208.

TOPICS FOR WRITTEN OR ORAL EXPLORATION

1. Have you ever moved to a new country or community? Describe the adjustments you had to make. Which family members found it easiest to move? Which found it most difficult? What did you miss most after you moved? How did you make new friends?

2. Make a list of all the activities you participate in outside of your home during one week. Discuss how being deprived of those experiences would affect your life, your development, your mental health.

3. What does Anne take with her when the family goes into hiding? What do these choices reveal about her? What would you take? Why?

4. How does Anne cope with her anxieties about being discovered? Find diary entries that reveal her anxieties and entries that explain how she handles them. What do you do when you are frightened? Anxious? What advice would you give Anne? What have you learned from her?

5. Many young people today live in violent neighborhoods and feel that they need to "hide" from the dangerous elements in their communities. How are their fears similar to Anne's? What are the differences? Write a diary entry from the point of view of such a young person.

6. If the Franks had not gone into hiding on July 6, 1942, Margot Frank would have been forced to leave her family and been sent to "destination unknown." Pretend that you are Anne and write a diary entry describing Margot's leave-taking.

7. Compare and contrast Miep Gies's account of the Franks going into hiding with Anne's diary entries on the subject. What does Miep see and know that Anne does not?

8. Pretend that you are a gentile friend of Anne Frank. Write several diary entries in which you describe how you feel about her disappearance. What do you think has happened to her? How do you feel about Jewish families being taken from their homes and deported?

9. Etty Hillesum's extraordinary letters from Westerbork reveal similarities between her spirit and Anne's. Select passages from Anne's diary and Etty's letters that express their feelings about maintaining "inner sunshine" in such devastating situations.

10. At the end of 1942, Etty Hillesum was helping others survive in Westerbork, while Anne Frank was already in hiding in the secret annex. Write a series of letters between Anne Frank and Etty Hillesum in which each young woman describes her present life and her feelings about what is happening around her.

11. Choose a diary entry in which Anne writes about an event occurring in the war. Research that event and write a report providing information Anne did not include.

12. Write a report about one of the world leaders Anne mentions in her diary.

13. Look at a newspaper account of a war or political struggle in some part of the world today. Imagine that you are a young teen living in that country and write a series of diary entries about the situation you are in.

14. Read Elie Wiesel's memoir *Night*, the story of his internment in Auschwitz. The memoir tells how Elie and his father stayed together in the concentration camp until the elder Wiesel died of starvation and disease. Write a response to the memoir in whatever form you feel best expresses your feelings.

15. After she was liberated from Auschwitz, Charlotte Delbo returned to France and wrote *None of Us Will Return*, the first part of her trilogy, *Auschwitz and After*. Delbo's descriptions of suffering in Auschwitz are graphic and poetic. Choose an excerpt from her memoir and respond to it in a nonverbal form: music, dance, visual art.

16. Write a dramatic scene from the point of view of one of the women who saw Anne Frank during the last seven months of her life.

17. Imagine that Anne had her diary with her in Auschwitz or Bergen-Belsen and write an entry based on one of the descriptions in Willy Lindwer's interviews.

18. Look at the photographs in *The Auschwitz Album* and write a narrative about any of the people in one of the photos. Imagine what they were like before Auschwitz. Imagine what they are thinking or feeling as they are being photographed.

19. Genocide continues to occur around the world today. Research one such event and prepare a report on where it is happening. What is the conflict? What is or is not being done to stop it? What is or is not being done to help its victims?

SUGGESTED READINGS

The Frank Family

Bettelheim, Bruno. "The Ignored Lesson of Anne Frank." In *Surviving and Other Essays*. New York: Alfred A. Knopf, 1979.

Gies, Miep, with Alison Leslie Gold. *Anne Frank Remembered: The Story of the Woman Who Helped to Hide the Frank Family*. New York: Simon and Schuster, 1988.

Lindwer, Willy. *The Last Seven Months of Anne Frank*. New York: Random House, 1991.

Merti, Betty. *The World of Anne Frank: Readings, Activities, and Resources*. Portland, Me.: J. Weston Walch, 1984.

Related Works

Czerniakow, Adam. *The Warsaw Diary of Chaim A. Kaplan*. Briarcliff Manor, N.Y.: Stein and Day, 1978.

Delbo, Charlotte. *Auschwitz and After*. Translated by Rosette C. Lamont. New Haven: Yale University Press, 1995.

Denes, Magda. *Castles Burning: A Child's Life in War*. New York: W. W. Norton, 1997.

Des Pres, Terrence. *The Survivor: An Anatomy of the Death Camps*. New York: Oxford University Press, 1976.

Drucker, Olga Levy. *Kindertransport*. New York: Holt, 1992.

Felstiner, Mary Lowenthal. *To Paint Her Life: Charlotte Salomon in the Nazi Era*. New York: HarperCollins, 1994.

Hillesum, Etty. *An Interrupted Life: The Diaries of Etty Hillesum*. Translated by Arno Pomerans. New York: Pantheon Books, 1983.

———. *Letters from Westerbork*. Translated by Arno Pomerans. New York: Pantheon Books, 1986.

Klein, Gerda Weissman. *All but My Life*. New York: Hill and Wang, 1957.

Korczak, Janusz. *Janusz Korczak, Ghetto Diary*. New York: Holocaust Library, 1978.

Leitner, Isabella. *Fragments of Isabella: A Memoir of Auschwitz*. New York: Dell, 1980.

Levi, Primo. *Survival in Auschwitz*. Translated by Stuart Woolf. New York: Macmillan, 1987.

Lewin, Abraham. *A Cup of Tears: A Diary of the Warsaw Ghetto*. Edited by Antony Polonsky; trans. by C. Hutton. Cambridge, Mass.: Basil Blackwell, 1988.

Ringelbaum, Emmanuel. *Notes from the Warsaw Ghetto: The Journal of Emmanuel Ringelbaum*. Edited and translated by Jacob Sloan. New York: Schocken Books, 1974.

Senesh, Hannah. *Hannah Senesh, Her Life and Her Diary*. New York: Schocken Books, 1973.

Spiegelman, Art. *Maus*. 2 vols. New York: Pantheon, 1991.

Wiesel, Elie. *Night*. New York: Bantam, 1982; Avon, 1972.

Wilkomirski, Binjamin. *Fragments: Memories of a Wartime Childhood*. New York: Schocken, 1996.

4

The Jews in Holland

The Jews who lived in the Netherlands had not suffered from the kinds of overt anti-Semitic attacks and intolerance prevalent in other European countries. For centuries, the Dutch government had served as a model of tolerance to other nations. Its Union of Utrecht in 1579 declared that all Dutch citizens, including Jews, had the right to practice their religion freely. Yet, for the most part, the Dutch people lived in communities made up of those of the same religion or denomination, Catholic, Protestant, and Jewish; so that while there was tolerance for religious differences, there was not an especially strong bond of shared experiences among the different denominations.

JEWISH REFUGEES IN HOLLAND

Unfortunately, this religious tolerance was tested and found wanting when increasing numbers of desperate Jewish refugees from Germany began entering the Netherlands in the 1930s. Non-Jews worried that the refugees would be an additional burden on the already depressed economy, and Dutch Jews were afraid that increased immigration would encourage anti-Semitism.

Economics played an important role in limiting the number of Jews who were allowed to take up residency in Holland. Like many other nations, including the United States, the Netherlands was unwilling to share its resources and provide safe havens for Jews increasingly frantic to escape Nazi persecution. Otto Frank and his family were among the fortunate Jews who were allowed to immigrate to Holland in 1933. Mr. Frank had the advantage of having Dutch friends and business associates who could help him establish a new life in Holland, and more important, he had money to bring with him which would ensure that he and his family would not be dependent on the Dutch government for financial support. In contrast, German Jews without financial resources or a sponsor in the Netherlands were not allowed to cross the border. Thus, it soon became clear to Jews trying to escape Nazi Germany that they were welcome in Holland as long as their numbers were limited and as long as they did not require special aid.

After 1938 German Jews could no longer enter Holland as emigrants. The borders between Germany and Holland were closed to legal immigration, and a detention camp, Westerbork, was built in 1939 to house refugees who continued to try to escape from Germany. This limited gesture of protection was maintained by the financial support of the Dutch Jewish community rather than by the Dutch government. By 1942 Westerbork had become the infamous transit camp from which more than 100,000 Jews, both Dutch and German, were sent to concentration camps, and, for the vast majority, to their doom.

GERMANY INVADES

Of the 140,000 Jews living in the Netherlands in 1940 when the Germans invaded, 24,000, including the Franks and the Van Pels family, were refugees from Hitler's Germany. The largest community of Jews, 90,000, lived in Amsterdam. Most Jews were poor and had neither financial nor political resources available to escape from Holland when it became clear that the Germans were imposing anti-Semitic measures in the Netherlands just as they had in all of the other countries they had already invaded. In addition, the Dutch landscape made it particularly difficult for Jews to escape. Holland is a flat country, without forests or mountains, and there were few places where fleeing Jews could take refuge. Nor could Jews hope to find safety in bordering countries, since Belgium and Germany were both already occupied by the Nazis.

THE NAZIS TAKE OVER

Four days after the Germans invaded Holland, Queen Wilhelmina and her entire government fled to Great Britain. The Dutch people were left without leadership and completely at the mercy of the Nazis, who quickly instituted their own anti-Semitic policies. Reichskommissar Artur Von Seyss-Inquart became the highest German official in the Netherlands. He was aided by four Generalkommissars who were in charge of Security and Police, Political Affairs and Propaganda, Administration and Justice, and Economy and Finance. With the aid of the Dutch Nationalist Socialist Movement (NSB), as well as members of the Dutch police and other willing collaborators, the Germans began identifying and persecuting the Jews in the Netherlands.

DUTCH REACTIONS TO NAZI POLICIES

Part of the German strategy was to use Dutch institutions to carry out Nazi racist policies. For the most part, the Dutch complied with German orders without immediately understanding the consequences of their actions. Many people, including Jews, did not intentionally collaborate with the Germans, yet their decisions to "cooperate" with Nazi requirements and rules ultimately cost countless lives. For example, in October 1940, the Amsterdam City Council, under the orders of the Germans, sent out two different kinds of forms to the heads of all education departments. Form A was to be filled out by Aryans; Form B was for non-Aryans. Every civil servant received two forms and needed to choose which one to fill out. Although many people, according to historian Jacob Presser, "wavered, angry and disconsolate" as to whether or not to sign, in the end, the forms were signed, thereby making it possible for Jews to be identified. This obedience to bureaucratic regulations aided the Germans. If a large number of Dutch citizens had refused to fill out either form and had not identified themselves according to the categories Aryan and non-Aryan, it would have been more difficult for the Germans to isolate the Jewish people. More important, the refusal would have sent a strong message to the Nazis that the Dutch were unwilling to abide by German anti-Semitic policies. But that did not happen.

Of course, there were courageous Dutch men and women who

resisted even the earliest German orders. One law professor drafted a petition to Seyss-Inquart in which he stated that he and his colleagues, as well as the majority of Dutch teachers, were against the identification of their fellow countrymen by race. He wrote: "It is a matter of indifference whether a scholar is Jewish or not. . . . In the Dutch view, all learning is service to a single, universal truth, involving all mankind, and it is from this service that education derives its moral value and social importance."[1]

RESPONSE OF THE DUTCH CHURCHES

The Dutch Churches also responded to German anti-Semitic measures to varying degrees. For the most part, their statements and petitions were not effective in changing policies or rallying non-Jews to protest en masse; in some cases, in order to save some of its own Jewish Christian members from deportation, the Dutch Reformed Church agreed not to publicize a protest against the deportation of Jews. Thus, in order to protect its own "Jews," the Church was complicit in helping the Germans implement their deadly actions against the "other" Jews. In many Protestant churches, worshippers were told that the anti-Semitic measures were "in direct conflict with the concept of Christian charity."[2] However, not all Protestant churches participated in this proclamation, and although it was an important expression of the Church's position, it did nothing to change German policy.

Unfortunately, there were far too many Dutch citizens who simply stood by while Jewish men, women, and children were dragged from their homes and rounded up on the streets. Dutch gentiles watched as Jewish children were taken from their classrooms and as the sick and aged were taken from their beds. While it is true that many in the Dutch community pinned yellow bits of cloth onto their clothes to express sympathy with their Jewish countrymen who were forced to wear yellow stars, these gestures of mass protest were relatively safe. The demonstrators remained anonymous in the crowd. Significantly more risky, but also far more effective, were individual acts of protection, rescue, and sabotage. Thus, while it is clear that both perpetrators and rescuers were active participants in the horrifying events that unfolded during the Holocaust, it is important to recognize that the majority of bystanders also "acted" when they chose not to resist Nazi policies or not to help save their Jewish friends, neighbors, and fellow countrymen.

THE DUTCH BOYCOTT

The earliest measures against the Jews were meant to impoverish, humiliate, and isolate them from the rest of the Dutch community. Many Jews lost their jobs, had to give up their businesses, and had their property confiscated. Eventually, Jews were banished from all parks and outdoor sports arenas and forbidden to use public transportation. As the decrees against the Jews continued to accumulate and escalate, the Dutch finally realized that their country and their way of life were being controlled and corrupted by the German invaders. A general strike was called in Holland on February 25, 1941, to protest the way the Jews were being treated. For three days all public transportation and industry stopped, and the morale of the entire Dutch population was lifted as the nation demonstrated its disdain for Nazi policies. Unfortunately, the Germans retaliated swiftly and brutally, terrorizing anyone who tried to oppose their actions. Eventually, all Dutch Jews were required to move into Amsterdam, where they could more easily be controlled and rounded up for deportation.

THE DUTCH POLICE

The Dutch police had initially resisted cooperating with German orders to arrest Jews who violated Nazi policies; however, by the end of August 1942, only a few weeks after the Franks had gone into hiding, Dutch policemen were actively removing Jews from their homes and grabbing them off the streets of Amsterdam. Under threat of losing their jobs and pensions, or even being arrested as saboteurs, many Dutch policemen obeyed German orders as decreed by H. Rauter, German Chief of Security and Police. In a letter to his superiors, Rauter proudly reported: "The new Dutch police units are behaving excellently on the Jewish question; day and night they are arresting Jews by the hundred. The only danger involved in this is the fact that here and there a police officer's hand strays and he enriches himself out of Jewish property."[3] Still, enough police were so uncooperative and resistant to Nazi orders that in 1943 an auxiliary police force made up of volunteer Dutchmen took over the job of rounding up Jews for deportation. In Amsterdam alone, more than one thousand Dutch citizens signed up for the job.

THE JEWISH COUNCIL

Just as the Germans used their Dutch counterparts to accomplish their anti-Semitic policies, they also used the Jewish community to aid them in manipulating and vanquishing the Jews. The Germans insisted that the Jewish community select a group of representatives who would be the liaisons between the Nazis and the Jews. Leading rabbis and administrators were chosen or volunteered to become members of the Jewish Council. These men were responsible for making sure that all German orders were implemented. Needless to say, the members of the Jewish Council often found themselves having to make impossible choices and decisions. Among its other duties, the Jewish Council was responsible for informing the Jewish community that men and women between sixteen and forty would be required to go to Germany in "police-controlled labour contingents."[4] The Germans insisted that the Council distribute and collect the forms that identified those eligible for forced labor, and it was up to the Council to inform the Germans how many Jews per day they could "process."

In July 1942, Margot Frank was among those who received a postcard from the Jewish Council informing her of her selection for labor in Germany. Often, Jews were simply rounded up in the streets and in their homes whenever one of these orders for several hundred Jewish "volunteers" to go "East" was instituted. At other times, however, it was up to the Jewish Council to decide who would be among those chosen. Frantic parents and spouses would petition the Council to exempt a member of their family, but in the end, a certain number of victims were required, and the Council was responsible for making those selections. Council members feared that if they disobeyed German orders, even harsher actions would be taken against the Jews, and so they acquiesced to increasingly demonic Nazi demands.

Although it is inconceivable that the Jewish Council knowingly sent so many of their fellow Jews to their deaths, it is important to understand that for the first year or more after the Germans began sending Jews to labor camps, and then concentration camps, most people could not imagine that thousands of men, women, and children were systematically being exterminated at Mauthausen, where they were told they were being sent to "work." Those remaining in the Netherlands were told, and wanted to believe, that their loved ones were helping the Germans in the war effort. To maintain this charade, the Germans allowed Dutch Jews to send mail and packages to those in the camps, and even after news began filtering back that people were dying in huge numbers, most people could not imagine that their family members and friends were being annihilated simply because they were Jews.

The evil of the Nazi policies was compounded by the fact that they made the Jewish Council responsible for orchestrating the deaths of their own people. Historians and survivors have questioned the role of the Jewish Council in the Netherlands and other countries invaded by the Germans. Were they complicit in the extermination of the Jews? Could they have refused to obey German orders? Did they end up making choices to save their own and their families' lives? These are extremely difficult questions to answer. At all times, the Germans were willing to kill anyone who disobeyed their orders. Any refusal to comply with their demands resulted in additional suffering and terror. For the most part, members of the Jewish Council continued to hope (or convinced themselves) that they could limit the number of deaths if they cooperated with their captors. In the end, they could save very few.

THE DOCUMENTS

The documents included in this chapter focus on specific Nazi actions against the Dutch Jews. Jacob Presser was an eyewitness and victim of Nazi persecution; after the Holocaust he wrote a detailed history, *The Destruction of the Dutch Jews*, which provides invaluable information about the daily humiliations, deprivations, and terrorism inflicted on the Jewish population. The transcript from the communications regarding the "Final Solution of the Jewish Question in the Netherlands" also focuses on the particular strategies formulated to rid the Netherlands of its Jews.

NOTES

1. Jacob Presser, *The Destruction of the Dutch Jews: A Definitive Account of the Holocaust in the Netherlands*, translated by Arnold Pomerans (New York: E. P. Dutton, 1969), 21.

2. Ibid., 23.

3. Ernst Schnabel, *Anne Frank: A Portrait in Courage*, translated by Richard and Clara Winston (New York: Harcourt, Brace and World, 1958), 69.

4. Presser, *Destruction of the Dutch Jews*, 136.

THE RAIDS OF JULY AND AUGUST

FROM JACOB PRESSER, *THE DESTRUCTION OF THE DUTCH JEWS:
A DEFINITIVE ACCOUNT OF THE HOLOCAUST IN THE
NETHERLANDS* (1969)

Unlike many of the history texts written after World War II, *The
Destruction of the Dutch Jews* was written by a historian who had
himself witnessed and survived the Holocaust. Jacob Presser was
commissioned in 1950 by the Netherlands State Institute for War
Documentation to write the history of his country during a period
when murder was committed "on a scale never known before,
with malice aforethought and in cold blood." Focusing only on his
own country and his own countrymen, Presser described in passionate and intimate detail the process of destruction that led to
the deaths of over 100,000 Dutch Jews.

At times, Presser's personal feelings took precedence over "historical" objectivity. We are reminded that the writer was himself a
victim of Nazi persecution and lost many of his loved ones in the
Holocaust. Because he wrote his book so soon after the end of the
war, Presser was able to interview a large number of eyewitnesses
(both Jews and non-Jews) and was able to retrace the routes of
those who were driven from their homes in the Netherlands to
concentration camps in the East.

After 700 Jews were rounded up and arrested in Amsterdam, the
Jewish Council was given the responsibility of providing 4,000 Jews
to be sent to labor camps in exchange for the 700 Jewish prisoners.
Presser wrote in his account:

> Meanwhile, the 700 men and women were being detained in the
> courtyard of Security Police Headquarters; Blumenthal placed the
> women in the centre and made the men march round them.
> German female employees hung out of the windows taking snaps
> for their albums and, judging by their screams of laughter, were
> having a highly enjoyable time. (144)

As the raids of July 1942 continued, more trains were required
to carry the unfortunate Jews away from their homes. In his book,

Presser provided the precise train schedules and the exact numbers of Jews on each train, but he concluded the section with a
personal rather than a historical comment:

> The reader would be wrong to assume that all Jews were allowed
> to go to the station in trams. Boys and girls of sixteen had to go on
> foot from whatever distance. "There was no moon, the darkened
> city was black. The children's parents were not allowed to wave
> them goodbye, not even from the doorway. Once the door had shut
> behind these children, they had been seen for the last time." (149)

Jacob Presser saw firsthand the terror and helplessness of his
young students as the round-ups continued in 1942:

> There can be only very few surviving Jews who do not remember
> that black Friday of October 2, 1942. Something had leaked out
> early in the morning, and as the day went on rumour mushroomed
> until, by evening, there was panic in many Jewish circles. . . . The
> writer recalls very vividly how the headmaster of his school assem-
> bled the pupils at lunchtime and then ordered them to go home
> and to pack their rucksacks, how these children scattered in all di-
> rections as if a bomb had exploded, how frightened passers-by
> stopped to ask them what was happening, and how another long,
> long vigil began. . . . husbands were dragged away from their wives,
> women from their children, children from their parents, in a pro-
> cess of organized chaos. The writer remembers one of his pupils
> being snatched up, while the boy's mother, who was a neighbour,
> screamed into the night from her balcony. On Monday morning,
> when lessons at the school were resumed, there were many more
> empty benches than usual. (173)

ORDERS FOR THE "FINAL SOLUTION" IN THE NETHERLANDS

The following documents illustrate the excruciating attention paid by the Nazis to every possible definition of *Jew* so as to include as many victims as possible in the "Final Solution of the Jewish Question in the Netherlands." Note that the May 5, 1943, directions are "Secret."

In the letter from Reichskommissar Seyss-Inquart to Party Chancellery Chief Bormann, the "Jewish question" Seyss-Inquart refers to is a euphemism for the elimination of the Jewish population in the Netherlands. Seyss-Inquart is particularly concerned about how to deal with Jews who are married to non-Jews. He goes into great detail regarding the possible solutions to this vexing situation.

FROM RAUL HILBERG, ED., *DOCUMENTS OF DESTRUCTION: GERMANY AND JEWRY, 1933–1945* (CHICAGO: QUADRANGLE BOOKS, 1971).

Israel Police document 1356

The Commanding Officer of Security Police and Security Service in the Occupied
Dutch Territories B 4 [Jewish Affairs]
to Central Office for Jewish Emigration in Amsterdam (2 copies)
Westerbork camp
Concentration camp Hertogenbosch
All field offices [of Security Police and Security Service]
May 5, 1943
Secret
Subject: Final Solution of the Jewish Question in the Netherlands
On the basis of the latest instructions by SS-Major General Rauter and the discussions held with representatives of the Reich Security Main Office, the following actions are to be carried out during the next few months in the Jewish work:

1. *General Policy*:
The Reichsführer-SS [Himmler] wishes that this year everything

by way of Jews should be transported to the East so far as humanly possible.

2. *Next Trains to the East*:

Inasmuch as a synthetic rubber plant, destroyed by bombs in the West, is to be built anew in Auschwitz, a maximum number of Jews from the West will be needed there, especially during May and June. It was agreed that Jews readied for transport should be shipped out in several trains by the first half of this month—in short, Westerbork camp is to be emptied rapidly. The goal for May is 8000. Train agreements will be made by the Commanding Officer, Security Police and Security Service, The Hague, with the Reich Security Main Office.

3. *Camp Hertogenbosch*:

Inasmuch as the Reich Security Main Office is demanding another 15,000 Jews for June, preparations have to be made as rapidly as possible so that the inmates of camp Hertogenbosch may also be claimed.

4. *Amsterdam*:

The foregoing goal is covered by the intention of the SS-Major General [Rauter] to order the evacuation of Jews from the city of Amsterdam as soon as current political opposition has been beaten down. Two phases are foreseen: the Jews are to be induced to report to concentration camp Hertogenbosch voluntarily. The Central Office [for Jewish Emigration] should have deliberations on whether the evacuation should [then] advance section by section (first south and west, then center or ghetto) or according to other criteria, for example, alphabetically. During the evacuation most of the [personnel of the] Jewish Council would have to move first. No attention is to be paid to the Jew economy (distribution of Jewish stores in sections of the city).

5. *Armament Jews*:

It is absolutely necessary to insist on the promise of the [Armed Forces] Armament Inspectorate etc. to reduce its Jewish labor forces already during May. Insofar as armament enterprises are not transferred to Hertogenbosch, the armament Jews and their families can immediately be removed to Westerbork.

6. *Portuguese Jews*:

All Portuguese Jews (so far as there are no special reasons for leaving them behind) are to be quartered in special barracks of camp Westerbork, where they can be examined for their descent by SS-Major General Rauter and the leader of the [SS] Race and Resettlement Main Office.

7. *Barneveld*:

For the moment the final lists are to be examined for negative indications and the camp is to be inspected. An early transfer of all inmates to Theresienstadt should follow.

8. *A-B List*:

The Reichsführer-SS [Himmler] intends to set up a camp in Germany for ca. 10,000 Jews of French, Belgian, and Dutch nationalities whose connections abroad would make them suitable hostages. Eventually they might be allowed to emigrate in exchange for German returnees.

9. *Mixed Marriages*:

a) Jewesses over 45 will be called up in groups to Amsterdam and freed from wearing the Jewish Star, so that word may get around that Jewish partners in mixed marriages are being allowed to remain if they can no longer have children.

b) Jews in mixed marriages without children are to be transferred to a camp.

c) For the remaining Jews and Jewesses the aspired goal is voluntary sterilization which is to be carried out in Amsterdam. In case of refusal, forced sterilization should follow in camp Hertogenbosch.

d) Inquiries into the economic activities and professional commitments of male Jews in mixed marriages are to be made quickly. Report is to be submitted to the Reich Commissar [Seyss-Inquart].

e) At the very least, all the mixed couples in which the husband is a Jew are to be concentrated without regard to sterilization. SS-Major General [Rauter] envisages some town in the east or southeast of the country for them, since he wants Amsterdam free of Jews for purposes of police control.

10. *Rewards per Head*:

If a large number of Jews are brought in, one might consider as a reward also a grant of immunity [to former Dutch prisoners-of-war] from return to a prisoner-of-war camp. If need be, this matter is to be discussed with Armed Forces Commander, Netherlands.

11. *Foundlings*:

An attempt must be made to have all cases reported to Security Police. A special institution is foreseen for the reception of foundlings, where on the basis of available reports they can be certified as to their biological inheritance.

I request that all necessary preparations be made for these actions despite current political unrest. Detailed instructions will follow.

signed Dr. Harster
SS-Brigadier General
and Brigadier General of Police

Israel Police document 1439

Reich Commissar for the Occupied Netherlands Territories,
The Hague
to Party Chancellery Chief Bormann
copies to General Commissars in Netherlands and Plenipotentiary Dr. Schröder
February 28, 1944

Dear Party Comrade Bormann:

We have cleaned up the Jewish question in the Netherlands, insofar as now we only have to carry out decisions that have already been formulated. The Jews have been eliminated from the body of the Dutch people and, insofar as they have not been transported to the East for labor, they are enclosed in a camp. We are dealing here first of all with some 1500 persons who have not been transported to the East for special reasons such as interventions by churches or by personalities who are close to us. In the main I have warded off the interference of the churches in the whole Jewish question in that I held back the Christian Jews in a closed camp where they can be visited weekly by clergy. About 8–9000 Jews have avoided transport by submerging [in hiding]. By and by they are being seized and sent to the East; at the moment, the rate of seizures is 5–600 a week. The Jewish property has been confiscated and is undergoing liquidation. With the exception of a few enterprises which have not yet been Aryanized, but which have been placed under trusteeship, the liquidation is finished and the property converted into financial papers of the Reich. I count on a yield of ca. 500 million Guilders [more than $250,000,000]. At some appropriate time the future utilization of this money is to be decided on in concert with the Reich Finance Minister; however, the Reich Finance Minister agrees in principle to the use of these funds for purposes in the Netherlands.

The question of Jews in mixed marriages is still open. Here we went further than the Reich and obliged also these Jews to wear the star. I had also ordered that the Jewish partner in a childless mixed marriage should likewise be brought to the East for labor. Our Security Police processed a few hundred such cases, but then received instructions from Berlin not to go on, so that a few thousand of these Jews have remained in the country. Finally, Berlin expressed the wish that the Jews in mixed marriages be concentrated in the Jewish camp Westerbork, to be employed here in labor for the moment. Herewith we raise the problem of mixed marriages. Since this matter is basic I turn to you. The following is to be considered with respect to marriages in which there are children: if one parent is brought to a concentration camp and then probably to labor in the East, the children will always be under the impression that we took the parent away from them. As a matter of fact, the offspring of mixed marriages are more troublesome than full Jews. In political trials, for example, we can determine that it is precisely these offspring who start or carry out most of the assassination attempts or sabotage. If we now introduced a measure that is sure to release the hatred of these people, then we will have a group in our midst with which we will hardly be able to deal in any way save separation. If, in short, there is a plan which is aimed at the removal of Jewish partners from mixed marriages with children, then the children of these marriages will sooner or later have to travel the same road. Hence I believe that it may be more appropriate not to start on this course, but to decide in each instance whether to remove the whole family or—with due regard to security police precautions—to permit the Jewish member to remain in the family. In the first case, the couple, complete with children, will have to be segregated, possibly like the Jews in Theresienstadt. But in that case one must remember that the offspring will get together to have more children, so that practically the Jewish problem will not be solved lest we take some opportunity to remove this whole society from the Reich's sphere of interest. We are [now] trying the other way in that we free the Jewish partner who is no longer able to have children, or who allows himself to be sterilized, from wearing the star and permit him to stay with his family. These Jews—at the moment there must be 4–5000 in the Netherlands—remain under a certain amount of security police control with respect to residence and employability. For example, they are not permitted to direct an enterprise which has employees or occupy a leading position in such an enterprise. There are quite a few volunteers for sterilization. I believe also that we have nothing to fear any more from these people, since their decision indicates a willingness to accept conditions as they are. The situation with the Jewish women is not so simple, since the surgical procedure is known to be difficult. All the same I believe in time this way will yield results, provided one does not decide on the radical method of removing the whole family. For the Netherlands then, I would consider the following for a conclusion of the Jewish problem:

1. The male Jewish partner in a mixed marriage—so far as he has not been freed from the star for reasons mentioned above—is taken for

enclosed labor to Westerbork. This measure would signify no permanent separation, but action of a security police nature for the duration of exceptional conditions. These Jews will be employed accordingly and will also receive appropriate wages with which they can support their families who will remain behind. They will also receive a few days' leave about once in three months. One can proceed with childless female partners in mixed marriages in the same way. We have here in the Netherlands 834 male Jews in childless mixed marriages, 2775 [male] Jews in mixed marriages with children, and 574 Jewesses in childless mixed marriages. Under certain circumstances these Jews can return to their families, for example, if they submit to sterilization, or if the reasons for separation become less weighty in some other way, or if other precautions are taken or conditions develop which make separation no longer seem necessary.

2. The Jewish women in mixed marriages with children—the number involved is 1448—should be freed from the star. The following considerations apply here: it is impossible to take these Jewish women from their families—the Reich Security Main Office agrees—if there are children under 14. On the other hand the women with children over 14 would in most cases have reached an age which would entitle them to request freedom from the star because it is hardly likely that they will have more children.

3. I am now going to carry out the Law for the Protection of Blood [prohibition of intermarriage and extramarital relations between Aryans and non-Aryans] in the Netherlands, and

4. make possible divorce in mixed marriages by reason of race difference.

These four measures together will constitute a final cleanup of the Jewish question in the Netherlands. Since this regulation could in a certain sense produce a precedent for the Reich, even while in the long run the regulation of mixed marriages in the Reich will also apply in the Netherlands, I am informing you, Mr. Party Director, of my intentions in the hope that I may have your reactions. I wrote in the same vein to the Reichsführer-SS [Himmler].

With best regards

                              Heil Hitler!
                              Your
                              Seyss-Inquart

Translated by Arnold Pomerans. New York: E. P. Dutton, 1969, pp. 145–151.

TOPICS FOR WRITTEN OR ORAL EXPLORATION

1. What was happening to Anne Frank in the secret annex at the time the Commissar was sending his letter about the "Jewish question" to The Hague? Find her diary entries and write a letter from Anne to the Commissar.

2. Why is Seyss-Inquart so concerned about what to do with Jews in mixed marriages? What are some of the problems that could arise as a result of these restrictions?

3. Find words and phrases in Seyss-Inquart's letter that hide the true horrors of the situation. Rewrite a section, substituting words that more accurately convey the subject of his letter.

4. How do the Nazis involve the Jews in their own destruction? What is the dilemma the Jewish Council confronts?

5. Write a scene in which members of the Jewish Council are confronted by their Jewish friends who have come to ask for help in escaping Nazi orders.

6. Write a diary entry from the point of view of a member of the Jewish Council.

5

Children in the Holocaust and Their Rescuers

Anne Frank was only one of the approximately 1.7 million Jewish children in Nazi-occupied Europe who suffered the miseries and atrocities of the Holocaust. Since most children's fates were not documented, it can only be estimated that as many as 1.5 million Jewish children did not survive. A much larger percentage of children than adults perished in the Holocaust. For example, of Poland's 1 million Jewish children, only 5,000 survived. Among the 35,000 Dutch survivors, only 10 percent, 3,500, were children. Most children were not able to save themselves by doing forced labor, and, of course, very young children were immediately gassed upon arrival in the death camps.

There are only broad estimates of between 10,000 and 500,000 children hidden during the Holocaust; but even by going into hiding, many of them did not survive the genocide. Depending on the extent of the Nazi occupation and anti-Semitic sentiment in their homelands, Jewish children were sometimes hidden in orphanages, convents, and boarding schools. Some countries, including Belgium and the Netherlands, had special underground networks to rescue and hide Jewish children; for, unlike their parents, Jewish children did not need to have identifying documents and were therefore more easily assimilated into gentile families who could pass the youngsters off as visiting relatives or needy children from other parts of the country.

The Diary of a Young Girl presents only one version of what it meant to be in hiding. The vast majority of children were forced to leave their parents and siblings, because rescuers were more likely to accept one or two children rather than an entire family; also, by splitting up the family, if one of its members was discovered, the others, hidden somewhere else, still had a chance of surviving.

THE TRAUMAS OF HIDING

Although many of the Jewish children who went into hiding were treated like members of the family they joined, they also felt an enormous sense of loss and helplessness. Many did not know the fate of their parents and siblings. Many had to assume new identities, dye their dark hair blond, pretend to be Christian, and remember not to give themselves away by saying or doing anything suspicious. In order to prevent having to reveal their circumcisions, some boys pretended to be girls.

In some cases, children were exploited as cheap labor or abused by their "protectors." Many children were continually moved from place to place, and so they constantly had to readjust to new situations and new caretakers. Deprived of the normal stability of their families and homes, the children who were fortunate enough to go into hiding were always aware of their "otherness." Most of all, they were constantly in fear of being discovered and taken away to an unknown but horrible fate.

After the war, hidden children had heartbreaking circumstances to confront. Many did not have their parents return for them. Some did not know for certain what had happened to their mothers and fathers, and so it was difficult to put closure on their losses. Many of these orphans remained with the families who had protected them, but even that was often problematic. The Jewish relief agencies tried to resettle the children in Israel, hoping to reconnect them with their Jewish heritage and at the same time increase the population of the brand new Jewish homeland. Children who had already suffered so much trauma and loss now had to readjust once again to a new country, a new language, new relationships.

Some Jewish children who had been very young when they had

gone into hiding did not even know that the families they lived with were not their natural parents. When "strangers" showed up after the war to claim their precious offspring, these young survivors found themselves in the arms of people they did not recognize or remember. Sometimes children did remember, but felt such pain at having been "abandoned" that they refused to acknowledge or reconnect with their biological parents. In short, while surviving as a hidden child required the selflessness of Jewish mothers and fathers as well as the generosity and courage of non-Jews, it was traumatic for all of the participants. Parents gave their children to anyone who could save them from deportation, not knowing how the children would be treated or where they would eventually end up. The Dutch families often became deeply attached to the children, but most of the time had to return them after the war. And of course, no matter what the ultimate resolution, the hidden children endured tremendous danger, confusion, and anxiety during those weeks, months, and even years that they were forced to live like criminals on the run or in hiding. Bereft of their childhoods, those who survived could not simply celebrate their good fortune. The Holocaust also left them with a legacy of loss.

DUTCH COLLABORATORS AND BYSTANDERS

Three thousand three hundred seventy-two Dutch Christians, including Miep and Henk Gies, have been honored as "rescuers" or "righteous gentiles" by Yad Vashem, the Holocaust Memorial in Israel. Yet, despite its claim to more righteous gentiles than any other country, the Netherlands also lost more of its Jewish population during World War II than any other Western European country, including Germany. Over 115,000 of the 140,000 Jews in Holland perished in the war.

Most people would like to believe that many Dutch citizens were like Miep and Elli, Mr. Victor Kraler and Mr. Jo Koophius, devoted to their Jewish friends and constantly providing them with not only material necessities, but also the psychological and emotional connections that made life in hiding bearable. Of course, there were others who were as brave as the Franks' protectors, but it is important to recognize that more than 80 percent of the entire Jewish population would not have died at the hands of the Nazis if so many of their fellow Dutchmen had not been accomplices, collaborators, or willing bystanders to the round-ups and deportations of the Jews. This was true throughout Europe as well. While millions of Jews needed protection from the Nazis, fewer than one-half of 1 percent of the non-Jews under Nazi occupation helped to rescue Jews!

One contemporary Dutch journalist described the situation in Holland during the war as follows:

> Dutch civil servants supplied Jewish addresses. Dutch policemen forcibly removed them from their homes. Dutch tram conductors transported them to the train stations, and the Dutch Railways sent itemized invoices to the Nazi headquarters for adding extra trains to the Westerbork transit camp.[1]

DUTCH RESCUERS

Fortunately, there were Dutch men and women who did risk their lives to save their fellow Jewish countrymen. In *Children with a Star: Jewish Youth in Nazi Europe*, Debórah Dwork describes the variety of ways in which the Jews, and especially Jewish children, were rescued in Holland. One Dutch family of farmers, the Boogaards, managed to hide hundreds of Jews on their own farm and neighboring farms. The Boogaards also arranged for Jewish children to be "kidnapped" from the Jewish orphanage in Amsterdam. Maurits Cohen, a Dutch survivor, describes what happened to him when he was eight years old:

> On a certain day, we small children walked along the streets in Amsterdam. The underground came and took me out of the line of children into a urinal and they cut off the star—back on the street—and I was sent to [the] farmer [Boogaard]. I was not told in advance. It just happened.[2]

The Dutch NV, a resistance group that worked to sabotage the Nazi effort, also organized young men and women to find and escort Jewish children into hiding. A young man would appear at the home of a Jewish family and offer to take their child into hiding. Then a young Dutch woman would accompany the child on the train to a point outside of the city where the child would be hidden with a family. Understandably, it was not easy to convince parents to give their children to complete strangers. Parents had to choose between keeping their child with them and being deported together, or giving the child to strangers with the knowledge that they might never be reunited. One resistance worker said: "The parents cried tremendously most of the time, which was very depressing. But I think the people who did it had a lot of courage. It took very much courage."[3]

THE DOCUMENTS

This chapter includes excerpts from the diaries of children in the Holocaust as well as excerpts from the memoir of a young Polish boy's Holocaust experience. Also included are interviews with Dutch rescuers who saved the lives of numbers of Jews.

NOTES

1. *Anne Frank in Historical Perspective: A Teaching Guide for Secondary Schools* (Los Angeles, Calif.: Martyrs Memorial and Museum of the Holocaust of the Jewish Federation Council of Greater Los Angeles, 1995), 24.

2. Debórah Dwork, *Children with a Star: Jewish Youth in Nazi Europe* (New Haven: Yale University Press, 1991), 37.

3. Ibid., 52.

EVA HEYMAN OF HUNGARY

The following excerpts from diaries written by children from Hungary and Lithuania give us additional perspectives on the traumatic experiences of young people during the Holocaust. They describe what was actually happening in the communities and on the streets of villages overrun by the Nazis. They tell about the everyday physical hardships of surviving under increasingly terrifying conditions. The young diarists reveal the relentless psychological stress they endured under Nazi oppression and write about the brutality they observed and suffered.

Eva Heyman's diary is remarkably similar to Anne Frank's writings in its honest and mature depiction of a young girl's life torn apart by the cruelties of anti-Semitism and hatred. Eva's passionate desire to live is one of the central themes of her diary, as she cries out on the page, "I don't want to die, because I've hardly lived!" In another entry she admits that, unlike her best friend Márta, who went with her father "to die in Poland," Eva would be willing to remain behind without her family, "without anybody at all, because I want to stay alive!" Her final entry is overwhelmingly sad. Without ever having known Anne Frank, Eva Heyman describes how desperately she wants to stay alive, even if it means hiding "in some secret cranny."

Tragically, Eva, like Anne, did not survive the Holocaust. The thirteen-year-old Jewish Hungarian girl was deported with her grandparents to Auschwitz, where they were all killed in October 1944. Eva's mother, Ági, did survive, but after getting her young daughter's remarkable diary published, she succumbed to her grief and committed suicide.

FROM THE DIARY OF EVA HEYMAN

March 31, 1944
Today an order was issued that from now on Jews have to wear a yellow star-shaped patch. The order tells exactly how big the star patch must be, and that it must be sewn on every outer garment, jacket or coat. When Grandma heard this, she started acting up again and we called the doctor. He gave her an injection. She is asleep now. Grandma doesn't

know yet that the telephones have been cut off. Ági wanted to telephone to the doctor but couldn't. Then Grandpa told her that the telephones had been taken away from the Jews, and he said that he would go and get the doctor.

April 1, 1944

We are the only ones in the neighbourhood who haven't been thrown out of our home yet. Until the order about wearing the star goes into effect, I'm moving to Anikó's house. Grandma Raćz has her attacks very frequently now. When that happens I start to shake, and Ági doesn't want me to see these attacks.

Aunt Bora was here today and asked Ági if I could stay with Anikó, because Anni is so unhappy, practically in a state of depression. God, today is April Fool's Day; on whom should I play tricks? Who thinks about that at all now? Dear diary, soon I'll be going to Anikó's house, and I'm taking along the little suitcase which Mariska packed and my canary in the cage. I'm afraid that Mandi will die if I leave her at home, because everybody's mind is on other things now, and I'm worried about Mandi. She's such a darling bird. Whenever I come near her cage she notices me right away and starts singing. Mariska will bring me to the Anikós, because she is an Aryan and with her I'll be safer in the street.

Dear diary, I'm taking you along to Anikó's house. Don't worry, you won't be alone; you're my best friend.

April 7, 1944

Today they came for my bicycle. I almost caused a big drama. You know, dear diary, I was awfully afraid just by the fact that the policemen came into the house. I know that policemen bring only trouble with them, wherever they go. My bicycle had a proper license plate, and Grandpa had paid the tax for it. That's how the policemen found it, because it was registered at City Hall that I have a bicycle. Now that it's all over, I'm so ashamed about how I behaved in front of the policemen. So, dear diary, I threw myself on the ground, held on to the back wheel of my bicycle, and shouted all sorts of things at the policemen: "Shame on you for taking away a bicycle from a girl! That's robbery!" We had saved up for a year and a half to buy the bicycle. We had sold my old bicycle, my layette and Grandpa's old winter coat and added the money we had saved. My grandparents, Juszti, the Ágis, Grandma Lujza and Papa all had chipped in to buy my bicycle. We still didn't have the whole sum, but Hoffmann didn't sell the bicycle to anyone else, and he even said that I could take the bicycle home. My father would pay, or Grandpa. But I didn't want to take the bicycle home until we had all the money. But in the meantime I hurried over to the store whenever I could and looked to see if that red bicycle was still there. How Ági laughed when I told her that when the whole sum was finally there. I went to the store and took the bicycle home, only I didn't ride it but led it along with my hands, the way you handle a big, beautiful dog. From the outside I admired the bicycle, and even gave it a name: Friday. I took the name from Robinson Crusoe, but it suits the bicycle. First of all, because I brought it home on a Friday, and also because Friday is the symbol of loyalty, because he was so loyal to Robinson. The "Bicycle Friday" would be loyal to "Éva Robinson," and I was right, because for three years it never gave me any trouble, that is, it never broke down, and there were no expenses for repair. Marica and Anni also gave their bicycles names. Marica's was called Horsie, and Anni's was called Berci just because that's such a funny name. One of the policemen was very annoyed and said: All we need is for a Jewgirl to put on such a comedy when her bicycle is being taken away. No Jewkid is entitled to keep a bicycle anymore. The Jews aren't entitled to bread, either; they shouldn't guzzle everything, but leave the food for the soldiers. You can imagine, dear diary, how I felt when they were saying this to my face. I had only heard that sort of thing on the radio, or read it in a German newspaper. Still, it's different when you read something and when it's thrown into your face. Especially if it's when they're taking my bicycle away. Actually, what does that nasty policeman think? That we stole the bicycle? We bought it from Hoffmann for cash, and Grandpa and all the others worked for this money. But you know, dear diary, I think the other policeman felt sorry for me. You should be ashamed of yourself, colleague, he said, is your heart made of stone? How can you speak that way to such a beautiful girl? Then he stroked my hair and promised to take good care of my bicycle. He gave me a receipt and told me not to cry, because when the war was over I would get my bicycle back. At worst it would need some repairs at Hoffmann's. . . .

• • •

April 9, 1944

Today they arrested my father. At night they came to him and put a seal on his door. For several days now I've known that a few hundred people are being held prisoner in the school in Körös Street, but until now they only took the very rich people.

I learned from Aunt Lili that my father has been taken away and locked up in the elementary school in Körös Street. Aunt Lili was terribly upset. Grandma Lujza sent her to us, because she has heard that it is possible to bring lunch to my father and they want me to bring the food, because if adults bring it the policemen don't allow them near the place, or they pretend that an accident happened and the food was spilled, while the prisoner goes hungry!

At twelve o'clock the meal was ready. I took potato soup, meatballs with pumpkin, and Linz pie. On the way many people stopped me to ask whether Grandpa was in prison and whether I was bringing him lunch. I said: No, I'm bringing it to my father. But I was very much afraid, because from their questions it occurred to me that Grandpa can also be put in prison, and then I really don't know what will become of us and what will I do with Grandma Raćz and Ági.

From the bridge I already saw a crowd standing and waiting in front of the elementary school building in Körös Street. When I got there, I saw that I knew nearly every single one of the people. And it seems that Grandma Lujza was right when she said that it is better for a boy or a girl to bring the meal. A crowd of boys and girls were standing and waiting in front of the school, holding food containers. While waiting to get in, I found out that my father was being held as a hostage.

While we waited, Aunt Ági explained to me that hostage means security, that is, my father has now become a security; only I don't understand how a human being can be a security. At last they let me go in to my father. Most of those securities sat in the yard on the ground. The sick ones lay in the classroom on the bare floor. Papa said that it wasn't so terrible, but it was boring and uncomfortable because there was no place to sit down alone, and he didn't feel like talking to anyone, so he had no choice but to pace back and forth in the yard of the elementary school. When I left him, it occurred to me that when I was going to elementary school, we children always used to be inside the gate and the parents would wait outside the fence to take us home after school. Now only adults, even old people, are inside the school fence, and we children are outside. There is no getting away from it: the world is topsy-turvy.

• • •

April 10, 1944
 . . . I haven't yet written in you, dear diary, what else happened when they arrested Papa. He was taken away at five o'clock in the morning and they put a seal on his door, but they forgot Juno, Papa's puppy, inside. The poor dog kept yelping inside till the neighbours nearly went out of their minds, but nothing could be done, because the apartment was sealed, and only the police can open such a seal. Aunt Lili, my father's sister, approached the police about the dog, and today my father's apartment was finally opened for a minute; dear diary, miracle of miracles: Juno was alive. It seems he discovered the giblets that were kept in the pantry. But we don't really know, because only the policemen could go into the apartment, and they brought the dog out. Now Juno is living with Grandma Lujza, but he is so sad that he hardly eats anything at all. That dog is so loyal to Papa, more so than a lot of people, says Ági.

Dear diary, Papa is kept in prison all the time, without any change. I still bring him lunch, and every day there are more and more prisoners there. Sometimes I wait for hours for my turn to come to bring in the food, and even then I don't always get to talk to him. When I'm coming home late, Ági already sits in the gate arch to hear my footsteps come up the street, because she's afraid that one day I'll become a security like my father. Life is really hard, dear diary; Good night.   (104–111)

• • •

May 29, 1944

And so, dear diary, now the end of everything has really come. The Ghetto has been divided up into blocks and we're all going to be taken away from here.

May 30, 1944

The people of Block One were taken away yesterday. All of them had to be in their houses in the afternoon. We've been locked up in here a long time, but now even those with special passes aren't allowed to go out anymore. We even know already that we can take along one knapsack for every two persons. It is forbidden to put in it more than one change of underwear; no bedding. Rumor has it that food is allowed, but who has any food left? The gendarmes took everybody's food away when they took ours. It is so quiet you can hear a fly buzz. Nobody cries. We don't even care that only Grandpa and Uncle Béla are allowed to take a knapsack.

Dear diary, everybody says we're going to stay in Hungary; the Jews from all over the country are being brought to the Lake Balaton area and we are going to work there. But I don't believe it. That train-wagon is probably awful, and now nobody says that we're being taken away, but that they deport us. I've never heard this word before, and now Ági says to Uncle Béla: Béluska, don't you understand? We are being deported! There's a gendarme pacing back and forth in front of the house. Yesterday he was in Rédey Park, from where the Jews are being deported. Not from the real railroad station, because then it would all be seen by the city, Grandpa says. As though the city cares at all. If the Aryans had wanted to, they could have prevented our being put in the Ghetto. But they were even glad about it, and now they also don't care what happens to us! That gendarme in front of the house, whom Uncle Béla calls a friendly gendarme, because he never yells at us and doesn't even speak familiarly to the women, came into the garden and told us that he will have to leave the gendarmerie, because what he saw in Rédey Park isn't a fit sight for human beings. They stuffed eighty people into each wagon and all they gave them was one pail of water for that many people. But what is even more awful is that they bolt the wagons. In this terrible heat we will suffocate in there! The gendarme says that he doesn't understand these Jews: not even the children cried; all of them were like zombies; like robots. They walked into the wagon so mechanically, without making a sound. The friendly gendarme didn't sleep all night, even though—he said—he usually falls asleep as soon as his head touches the pillow. It was such an awful sight that even he couldn't fall asleep, he said. And after all, he's a gendarme! Ági and Uncle Béla are whispering something to each other about our staying here in some kind of typhoid hospital, because they plan to say that Uncle Béla has typhoid fever. It's possible, because he had it when he was in the Ukraine. All I know is that I don't believe anything anymore, all I think about is Márta, and I'm afraid that what happened to her is going to happen to us, too. It's no use that everybody says that we're not going to Poland but to Balaton. Even though, dear diary, I don't want to die; I want to live even if it means that I'll be the only person here allowed to stay. I would wait for the end of the war in some cellar, or on the roof, or in some secret cranny. I would even let the cross-eyed gendarme, the one who took our flour away from us, kiss me, just as long as they didn't kill me, only that they should let me live.

Now I see that friendly gendarme has let Mariska come in. I can't write anymore, dear diary, the tears run from my eyes, I'm hurrying over to Mariska . . . (End of diary) (123–125)

Laurel Holliday, ed., *Children in the Holocaust and World War II: Their Secret Diaries* (New York: Simon and Schuster, 1995).

YITSKHOK RUDASHEVSKI OF LITHUANIA

Yitskhok Rudashevski lived in Vilna, a town on the Lithuanian-Russian border. In 1941, when Yitskhok was fourteen, Vilna was invaded and occupied by the Germans. Like countless other Jews throughout Europe, Yitskhok and his family were tormented by Nazi regulations aimed at demoralizing and marginalizing the Jewish victims. Nevertheless, even after the family was taken from its home and forced to live in the Vilna Ghetto, the young teen refused to surrender his spirit to German restrictions. Yitskhok and his friends continued to study academic subjects and participate in cultural activities created in the ghetto.

From June 1941 until April 1943, Yitskhok kept a diary of the "heart crushing" events in Vilna. He recorded how Jews who held yellow certificates were promised "life," while Jews with white certificates desperately sought any way to escape from certain deportation and death. To avoid being captured, Rudashevski's family went into temporary hiding with a large number of other Jews. Like the Franks, they fled to a warehouse which had a hiding place "blocked ingeniously by a kitchen cupboard." They were packed together in the stifling space, where even a child's cry could mean discovery and death.

For many increasingly unbearable months, the Jews of Vilna, including the Rudashevskis, tried to survive in the ghetto. They foraged for food, traded whatever they had for something they needed more, and always waited to be rescued from extermination by the Allies, whose maneuvers were followed with desperate interest.

On the occasion of his fifteenth birthday, and despite the extreme misery and relentless terror in the Vilna Ghetto, Yitskhok Rudashevski was able to write a hopeful entry in his diary. Much like Anne Frank, the young teen believed he would have a "new life." Also like Anne Frank, Yitskhok and his family were discovered in their hideout, in October 1943. The entire family was slaughtered at Ponar, the site of the execution of thousands of Jewish victims.

Yitskhok's diary was discovered by his young cousin who had escaped from the Germans on the way to Ponar. After the war, she returned to the hiding place she had shared with the Rudashevskis and found the diary, written in Yiddish. It is now preserved at the Yivo Institute for Jewish Research in New York.

FROM THE DIARY OF YITSKHOK RUDASHEVSKI

Wednesday the 10th of December [1942]

It dawned on me that today is my birthday. Today I became 15 years old. You hardly realize how time flies. It, the time, runs ahead unnoticed and presently we realize, as I did today, for example, and discover that days and months go by, that the ghetto is not a painful, squirming moment of a dream which constantly disappears, but is a large swamp in which we lose our days and weeks. Today I became deeply absorbed in the thought. I decided not to trifle my time away in the ghetto on nothing and I feel somehow happy that I can study, read, develop myself, and see that time does not stand still as long as I progress normally with it. In my daily ghetto life it seems to me that I live normally but often I have deep qualms. Surely I could have lived better. Must I day in day out see the walled-up ghetto gate, must I in my best years see only the one little street, the few stuffy courtyards?

Still other thoughts buzzed around in my head but I felt two things most strongly: a regret, a sort of gnawing. I wish to shout to time to linger, not to run. I wish to recapture my past year and keep it for later, for the new life. My second feeling today is that of strength and hope. I do not feel the slightest despair. Today I became 15 years of age and I live confident in the future. I am not conflicted about it, and see before me sun and sun and sun. . . .   (172–173)

· · ·

Sunday the 7th of February [1943]

We have good news. The people in the ghetto are celebrating. The Germans concede that Stalingrad has fallen.

I walk across the street. . . . People wink at each other with happy eyes. At last the Germans have suffered a gigantic defeat. The entire 9th German army is crushed! Over three hundred thousand Germans killed. The staff taken prisoner. Stalin's city is the enemy's grave. The winter offensive of the Soviets produces splendid results.

I walk in the street. . . . Winter is beginning to take leave of the little ghetto streets. The air is warm and sunny. The ice on the streets melts and oozes and our hearts are filled with spring. The snow within us melts too, and such a sunny feeling envelops us. Liberation is near. I feel its proximity with all my blood.

Sunday the 14th

All is well. All is gay. The Soviet offensive is proceeding admirably. Kharkov and Rostov have been occupied. Goebbels, the German minister of propaganda, delivered a speech full of pessimism. We were delighted at his calls for help: he appeals to all cultural nations to help Germany against the Soviets because things are in a critical state. This time Goebbels said a great truth, that if the German front collapses, Bolshevism will flood the world. And he is not even ashamed to say that the German front is on the point of falling, that one must exert all one's strength before it is too late.

Thursday the 18th

I am busy for hours at a time. It is so hard to accomplish something at school and in the club, and at the same time to be involved with cooking and cleaning. First of all reports sneaked up on us. At school we are now covering the theme Vilna in geography. I am preparing a report "On Jew[ish] Printing in Vilna." For several months now there is no light in the evenings. In the evenings we lie around in the workroom, the reading room. I often reflect, this is supposedly the ghetto yet I have such a rich life of intellectual work: I study, I read, I visit club circles. Time runs by so quickly and there is so much work to be done, lectures, social gatherings. I often forget that I am in the ghetto.

Thursday the 25th of March

A command was issued by the German regime about liquidating five small ghettos in the Vilna province. The Jews are being transported to the Vilna and the Kovno ghetto. Today the Jews from the neighboring little towns have begun to arrive. It is rainy and gray outside. Sadly the peasant carts ride into the ghetto like gypsy covered wagons. On the carts Jews with children, their bag and baggage. The newly arrived Jews have to be provided with dwellings. The school on Shavler 1 has been pre-empted for the newly arrived Jews. The school on Shavler 1 was moved into the building of our school. They are teaching in two shifts. Today we went to class in the evening. Our studies somehow no longer have any form. We are all depressed. We are in a bad mood.

Sunday the 28th

The mood in the ghetto is a very gloomy one. The crowding together in one place of so many Jews is a signal for something. The transportation of food through the gate has become very difficult. Several people have already been arrested on Lukishki. People walk around gray and worried. Danger is hovering in the air. No! This time we shall not permit ourselves to be led like dogs to the slaughter! We have been discussing this lately at our [. . .] and are prepared at any moment. We have to improve ourselves. This thought strengthens our nerves, gives us courage and endurance.

Monday the 5th [April]

Sunday at 3 o'clock the streets in the ghetto were closed off. A group of 300 of the Jews from Sol and Smorgon have left for Kovno with a large transport of provincial Jews that arrived at the railway station. As I stood at the gate I saw how they were packing their things. Gaily and in high spirits they went to the train. Today the terrible news reached us: 85 railroad cars of Jews, around 5000 persons, were not taken to Kovno as promised but transported by train to Ponar where they were shot to death. 5000 new bloody victims. The ghetto was deeply shaken, as though struck by thunder. The atmosphere of slaughter has gripped the people. It has begun again. Once more the sparrow hawk spurs are in evidence. People sit caged in as in a box. On the other side lurks the enemy which is preparing to destroy us in a sophisticated manner according to a plan, as today's slaughter has proved. The ghetto is depressed and mournful. We are unprotected and exposed to death. Again there hovers over the little Vilna ghetto streets the nightmare of Ponar. It is terrible, terrible. People walk around like ghosts. They wring their hands. Toward evening an urgent gathering. The situation has been confirmed. We have no one to depend on. The danger is very great. We believe in our own strength. We are ready at any moment.

Tuesday the 6th

The situation is an oppressive one. We now know all the horrible details. Instead of Kovno, 5000 Jews were taken to Ponar where they were shot to death. Like wild animals before dying, the people began in mortal despair to break the railroad cars, they broke the little windows reinforced by strong wire. Hundreds were shot to death while running away. The railroad line over a great distance is covered with corpses. We did not study in school today. The children run away from their homes where it is terrible to stay on account of the mood, on account of the women. The teachers are also despondent. So we sit in a circle. We rally our spirits. We sing a song.

In the evening I went out into the street. It is 5 o'clock in the afternoon. The ghetto looks terrible: heavy leaden clouds hang and lower over the ghetto.   (180–183)

Laurel Holliday, ed., *Children in the Holocaust and World War II: Their Secret Diaries* (New York: Simon and Schuster, 1995).

YEHUDA NIR OF POLAND

There were as many versions of "hiding" as there were victims of Nazi anti-Semitism. Some Jews were forced to hide for months in pits dug into the ground; some hid in haylofts, not able to make a sound or move for hours at a time. Some Jews even managed to hide in the midst of Nazi-occupied communities by passing as gentiles. Yehuda Nir, a Polish Jewish boy, his mother, and his older sister were able to survive the Holocaust by getting false papers that claimed that they were Polish Catholics.

Yehuda Nir was born in Lwów, Poland, in 1930. By the time he was nine, his country had been invaded by the Germans, and the Jewish boy became one of the 3.5 million Polish Jews targeted for extermination. After his father was rounded up and executed along with hundreds of other Jewish men, Yehuda, his mother, and his sister moved from place to place in Poland, working for Polish and German gentiles. They often were separated from each other.

While his mother and sister were light-haired and blue-eyed, and therefore could more easily pass as non-Jews, Yehuda's darker hair and brown eyes made him more vulnerable to being identified and deported. In addition, as a circumcised Jewish male, the young boy was in constant fear of being discovered; anyone who was suspicious of his background could have insisted that he strip off his clothes and would have had proof of his Jewish heritage. Yet, by dying his dark hair yellow and dressing in a uniform that looked like those worn by Hitler Youth, Yehuda Nir managed to outwit both the German and Polish perpetrators.

At one point during the war, the thirteen-year-old veteran of subterfuge and suffering joined a volunteer resistance army. His job was to deliver grenades to the Polish fighters by carrying the ammunition through the underground mazes of Warsaw. Although the young teen knew that at any moment he could be blown up by the materials he carried or by the gunfire aimed at him by snipers, he was determined to fight for his survival.

Yehuda Nir wrote his memoir many years after the events he describes. After meeting "the only other child survivor" of his grammar school in Lwów, Nir began to think about his Holocaust experiences and decided to write them down. Today, Yehuda Nir is a professor of psychiatry in New York.

FROM YEHUDA NIR, *THE LOST CHILDHOOD: A MEMOIR* (1989)

The Germans entered a week later, on June 30, 1941, my mother's thirty-eighth birthday. They were busy chasing the Russian army and left the policing of the city to their local friends the Ukrainians, who went at it with a vengeance. Within days the Ukrainians had organized a police force and started arresting Jewish men on the street and sending them to the city jails. My uncle Schmerl was among the first arrested, but he escaped several days later while being transferred to another prison. Although he had been in jail for only two days, his stories were full of terror. This was my first direct encounter with Nazi brutality, and I was overwhelmed with fear. Schmerl returned bruised, haggard, *changed*. With mounting apprehension, we listened to his horrifying tales of the abuse he had experienced, the innocent people he had seen killed, the conditions in jail.

After listening to Schmerl, my father ordered a "total alert." None of us, especially the men, were to leave home. My mother was now officially in charge. If food was available, she or I would do the shopping. Lala was too attractive to go out; she would be easy prey for the Germans or the Ukrainians. No one talked about it, but we all felt that our days were numbered. We were trapped, afraid to leave our third-floor apartment.

The Germans' first decree required all citizens to turn in their radios within twenty-four hours. Disobedience would be punished with death by hanging. This order put an end to our contacts with the outside world, our only source of moral support and strength. Together, my mother and I carried our Telefunken to the police station. My father watched us silently, his sad, deep brown eyes telling his feelings. He tried to crack a smile of encouragement when we awkwardly lifted the large box, but the smile didn't materialize. He looked about to cry. We were carrying out a part of him.

This was probably the last week of my father's life. The German army was preoccupied, probably overwhelmed by the ease of its victory on the front, and was not interfering with the attacks of the Ukrainian police on the Jews. This was not yet the era of the "Final Solution," but the Germans were pleased to give the Ukrainians—originators of pogroms, virulently anti-Semitic since the seventeenth century—a free hand. It was a green light for murder. The Ukrainians were aware that this was only a temporary arrangement, that the Gestapo would take over as soon as the

Germans caught up with the moving front, so they had to hurry. Hundreds of Jews were rounded up daily, marched to the woods, and executed with machinegun fire. We had been aware of the police brutality since my uncle's arrest, but we did not know about the mass executions until much later. The bloodbath reached its climax on "Petlyura day." [Petlyura was a Ukrainian official killed in 1926 in Paris by a Jewish student.] When the police came for my father and my uncle that morning, we hoped that it was just a temporary arrest. My father didn't resist, and I followed him to the local police precinct where all the Jews were being held. Two hours later the police came for my mother. She was lying on the living-room couch, sad but not crying. When the Ukrainians arrived, she refused to go, claiming to be ill. "You'll have to carry me out if you want me," she said. Had she said this a year later, they would have shot her on the spot, but in July 1941 their procedures of arrest were in disarray and they let her stay.

My mother's passive resistance on that day was a decisive factor in my surviving the war. Had she gone with them, I would never have seen her again. The police were back an hour later to take Lala. This, however, was for a specific assignment: to wash the toilets at the police station. I was ignored; I guess they couldn't figure out what to do with an eleven-year-old boy.

Worried about my father, I followed Lala to the local precinct. My mind was racing. I was overwhelmed by the rapid flow of events. My father and my uncle arrested, my mother sick and resisting the police, my sister washing toilets for the police—what would come next? As we approached the building, I spotted a column of men, six abreast, marching out of the police yard surrounded by Ukrainians with submachine guns. My father was next to his brother in the row before the last. Our eyes met. He seemed surprised to see me on the street, and didn't notice Lala.

I followed the column for a little while. Father turned around once and gave me a faint smile, like the one I had seen on his face a week before when we carried out the radio. I waved to him, but failed to catch his eye. One of the policemen noticed, however, and, aiming the submachine gun at me, forbade me to follow the column. I stood in place for several minutes until the prisoners were gone.

I would never see my father again.

With tears rolling down my cheeks, I slowly returned home. Lala came back late in the afternoon, exhausted and frightened. She had seen all the people at the station who were arrested with my father, and she had witnessed the brutal treatment they received. She had heard the first rumors about my father's fate: the men were being loaded on freight trains and sent to a coal mine in Austria. These rumors, with some variations, persisted for many months. Hundreds of Jewish men had been apprehended on Petlyura day, and their families had no information on their whereabouts. Later, we found out that the Ukrainians had walked the men to a forest near Lwów called Piaskowa Gora, lined them up, and executed them with machine guns. My father had been murdered the day he was arrested.

But for years we didn't know whether my father was dead or alive. We thought of him not as dead, but away. I had recurrent dreams of his return, of accidentally meeting him on the street or on a train. My father never died; he just faded away, was carried off into nowhere. It was as if he were dead and alive at the same time. Even after the war, in 1945, when we found out that he had definitely been killed on the day of his arrest in July 1941, we continued to search for him through the Red Cross.

With Father's arrest, our life-style changed rapidly. The leader was gone and the surviving members of the family unit had to reshuffle their positions. Leading was not my mother's style; she chose instead to be the senior member of a triumvirate. From then on, decisions were made jointly, based on available information and alternatives for action. Age and experience did not matter, since we were all new to this brutal game of survival.

San Diego, Calif.: Harcourt Brace Jovanovich, 1991, pp. 22–26.

Young children were especially vulnerable during the Holocaust. Too small to be used as slave labor, they were immediately gassed with their mothers upon arrival at the death camps. Children who were fortunate enough to be hidden always risked being discovered and sent to their deaths. Nir's six-year-old cousin, Julek, was one of those innocent victims of atrocity who was executed by the Germans while in hiding with his grandparents.

• • •

Sonia could not keep her son Julek in her professional apartment, so she sent him to her parents in Stanislawow. In May 1942, six-year-old Julek was executed with his grandparents in the Jewish cemetery of Stanislawow. The Germans had gathered all the people who didn't work—hundreds of women and children—and shot them with machine guns.

The image of this child before a machine gun was intolerable to us all. Little Juleczek, as we used to call him affectionately, had been the darling of the family. Delicate, like his father, his blond hair in a curled pompadour, he symbolized the pampered, well-bred, new generation of our family, its growing affluence and well-being.

My aunt and uncle were numb with grief. They must have felt guilty for not having kept the child with them, although they couldn't be blamed. It had seemed, at the time, that people in smaller towns were safer. But Arthur stopped shaving and entered a period of mourning that he maintained until he was killed two years later in a concentration camp. He also stopped talking. Sonia had to continue to work and to maintain her composure while her heart was torn with grief. As the closest in age to Julek, I felt particularly vulnerable. The feeling of protection I had been afforded by the idea that I, as a child, could remain unnoticed was shattered by the bullet that killed my little cousin. Suddenly I felt that I might be next. Age no longer offered protection. Nothing did.

Julek's murder and the move to the ghetto were catalysts for our plans to escape. Ludwig was the key to our survival. We were totally dependent on his skills, talents, courage, and imagination. He had already taken the first step: he had obtained baptismal certificates for his mother and his younger sister Marysia, and escorted them on a train to the small resort town of Swoszowice, near Kraków. Even with Aryan papers, we felt, it was perilous to stay in Lwów. There was a strong possibility of our being recognized by gentiles as former neighbors or acquaintances, and reported to the police. It was not uncommon for the Pole who recognized a Jew on the street to blackmail the victim; take all his money and then turn him over to the Germans. Although their hatred of the Germans was centuries old, many Poles eagerly helped in the liquidation of the Jews. These blackmailers were not motivated by greed alone; for them it was a labor of love.   (42–43)

After five grueling years under German occupation, the Polish people were desperate to regain their freedom. Resistance groups and armies fought back with whatever weapons they could collect or fabricate. The sense of excitement and elation created by striking back at the Germans made even the most dangerous missions worth the risks. Inspired by other Jewish resistance fighters, Yehuda Nir joined the Polish armed forces. He was determined "to kill at least one German before I was killed. It made no sense to sit and wait. I still remembered vividly the group of five Jews who had escaped with guns from the burning Warsaw ghetto."

• • •

I was given a hand grenade and made a courier. I was assigned to deliver messages, supplies, ammunition, and food to outposts all over the inner city. This was a dangerous task because it entailed continuous exposure to the enemy, particularly snipers. The standard means of communication—radios and field telephones—were in very limited supply, so couriers were crucial to the war effort.

I didn't reveal my true identity. I was concerned about the possibility of being taken prisoner of war by the Germans, and I knew that I had a better chance for survival if they didn't know I was a Jew.

• • •

. . . The courier unit had originally been composed of five members. One of my predecessors had been killed the day before I joined, and his funeral had taken place just two hours before my induction into the army. He was buried in the yard. Through the window Stefan showed me a small grave, one of several, with a plain wooden cross on it. The other missing courier was in the hospital. He had stepped on a mine and had both legs and his left arm blown off. The news about the dead boy didn't disturb me very much. Even seeing his grave at the doorstep was something I could cope with. I wasn't ready, however, for the second story. The possibility of being mutilated had never crossed my mind. My two companions noticed my reaction—I must have grown very pale—but they didn't make fun of it. They were mature for their age, seasoned by the war. Basia even offered me a glass of water.

After a short lull, the fighting exploded with increased vehemence. I was active around the clock. Until I joined the army I hadn't been aware that, in this type of house-to-house warfare, one of a courier's major tasks was moving ammunition to outposts through endless trenches, cellars, and tunnels. The assignments were both dangerous and exhausting. In the third week of the uprising we were already producing our own ammunition, Molotov cocktails and flame throwers: primitive but effective weapons. As it was difficult to travel through the underground maze, only small quantities of ammunition could be carried at a time. The courier who had been killed had tried to shorten the trip by walking on the street. A sniper's bullet had hit one of the Molotov cocktails he was carrying, setting him afire. Occasionally a Molotov cocktail exploded on its own, making our work even more dangerous. We were forbidden to use open routes except when carrying messages of extreme urgency. We were also directed never, under any circumstances, to let the Germans catch us with a message. If there was no other way to avoid being caught, we had to use the hand grenade, our only weapon, to destroy ourselves and the message.   (162, 164–165)

• • •

The sludge got deeper, to midcalf, and it was very slippery. I was afraid that I might fall and explode one of the Molotov cocktails. I tried to hold on to the rounded wall, but it was slippery too and offered limited support. To make things worse, the pipes were getting progressively narrower. By now I had to bend in order to walk without hitting my head. The tall men in the unit were bent double, some on their knees, carrying their heavy loads in front of them.

We almost failed to see the first open manhole in German-occupied territory. Walking at night offered some protection, as the Germans couldn't see us from above, but it also had the disadvantage of making it difficult to discern which manholes were open and which were not. Fortunately, the man leading our outfit (the captain was in the back helping the other fourteen-year-old, who had suddenly started to cry) saw a reflection of a star in the thick sludge and realized that it was from an open manhole. We froze, almost falling over one another. After retreating several yards, Captain Komarek followed the master plan. He threw an object into the sludge just under the cover and it made a loud splash. We heard voices from the street, and then there was a frighteningly loud explosion that blew us off our feet into the cold, muddy, filthy water. It must have been more than a hand grenade. The captain's next command came in a whisper, "Move quickly past the manhole." We proceeded in silence now, some of us on all fours. My heart was thumping rapidly. I could hardly catch my breath, waiting for the Germans to throw in the second grenade. They didn't. Instead, we heard an announcement in Polish, through a bullhorn, calling on us to surrender, assuring us that we would be treated according to the Geneva Convention. Such offers were traps. The Germans machine-gunned people the moment they emerged from the manhole.

• • •

Now we were faced with a new problem: the sludge was getting thicker and deeper, reaching my waist. My shortness, an advantage in the earlier tunnel, was now a serious handicap. Someone suggested that the Germans were trying to drown us in excrement by setting up a dam in the section under their control. This must have been on everybody's mind. Once verbalized, it somehow changed from a personal fear to a potential reality. Silence followed the remark. I assumed that everyone was feeling the same way, gripped by the fear of a horrible death, drowning in sewage. Being the shortest in the group, I thought of myself as the most vulnerable, but I cared less and less as time went by. I must have been getting intoxicated by the fumes.

By the time we approached the third manhole, the situation had reached crisis proportions. Two of the men, both in their early twenties, announced that they had had enough; they couldn't take it anymore. They wanted to surrender to the Germans.

The captain tried at first to dissuade them, calling their decision "insane, suicidal." They would not relent. Then he threatened to shoot them for disobedience, for treason. As might have been expected, they didn't care, and challenged him to go ahead. There was no way to stop them. One of the men took off his shirt, which must have been white at some point, and made a makeshift flag, using his arm as the flagpole. We all focused our flashlights on him, trying to help in his preparation for the climb to the surface. He and his colleague handed their guns to Captain Komarek, who, in turn, gave one to me and the other to the woman. We were the only ones who hadn't carried guns before.

The man with the white flag didn't say goodbye. Instead, he said "Long Live Poland!" a farewell I always associated with people about to be executed. He walked, cautiously, the few steps that separated us from the manhole, followed closely by his companion, who was holding onto him. They didn't use flashlights, to avoid being detected before their climb. It was a pathetic sight, two seasoned soldiers walking like helpless frightened children, each waving a white rag.

The man with the flag started to climb, his arm stretched above him. There was total silence until he was halfway out and then, suddenly, a short burst of machinegun fire. I didn't hear his scream; his head was above the ground. His body fell with a splash into the sewer, dragging in the second man, who sank to the bottom under the weight of the dead body. The captain motioned us to retreat. He was right this time. The Germans followed the shooting with a hand grenade, blowing both men to pieces.   (180–183)

RESCUERS IN HOLLAND

The testimonies of Jewish Holocaust survivors are being collected and documented with great care by such organizations as the Fortunoff Video Archive for Holocaust Testimonies at Yale University, and Steven Spielberg's Survivors of the Shoah Visual History Foundation. In addition to Jewish stories of displacement, terror, and enormous suffering, there are also the narratives of those who saved Jews from the Nazi perpetrators. Over the years, social scientists and theologians have tried to determine what circumstances or what personal characteristics were required for a person or even an entire community (Le Chambon in France) to risk their lives, and often the lives of their families, in order to save other human beings.

Many rescuers say they simply did what they felt was necessary when faced with a situation that required compassion. Some knew Jews personally and began by helping those friends. Some rescuers say they had been taught to care for others by their parents, and some, like Miep Gies, the Austrian-born woman who protected the inhabitants of the secret annex, had herself been rescued by a generous Dutch family during World War I. She understood how it felt to be a victim, and she was determined to help others who needed protection and aid.

Like Holocaust survivors' stories, each rescuer's story is unique. Yet these Dutch rescuers do share a modest courage and an ability to empathize with others which is beautifully expressed by one rescuer, Johannes DeVries, who says: "When you would close the door on someone like that and you heard later that he was destroyed, how would you feel the rest of your life? I think I would be destroyed myself."[1]

Marion P. Van Binsbergen Pritchard estimates that she saved about 150 Jews during the Holocaust. As a young graduate student in psychology, she formed a network of friends who helped find refuge and food for Jews, and she hid Jewish victims of Nazi persecution in her own home. After the war, Marion Pritchard continued to help the survivors of the Holocaust by working in a displaced persons' camp.

When she came to America as a young bride in 1947, Marion

Pritchard found that people were not interested in hearing about what had happened during the war. She stopped talking about her experiences but continued to find work that involved helping Jewish refugees "put their lives back together." Her three sons never knew about their mother's heroic deeds. She did not believe that telling them her history would influence her children to behave altruistically. Instead, she encouraged her children to question people's behaviors and motives. She believed that "children must be helped to develop their own sense of what is right by questioning." She also served as a role model for her sons, because "it will make a difference if a child sees their parents behave in a caring way about larger issues. . . . They'll see if their parents are racist, if they're anti-Semitic, if they support war and things like aid for the Contras, they'll probably grow up to do the same."

Marion Pritchard is still in contact with some of the people she rescued during the Holocaust.

Yad Vashem honored the 250 citizens of Nieuwlande, Holland, for their rescue of hundreds of Jews. Arnold Douwes and Seine Otten and his wife, Dirkje Jantje, found or provided shelter for Jews who were being rounded up for deportation to concentration camps.

Arnold Douwes did not wait to be asked for help. He traveled to Amsterdam looking for Jewish families. He would tell them, " 'Come with me. I know a wonderful farm where there is plenty of food and you'll be safe.' Was there such a place? Of course not." Douwes brought the Jews back to Nieuwlande and the Ottens. In all, the Ottens hid fifty Jews in their own home during the war, and together with Douwes placed many others in safe quarters.

Like that of many other "rescuers," Douwes's altruistic behavior was natural to him. He had already tried to help a victim of racism years before when he was living in the United States. He recalls, "One day during the thirties, I sat down at a lunch counter in Chicago, and there was a black man sitting there, but no one was serving him. I started talking to him and found out what was going on, so when my food came I gave it to him and I ordered another meal. The owner of the restaurant didn't like that, and he called the police and I was arrested."[2]

FROM GAY BLOCK AND MALKA DRUCKER, EDS., *RESCUERS:
PORTRAITS OF MORAL COURAGE IN THE HOLOCAUST* (1992)

Marion P. Van Binsbergen Pritchard

I was born in 1920. My father was a liberal judge in Amsterdam, and
a member of the board of regents of the prisons there. I learned tolerance
from him. He was more accepting of all people and their differences than
my mother, who was tiny, tough, cheerful, critical, self-confident, very
British and class-conscious. She wasn't the intellectual my father was, but
he wasn't brazen the way she was. When they returned from a trip
abroad, she would hide her cigarettes and he would declare every one
of his 150 cigars. Being a judge, he did the right thing while she played
her illegal radio with the windows open.

I think it was my parents' unusual way of child-rearing that provided
the motivation for me to behave the way I did during the war. I was never
punished and always encouraged to express my feelings, both the negative and positive ones, in words. And when I asked questions I got answers. I was never told I was too young or anything like that. I was treated
with respect and consideration from the time I was born.

I went to a private school where there were Jews in every class. In
Holland, the Jews were considered Dutch like everyone else. I wanted to
become a therapist so, at nineteen, I entered the school of social work
in Amsterdam, and was there when the Nazis occupied Holland in 1940.

The Germans didn't start attacking Jews immediately. It is much easier
to segregate a part of the population when the rest is with you. So they
began mildly, with propaganda. One example is a film we were required
to see in school called *The Eternal Jew*. We sat through it, laughed aloud,
and thought it was ridiculous, but what impressed me in retrospect is
that one of the students said to me the next day, "You know, that was
an awful movie, scurrilous, and I don't believe a word of it, but what it
has done is divided us into 'them' and 'us.' I wish it didn't, but now I
look at people and say, 'Huh, you're Jewish.' " And this was a person
who was determined to help Jews, but the split had been made. Then
there was the Aryan attestation. If you were Jewish you filled out one
form and if you were Aryan, as they call it, you filled out another. My
father refused to sign the form, as did I. He had read *Mein Kampf* and
believed Hitler would do what he said. But when I spoke that way to my
friends, especially my Jewish friends, they didn't want to accept it. Some
even became angry. But I'm action-oriented like my mother.

Even my twelve-year-old brother wanted to take action. He and his
friends put on the yellow star. My mother told him to take it off, but my

father supported my brother. The question is: when is a child old enough to take a stand? Anyway, my brother had a terrible experience which demonstrates the randomness of the German response. He was coming home from school and he and his friends were talking about the Germans and called them "lousy Krauts." The officers overheard them and took them to headquarters. They let my brother go after about forty-five minutes, but called the other boy's mother and gave her a choice. They told her that her son had been disrespectful to the occupying forces and asked if she wanted them to give him a beating or if she wanted her husband arrested. She was fixing lunch for the other kids, right? So she told them to give the boy the beating and they told her when to come pick up her son. Well, when she went to pick him up, he was dead. Twelve years old.

• • •

Just about this time, I witnessed a terrible thing. One morning on my way to school I passed a small Jewish children's home. I saw the Nazis loading children, from babies to about eight years old, onto trucks. They were all crying, and when they didn't move fast enough, a Nazi would pick them up by an arm or leg, or even hair, and throw them onto the trucks. I was so shocked by this treatment that I found myself in tears. Then I saw two women coming down the street try to stop them, and the Germans threw them into the trucks, too. I stood frozen on my bicycle. Before this I had known of the threats but I hadn't actually seen the Germans in action. When I saw that, I knew that my rescue work was more important that anything else I might be doing.

A friend of mine was hiding with her husband and was pregnant. The people keeping them couldn't have a baby in their apartment so I asked another couple, also friends of mine, to take the baby when it was born. They said they were already giving money to save Jews, and were paying for Jews to have plastic surgery, but they felt that taking a child was a bit much. But the next morning they had changed their mind. She pretended to be pregnant and fixed a nursery and hired a nurse. They had a nanny for their four other children, but decided to have nothing to do with the baby so they wouldn't get attached. The baby was premature and the nurse wasn't available, so I stayed for a week, taking care of him. Well, the baby was fine but the parents didn't survive. I heard at the end of the war that he had been totally accepted as a member of their household, and they were trying to decide whether to tell him about his parents. I thought it was wonderful, whether or not they told him, but the Zionists later informed me otherwise.

The nursery where the Germans placed all Jewish children who were on their way to Westerbork was next door to a teachers' college. The workers in the nursery along with the student teachers smuggled out more than 1,000 Jewish children in laundry hampers, knapsacks, and the like. These were average people you might never think would do this. So one can't know what one would do.

One day I was given a little girl to place in a home in northeast Holland. I was told this was sure thing, that if I took her there they would take her. When I arrived after a long train ride, the man at the station told me that the address was not available. I was tired, so he invited me to his house to rest before returning to Amsterdam. They were people of modest means, and in his house were his wife and four or five children. I fell asleep and when I woke up the woman was changing and feeding the baby and this was how these people made up their minds. We talk about moral decisions. These people just knew that this was the thing God would have wanted them to do. When the man walked me back to the station he apologetically explained that they had told the other children that this was my illegitimate baby and that my punishment would be that I could never see it again. It was a safe story so the villagers wouldn't be suspicious. And this is just one day.

In 1942 I was asked by friends in the resistance to find a place for a man, Freddie Pollak, and his three small children, aged four years, two years, and two weeks. I decided to move them into a large house in the country which belonged to an older woman whose son-in-law was a friend of Freddie's. In that year, I only came to live with them on weekends, but by 1943, I moved in full-time to take care of the children while Freddie worked on his thesis. Of course, I became very attached to the children, especially Erica, who was just a baby when we started. I maintained the fiction for the people in the neighborhood that they were my children, but some people knew, I'm sure. I didn't teach them prayers, but they had Christian names.

We had some floorboards removed under a rug, and built a hiding place in the basement in case of raids, which we had at times. One night four Germans and a Dutch Nazi policeman came to search the house. Everyone was in the hiding place and they didn't find it. But a short time later the Dutch Nazi returned alone. He had learned that Jews were often in hiding places, and that if you returned just after a raid you might catch them in the house. That's exactly what had happened. Erica had started to cry, so I let the children come up. When the Dutch policeman came back, I had to kill him with a revolver a friend had given me but I had never expected to use. I know I had no choice, but I still wish there had been some other way. An undertaker in town helped me dispose of the body by putting it in a coffin with another body. I hope the dead man's family would have approved.

There was no such thing as a routine day, even after I was hiding the

Pollak family. In the village of Huizen, near where we were living, was a house called "Het Hooge Nest." The people living there were Lientje Brilleslijper, the daughter of a Jewish family of circus artists and musicians, her Aryan, common-law German husband, Piet, and their daughter, Kathinka. Lientje and Piet had decided early that not only were they going to survive personally, but they would assist as many others as they could in the process. They invited all Lientje's Jewish relatives to join them. They also concentrated on keeping Jewish culture and tradition alive through their work as artists. Lientje was a dancer and singer, Piet was a musician. Another fifteen to twenty-five Jews were living in the house at various times. They were warned repeatedly that they were taking too many chances, but their response was always the same: "How can we refuse anyone who comes to us for shelter?" (33–37)

Arnold Douwes and Seine Otten

SEINE: Two Jewish boys, Peter [Isador Davids] and Herman [Lou Gans], did resistance work but they couldn't be seen out on the street very much. They stayed in our house for a long time. They worked with pen and ink and paint and paper drawing and writing all kinds of cards and pamphlets against the Germans to encourage the inhabitants of Nieuwlande. Herman especially was very clever drawing cartoons representing events that ridiculed the Germans. We sold these cards to get money for poor divers and for resistance efforts. A typical one shows a woman carrying packages, holding the hand of a child who's walking behind her. The message is from the New Testament and says in Dutch, "Never forget to be hospitable, for by hospitality some have entertained angels unawares." On the back it reads, "Help the people in hiding and buy this card for more than you can afford."

ARNOLD: Peter and Herman did more than stay inside and draw. Once we were taking a Jewish girl to a hiding place, and we had hired a taxi, which was unusual but necessary that night. A German soldier stopped us and asked for a ride, so we had to let him in. He never guessed what we were really up to.

In 1943 Johannes Post had to leave Nieuwlande because it wasn't safe, so I took over his work. I stole everything from ration cards to bicycles. I sent messages by carrier pigeon to England. I found hiding places for Jews, and I picked them up and took them. I worked twenty hours every day. Our greatest enemy, after the Nazis, was time. We never had enough hours in a day. We could never do enough. I didn't have a family like Seine. He risked more. I think only those with families should have gotten medals from Yad Vashem. Anyway, who needs a medal? I did my job and the Jews did theirs by keeping out of the hands of the Germans. That was their work, and it was very difficult. I could not have done it myself. Just imagine, for two years, to sit in a little hole or some damn place or other. It's enough to make you go mad, but they did what they had to do, and that's quite enough for me. Yes, they saved themselves and their families; they had the courage to sit it out for such a long time. Just imagine what that means.

SEINE: It was terrible sometimes, but we had a lot of fun, too. At night we'd be home after the eight o'clock curfew, and we'd all sit around the table and tell stories. Arnold's were the best. I'll tell you one: I was warned, early in 1944, that my name was on all the Nazi lists and I should get out of Nieuwlande. But I wouldn't leave without my wife and son. So on May 10, 1944, we went to a neighboring farm about six kilometers from home.

ARNOLD: On that night, Seine was gone and Nico [another member of the Resistance] and I were in the basement hiding place trying to put a message on a carrier pigeon's leg informing the Allied forces in England that there were Nazi V-2 rocket parts hidden underground at a nearby airfield. The Gestapo came to the house and searched for three hours, but all they found was the false hiding place in the attic. When they finally left, we let the pigeon go. The next day the Allies bombed the airfield and I got the message back from another pigeon: *"Carpe diem!"* That was a great day. We sent many messages like that. Still we didn't do enough. It's a disgrace that 100,000 Dutch Jews died in Auschwitz. Even in a place like Nieuwlande, it was hard to place Jews.

SEINE: Johannes Post was a real hero. Later on he formed a commando troop to rescue friends who had been captured. In July 1944, he was on such a rescue mission, but there was a traitor in his group and he was arrested. He and two of his comrades were condemned to death, and on July 16 he was executed. You should know that after the war a well-known Dutch writer wrote a book about Post. His wife is still alive and nearly ninety years old. He was a real hero. We were not heroes, not really. We had hope that it would come to an end without disaster.

ARNOLD: It wasn't a question of why we acted. The question is why things weren't done by others. You could do nothing else; it's as simple as that. It was obvious. When you see injustice done you do something against it. When you see people being persecuted, and I didn't care whether they were Jews or Eskimos or Catholics or whatever, they were persecuted people and you had to help them.

SEINE: People ask me if I taught my children to help other people. I don't think that's the point. Look, for the three months since my wife died my daughter has come here three or four times a day. She has cooked meals for me. And besides that, she goes once every fortnight to the old-age home to visit a man who has one leg and who is blind and deaf. I tell her this is nice of her, and she says, "No, it's my duty. It's so we don't feel alone in the world." And that is the whole point. Arnold lives an hour away, and he can't travel by himself, but still he has been to see me three times since my wife died.

ARNOLD: Seine helped me rescue Judith, the woman who became my wife. We went to Israel and lived on a *moshav* [a farm community]. We have three daughters who are still there. I think of the war every day.

SEINE: Perhaps ten or twenty years from now when we are no longer alive there won't be articles in the paper every week about the war, perhaps then the war will be forgotten. But not yet.

New York: Holmes and Meier, 1992, pp. 66–67.

NOTES

1. *Rescuers: Portraits of Moral Courage in the Holocaust*, Gay Block and Malka Drucker, eds. (New York: Holmes and Meier, 1992), 22.

2. Ibid., 62.

TOPICS FOR WRITTEN OR ORAL EXPLORATION

1. How do the additional diary excerpts by young teens help you to understand what happened during the Holocaust? Write a letter to Eva or Yitskhok in response to what you have learned about them from their diaries. Write a letter from Anne Frank to Eva and Yitskhok.

2. Read the diary of a young person that describes life in a different period in history. How much do you learn about the period? How much do you learn about the writer?

3. Yehuda Nir's narrative is a memoir. How is it similar to Anne Frank's diary? How is it different? What are some of the advantages of a memoir? Its limitations?

4. Choose one of Anne Frank's diary entries and rewrite it as if it had been written in memoir form by an older Anne Frank. What have you changed? Why?

5. Write a scene in which Eva Heyman, Yitskhok Rudashevski, Yehuda Nir, and Anne Frank meet. What is the setting? the year? What do they say to each other?

6. Have you ever risked your own safety or well-being to help another person? Why did you do it? How did you feel? Write a story describing the event and its consequences.

7. Miep Gies considered herself a "rescued" child. She attributed her willingness to help others to her personal history as an Austrian child saved by the Dutch after World War I. Read a biography or memoir about a rescuer. Write a profile of your subject focusing on the factors that made this person willing to risk his or her life to save others.

8. Oskar Schindler, the subject of Steven Spielberg's film *Schindler's List*, was a Polish businessman who rescued hundreds of Jews from extermination in Auschwitz. Raoul Wallenberg (Denmark), Chiune Sugihara (Japan), and Aristedes de Sousa Mendes (Portugal) also risked their own careers and lives to help thousands of Jews escape the Nazis. Wallenberg was imprisoned by the Russians after the war and is believed to have died in captivity. Sugihara and Sousa Mendes disobeyed their country's official orders and issued thousands of transit visas to desperate Jews trying to leave Europe. As a result of their insubordination, both men lost their government positions and lived in poverty for many years. Research any of these rescuers' stories and write a scene in which you recreate a confrontation between one of them and an official opposed to their actions on behalf of the Jews.

9. The civil rights movement was a dramatic example of how people of different races worked together to fight discrimination. Write a report

on a person or a group of people who participated in helping to bring about greater racial equality.

10. Not all situations require that people be rescued from Nazis or be hidden or smuggled to safety for their survival. What other kinds of contemporary situations challenge us to be "rescuers" of those who need our help? Make a list of these kinds of circumstances and then write a report on a person or group of people who have helped others in need.

SUGGESTED READINGS

Children in the Holocaust

Abells, Chana. *Children We Remember: Photos of Children from the Yad Vashem Collection*. New York: Greenwillow, 1986.

Dwork, Debórah. *Children with a Star: Jewish Youth in Nazi Europe*. New Haven: Yale University Press, 1991.

Fisher, Josey G., ed. *The Persistence of Youth: Oral Testimonies of the Holocaust*. Westport: Greenwood Press, 1991.

Greenfeld, Howard. *The Hidden Children*. New York: Ticknor and Fields, 1993.

Marks, Jane. *The Hidden Children: The Secret Survivors of the Holocaust*. New York: Fawcett, 1993.

Tatelbaum, Itzhak. *Through Our Eyes: Children Witness the Holocaust*. Jerusalem: I.B.T. Publishing, 1985.

Volavkova, Hana, ed. *I Never Saw Another Butterfly: Children's Drawings and Poems from Terezin Concentration Camp, 1942–1944*. New York: Schocken Books, 1993.

Memoirs and Diaries of Children in the Holocaust

Alland, Bronislawa. *Memoirs of a Hidden Child During the Holocaust*. Translated by George Alland. Lewiston, NY: Edwin Mellen Press, 1992.

Bauman, Janina. *Winter in the Morning: A Young Girl's Life in the War-saw Ghetto and Beyond, 1939–1945*. New York: The Free Press, 1986.

Flinker, Moshe. *Young Moshe's Diary: The Spiritual Torment of a Jewish Boy in Nazi Europe*. Jerusalem: Yad Vashem, 1965.

Heyman, Eva. *The Diary of Eva Heyman*. Translated by Moshe M. Kohn. New York: Shapolinsky, 1974.

Holliday, Laurel, ed. *Children in the Holocaust and World War II: Their Secret Diaries*. New York: Simon and Schuster, 1995.

Nir, Yehuda. *The Lost Childhood: A Memoir*. San Diego: Harcourt Brace Jovanovich, 1991.

Siegal, Aranka. *Grace in the Wilderness: After the Liberation, 1945–1948*. New York: Puffin Books, 1994.

———. *Upon the Head of a Goat: A Childhood in Hungary, 1939–1944*. New York: Farrar, Strans and Giroux, 1981.

Toll, Nelly S. *Behind the Secret Window: A Memoir of a Hidden Childhood During World War Two*. New York: Dial Books, 1993.

Victims, Survivors, and Rescuers

Bierman, John. *Righteous Gentile: The Story of Raoul Wallenberg, Missing Hero of the Holocaust*. New York: Anti-Defamation League, 1981.

Block, Gay, and Malka Drucker. *Rescuers: Portraits of Moral Courage in the Holocaust*. Rev. ed. New York: Holmes and Meier, 1992.

Brecher, Elinor J. *Schindler's Legacy: True Stories of the List Survivors*. New York: Plume, 1994.

Fogelman, Eva. *Conscience and Courage: Rescuers of Jews During the Holocaust*. New York: Anchor Books, 1994.

Hallie, Philip. *Lest Innocent Blood Be Shed: The Story of the Village of Le Chambon and How Goodness Happened There*. New York: Harper and Row, 1979.

Keneally, Thomas. *Schindler's List*. New York: Simon and Schuster, 1982.

Langer, Lawrence. *Holocaust Testimonies: The Ruins of Memory*. New Haven: Yale University Press, 1991.

Levi, Primo. *The Drowned and the Saved*. New York: Summit Books, 1988.

Lifton, Betty Jean. *The King of Children: A Portrait of Janusz Korczak*. New York: Schocken Books, 1989.

Linnea, Sharon. *Raoul Wallenberg: The Man Who Stopped Death*. Philadelphia: Jewish Publication Society, 1993.

Meltzer, Milton. *Rescue: The Story of How Gentiles Saved Jews in the Holocaust*. New York: HarperCollins Children's Books, 1991.

Oliner, Samuel P., and Pearl Oliner. *The Altruistic Personality: Rescuers of Jews in Nazi Europe*. New York: The Free Press, 1988.

Rittner, Carol, and Sandra Myers. *The Courage to Care*. New York: New York University Press, 1986.

Stadtler, Bea. *The Holocaust: A History of Courage and Resistance*. West Orange, N.J.: Behrman House, 1975.

Stein, André. *Quiet Heroes: Dutch-Canadian Rescuers of Jews*. Toronto: Lester and Orpen Dennys, 1988.

Tec, Nechama. *When Light Pierced the Darkness: Christian Rescue of Jews in Nazi Occupied Poland*. New York: Oxford University Press, 1986.

Related Works

Asscher-Pinkhof, Clara. *Star Children*. Detroit, Mich.: Wayne State University Press, 1986.
Forman, James. *The Survivor*. New York: Farrar, 1976.
Moskin, Marietta. *I Am Rosemarie*. New York: Dell, 1987.
Reiss, Johanna. *The Journey Back*. New York: Harper and Row, 1976.
———. *The Upstairs Room*. New York: Holt, Reinhart and Winston, 1974.
Van Stockum, Hilda. *Borrowed House*. New York: Farrar, 1975.

Video Documentary

Binford, Mira Beym. *Diamonds in the Snow*. New York: Cinema Guild, 1994.

6

Anti-Semitism in Modern Germany

The 6 million Jews who were annihilated during the Holocaust were victims not only of Nazi Germany's genocidal plan. Jewish men, women, and children were also killed or sent to their deaths by Austrians, Poles, Romanians, Ukrainians, French, Italians, and others. Although the Jews were not at war with any of these nations, nor a threatening majority in any of these countries, they were singled out to be discriminated against and scapegoated. Ultimately, two-thirds of all European Jewry died as a result of anti-Semitism in the middle of the twentieth century.

It is impossible ever to explain the reasons for the kinds of evil that occurred during the Holocaust; yet much of the justification for the systematic persecution of the Jewish people was rooted in prejudices and myths that go back thousands of years. Although anti-Semitism was an integral part of many European cultures, it was in Germany that it took its most diabolical form during the twentieth century. Over the course of many centuries, the myths about the "evil" Jews were so deeply ingrained in the psyches of generations of German citizens that when the economic and social upheavals following World War I disrupted the personal lives of many Germans, the most "obvious" culprits were the Jews. They were said to be plotting to control the world economy and ultimately planning to control the world. Of course, given the fact that the Jews were less than 1 percent of the entire population in Germany and had no way of waging war (much less defending themselves!) against their "Aryan" countrymen, this rampant and vicious anti-Semitism was clearly not based on reality. Instead, Adolf Hitler and his Nazi followers used the Jewish people as scapegoats. They projected their frustrations and anger onto the Jews, who had had a long and tragic history of being discriminated against, and even killed, for their religious beliefs.

The word *Holocaust* originally comes from a Greek word meaning "offering made by fire unto the Lord" or "whole burnt offering." In the second half of the twentieth century, however, the Holocaust has come to mean a particular event in human history, the systematic annihilation of 6 million Jews by the Nazis and their collaborators during World War II. During the Holocaust, many of the victims of Nazi genocide were burned alive, and often their bodies were destroyed in crematoria after they had been gassed in killing chambers. The Jews did not willingly die fighting for a just cause or offer themselves as martyrs to God. They were victims of hatred and prejudice. They were killed by other human beings who used poison gas, bullets, clubs, and attack dogs as well as the fires of the crematoria to eliminate 6 million innocent souls.

Although Hitler and his armies fought countless military battles during World War II, it was the painstakingly deliberate and well-organized destruction of the Jews that motivated Hitler's actions and inspired his most ambitious plans. He was determined to eliminate all traces of a race of people—their artifacts, their culture, and above all, their very being. He was determined to commit genocide.

PREJUDICE AND DISCRIMINATION

Unfortunately, anti-Semitism is only one form of prejudice. Racism, sexism, even ageism exist as forms of discrimination against people who are judged and often shunned based on their assumed characteristics and qualities. In this century, the Holocaust is the most stunning and ghastly example of how prejudice and hatred can overwhelm human reason and lead to unthinkable crimes against "others."

When we prejudge someone on the basis of his or her skin color, ethnic heritage, religion, gender, socioeconomic status, or any of a number of other characteristics, we are not seeing that person as a unique individual. We often make value judgments about that person based on our ideas about the group they happen to belong to. This is called stereotyping. Stereotyping often also sets up a comparative value system, leading to a "better than" and "worse than" way of thinking about ourselves and others. When we stereotype someone we create a barrier between that individual and ourselves. As a result, it is more difficult to identify and empathize with that person, and our ability to see the other person as having the same fears, problems, needs, and joys as ourselves is impaired.

Discrimination occurs when a prejudice is turned into action. For example, in the 1930s the Germans gradually made it more and more difficult for Jews to work and survive in Germany. Jewish businesses and shops were boycotted, and legislation was passed that prevented Jews from practicing their professions, working as civil servants, or teaching or attending the same schools as other Germans. Incrementally and methodically, the Jewish people were marginalized, humiliated, and left utterly vulnerable to the next stages of Nazi persecution.

In most everyday encounters, discrimination presents itself in less dramatic but nevertheless harmful forms. Clubs that bar membership to women or blacks or Hispanics, or landlords who make every effort not to rent to members of certain groups, are practicing discrimination. Even in the classroom, discrimination makes itself felt in the amount and kind of attention that is paid to boys as compared to girls. Whenever and however they happen, prejudice and discrimination distort and limit our ability to share and enjoy the world with a variety of people. In their worst forms, prejudice and discrimination create hatred, violence, and despair; and ultimately, they can destroy the very fiber of the society in which they are allowed to exist.

THE HISTORY OF ANTI-SEMITISM IN GERMANY

Anti-Semitism flourished in Germany for many hundreds of years before Adolf Hitler came to power in 1933. The earliest form of anti-Semitism was founded on the belief that the Jews had been responsible for the death of Christ. As a result of this myth, Jewish communities were often pillaged and destroyed, Jewish cemeteries were desecrated, and Jews were persecuted and killed. Even when there was no overt violence against the Jews, they had no civil rights and were ostracized socially, economically, and politically from the rest of German society.

Not only were the Jews considered "Christ killers," they also came to be stigmatized as usurers. Although Christians considered it sinful to charge interest on borrowed money, they needed moneylenders in their society. The Jews, excluded from working in many kinds of professions and crafts, had no choice but to take on the role of moneylenders in Germany. Yet, by performing this vital role, they became the target of gentile resentment and hatred. The non-Jewish population resented its dependence on Jewish moneylenders and accused the Jews of being sinners in league with the devil.

By 1350 the Jews were forced to live in separate walled-off sections of many German cities. To further set them apart from their Christian neighbors, German Jews were forced to wear a "Jewish hat," a pointed black hat which looked like a dunce cap. (Nearly six hundred years later, the Nazis required Jews to wear yellow stars on their clothes to identify themselves as Jews.) Isolated from the rest of the German people, and without political power, the Jews were exploited by the rulers of each German state. For example, Prince Ludwig the Bavarian proclaimed that "the Jews belong to us and the empire in body, soul, and earthly goods . . . we can do with them as we please and as we find convenient."[1]

As a result of this isolation, the Jewish people formed close-knit, vibrant communities of their own. Since they were not permitted to share the schools, orphanages, and other social institutions available to their German neighbors, the Jews created their own social and cultural institutions. They also created their own language, Yiddish, and nurtured countless teachers, writers, and rabbis over the centuries. Unfortunately, while this separateness helped develop a vibrant Jewish culture, it also intensified the differences and "otherness" of the Jewish people. As a result, anti-Semitism continued to flourish.

THE PROTESTANT REFORMATION

The Protestant Reformation, which began in 1517, ultimately brought new discrimination against the Jews. Martin Luther, a German monk, founded Protestantism after being excommunicated from the Catholic Church for protesting against its corruptions. Hoping to convince Jews to convert to his form of Christianity, Luther at first encouraged his followers to treat the Jews "in a brotherly manner." However, by 1543, having been unsuccessful in converting Jews, Luther issued a document, *Concerning the Jews and Their Lies*. The historian Paul Johnson called this document "the first work of modern anti-Semitism, and a giant step forward on the road to the Holocaust."[2] Luther wrote:

> First, their synagogues or churches should be set on fire, and whatever does not burn should be covered or spread over with dirt so that no one may ever be able to see a cinder or stone of it in order that God may see that we are Christians, and that we have not wittingly tolerated or approved of such public lying, cursing and blaspheming of His Son and His Christians. . . . Secondly, their homes should likewise be broken down and destroyed. For they perpetuate the same things there that they do in their synagogues. For this reason they ought to be put under one roof or in a stable, like gypsies, in order that they may realise that they are not masters in our land, as they boast, but miserable captives. . . . Thirdly, they should be deprived of their prayerbooks and Talmuds. . . . Fourthly, their rabbis must be forbidden under threat of death to teach any more.

He ended his diatribe thus: "Dear princes and nobles who have Jews in your domains, if this advice of mine does not suit you, then find a better one so that you and we may be free of this insufferable devilish burden—the Jews."[3] Luther also attacked the Jews for being usurers, what he called "no greater enemy of man, after the Devil," and urged his followers "to break on the wheel and kill . . . hunt down, curse and behead all usurers!"[4]

The vocabulary Martin Luther used to describe usurers ("enemy" and "Devil") had originally been used to describe the Jews as "Christ killers." Now, Luther used this hate-inspiring language to blame the Jews (since *usurer* was a code word for Jew) for their work as moneylenders. Slowly, but critically, a shift was occurring away from anti-Semitism based on religious differences toward anti-Semitism based on what eventually came to be considered inherent *racial* differences.

GERMAN NATIONALISM

Germany's defeat in the Napoleonic Wars at the beginning of the nineteenth century left the German people without economic, military, or political power. In reaction to this demoralization, and in order to develop a strong sense of nationalism, Germans were encouraged to look back to the folkways and folklore of their past. As they turned to the literature and myths of the pre-Christian pagan era and the romantic chivalry of the Middle Ages, they confirmed their own heroic past and created an image of the ideal German, a brave and loyal citizen who was racially "pure."

German philosophers fueled this nationalism in their writings. One philosopher argued against giving Jews their emancipation, saying, "The only way in which [one] could concede giving rights to Jews . . . would be 'to cut off all their heads in one night, and to set new ones on their shoulders, which should not contain one Jewish idea.' "[5]

Nationalism also nurtured the concept of the Germans as a *Volk*, a people who shared not only common roots through their culture, language, and history, but who also shared an "essence." Germans were encouraged to think of themselves as part of a larger unit than their families and to live for the betterment of the *Volk*. According to German propaganda, anyone who did not share in the heritage of the *Volk* was an outsider and was not only different, but also inferior. Jews were clearly in this category. This idealization of the German past and the need to protect and nurture its values would become Hitler's excuse to eliminate the Jews in the 1930s.

Discrimination against Jews was reinforced by journalists, academics, and political leaders. For example, Friedrich Rühs, a professor of history at the University of Berlin, argued in his essay "The Claims of the Jews for Civil Rights in Germany" against giving the Jews the same rights as their Christian neighbors. He recommended branding Jews with a "distinctive badge," restricting the number of Jews in each community, and prohibiting Jews from immigrating to Germany in order to protect German interests.

The conclusion to Rühs's, essay used benign prose to hide malevolent anti-Semitism: "The truly moral life . . . can only be a Christian life." Therefore, Rühs proposed, "everything should be done to bring them by kindly methods into Christianity and thereby to actual assumption of German national characteristics, in order to effect the gradual disappearance of the Jewish people in this manner."[6] Rühs's "kindly methods" were meant to slowly eliminate the Jews from Germany. His writings, as well as those of many other anti-Semitic Germans, set the stage for Adolf Hitler, who in the next century also would call for and implement the "disappearance of the Jewish people." Tragically, Hitler's methods were meant to eliminate all Jews for all time, not by converting them to Christianity, but by starving, torturing, gassing, and burning them to death.

In addition to growing nationalism, Germany's political and economic organization also made life for the Jews particularly difficult. Until it was unified in 1871, Germany was comprised of thirty separate states, each ruled by autocrats who had unlimited power over the people. The Jews were at the mercy of the harsh restrictions and taxations imposed by these rulers, who hoped the Jews would convert to Christianity in order to escape taxation. In one German city taxes were levied against the Jews "for the poorhouse and cemetery; for New Year presents; for a goose at the Feast of Saint Martin, for the arch-priest; for ringing the bells in the parish of St. Emeran."[7] Because they were burdened with every conceivable tax to support the rest of the state, most of the Jewish population lived in poverty. Jews were also required to pay exorbitantly high taxes in order to marry or have a child; as a result, many Jews were condemned to living without families. There were also restrictions on where they could live and the kinds of property they could own. Without the civil rights and equal protection under the law they had briefly enjoyed during Napoleon's reign, the Jews owed their allegiance and much of their income to the rulers of the German states. All of these restrictions and taxes condemned the vast majority of Jews to live at the edge of desperation, and because of their extreme poverty they were seen as undesirable members of society.

Not surprisingly, one reaction to loss of Jewish emancipation was conversion to Christianity. Just as Rühs had urged in his writings in 1815, some Jews chose to be baptized in order to gain a foothold in the secular German world. As Christians they could practice law, enter larger social spheres, and even become part of the political process. Many "converted" Jews went on to become extremely distinguished entrepreneurs, artists, and scientists, including the poet Heinrich Heine and the political economist Karl Marx.

A NEW FORM OF RACISM

Ironically, the short-lived emancipation of the Jews in the early part of the nineteenth century created new problems and hostilities. To encourge assimilation and thereby eventually "eliminate" the Jews from the country, German law required Jewish citizens to use the German language or a language other than Yiddish for all of their legal transactions. Jews were also required to take German family names. (In the twentieth century, Hitler reversed this law and ordered all Jews to have their identification papers stamped with the name Israel for men and Sarah for women so that Jews whose names did not "sound" Jewish could be detected.) Because they were now more free to participate in the activities of the communities in which they lived, the Jews were also more frequently in contact with the gentile populations, who continued to discriminate against them. The deep-seated biases against the Jewish people did not disappear; instead, new explanations for the old prejudices were presented in the "scientific" theories that developed.

In 1859 Charles Darwin, a British biologist, published *The Origin of Species*, in which he argued that species are always competing for limited resources and therefore must change and adapt to their environments in order to survive. Those that are most successful in this process go on to reproduce themselves. Herbert Spencer, a fellow Englishman, applied Darwin's theory to human development, proposing that human beings also competed and struggled with each other for the necessities of life. Spencer described the results of this process as "the survival of the fittest." He believed that this selection among humans was a "natural" process, and therefore the less "fit" were doomed to extinction, while the "fittest" humans had the right to rule. This theory came to be known as Social Darwinism.

A variety of studies in linguistics, phrenology, and anthropology all fueled the growing racism in Germany during the middle and late 1800s. The Jews were now considered different and inferior not because of their religious beliefs and practices (the old anti-Semitism), but because *inborn* qualities made Jews wicked, materialistic, and cowardly. This shift away from an anti-Semitism based on conflicting religious beliefs to an anti-Semitism rooted in racism, the belief that the Jews had intrinsically different physical, moral, and intellectual characteristics, made it easier to condemn the Jews as being inherently inferior and dangerous to the welfare of the German nation.

As Germans became more secular and nationalistic, discriminating against Jews because of their religion became less relevant. A new way of expressing hatred for the Jew was required. Racial difference became a more effective weapon against the Jews. The word *anti-Semitism* officially came into existence in 1879. This "scientific" term was based on racial theories about the "Semitic" and "Aryan" races and did not even include the term *Jew* in its formulation. Wilhelm Marr, a German journalist and anarchist who blamed the Jews for Germany's economic and social crises, founded the first Anti-Semitic League in Europe. Marr argued that their "racial qualities" had enabled the Jews to become far more powerful than the German people and that, as a result, "Germanism was lost." Needless to say, this kind of rhetoric did nothing to help the Jews become more accepted or integrated into German society.

MODERN ANTI-SEMITISM

As the nineteenth century was coming to a close, European society was changing rapidly and dramatically. The Industrial Revolution forced people to leave their farms and move into crowded cities in order to support themselves. Rigid class systems were breaking up, and power and wealth were being redistributed. Within this historical context, and with equal rights finally granted in 1869, the Jewish population in Germany had taken advantage of their new freedoms and opportunities in the professions and had become successful in business, journalism, and academics. With their increasing visibility in all areas of commerce, the Jews became a target for those who wished to return to a simpler society rooted in agriculture, crafts, and small businesses. Since the Jews were seen as being at the forefront of the changes in the expanding industrial and social fabric of the country, they were blamed for all the complex problems that accompanied those changes. "The

Jewish conspiracy" became the explanation for everything that was wrong in Germany.

ANTI-SEMITIC PROPAGANDA

The German population was continually barraged with literature about the evils of the Jew. Popular fiction reinforced the stereotypes of the Jew as a traitor and as an undesirable alien in German society. Even more dangerous were the writings of well-educated academicians who were quoted as "experts." One historian, Heinrich von Treitschke, published essays in 1881 in which he expressed his alarm over the growing Jewish populations in major cities and in educational institutions. He claimed that the Jews were an "alien element which has usurped too much space in our life." He stirred up feelings of fear and envy by writing, "If one considers that the most beautiful and most magnificent house of worship in the German capital is a synagogue, a fact which, of course, does not reflect on the Jews but on the Christians—then it can absolutely not be denied that the Jews are more powerful in Germany than in any other Western European country."[8] In the same year, a quarter of a million Germans signed an "Anti-Semites Petition" demanding that Jews be excluded from all government and teaching positions.

Anti-Semitism became more and more institutionalized as Germany increasingly suffered social and economic difficulties and the Jews continued to be blamed for the country's problems. Jews were attacked, riots broke out, and synagogues were burned. In 1882 the first International Anti-Jewish Congress met in Dresden, and other such gatherings were held in 1886 and 1889.

GERMANY AFTER WORLD WAR I

The loss of World War I brought to an end Germany's sense of itself as a glorious power. Forced to sign the Treaty of Versailles after their defeat, the Germans were stripped of their military and naval might, were required to pay huge reparations to the Allied governments, and were occupied by Allied forces to ensure that they complied with the treaty. Humiliated and shocked by this reversal in status, the German people were eager to find explanations and scapegoats for the decline of their military and economic power. Although many Jews, including Otto Frank, had served with distinction in the German army during World War I, the Jews were blamed for Germany's defeat; once again there was a resurgence of anti-Semitic propaganda and policies.

HITLER'S RISE TO POWER

Intellectually, socially, and psychologically, Adolf Hitler was poorly prepared for any significant position in society. Born in Austria in 1889, Hitler was one of six children, four of whom died in childhood. His father died when Hitler was fourteen, and his mother died four years later. Hitler dropped out of high school and was rejected twice by the Vienna Academy of Fine Arts, where he hoped to train as an artist. Alone in Vienna, without a home, job, or friends, Hitler lived in poorhouses and ate in soup kitchens. He did not fit into the cosmopolitan, sophisticated city, and he especially felt uncomfortable in the midst of so many different nationalities of people.

In 1913 Hitler moved to Munich, Germany, and joined the German army the following year. He served as a dispatch runner in World War I and was wounded twice, including by poison gas in 1918. Stunned and outraged by Germany's defeat, Hitler returned to Germany. He fervently believed that the Aryan people were superior to all others, and he could not accept the fact that Germany had lost the war. He, like many Germans, needed to find an explanation for the political and economic humiliation their once-great nation now suffered. In Munich, Hitler saw high unemployment, poverty, and violence. He also became aware that the newly formed democratic government, the Weimar Republic, was not effective in solving the country's problems. Although he had no experience in government or leadership, Hitler decided to go into politics to redeem Germany and reclaim its rightful place as a great world power.

THE NAZI PARTY

In 1919 Hitler joined a small group of disgruntled war veterans, the German Workers' Party, and by 1920 he had renamed it the National Socialist German Workers' (Nazi) Party. Hitler believed that in this new and still pliable group he could assert his power and create a movement that would change the fate of Germany. From the beginning, Hitler and his Nazi Party were determined to reclaim Germany for the Aryan people.

The swiftest and most complete "Aryanization" required immediate measures. The Nazi Party developed a twenty-five Point Program which specified that no Jew could "be a member of the nation." Jews were also to be deprived of the right to vote or hold political office. These points, among others, revealed the direction the Nazi Party would take in relation to its "aliens." In addition, the German people would be influenced through Nazi control of the educational system and the press. At the same time, everything would be done to eliminate, or at least limit, the power of non-Aryans, especially the Jews.

Ironically, although a number of German Jews did hold important positions in many of the more visible areas of commerce, science, culture, and education, the Jewish people were only 1 percent of the entire German population, and the vast majority of Jews were not in positions of power or influence, nor did they have significant wealth. The Nazi obsession with Jewish "power" was a complete distortion of what was actually happening in Germany after the war.

One historian, James Parkes, analyzed the Nazis' use of the Jews as scapegoats after World War I as follows:

> Germany was far too weak in the early days of the Nazi movement for public attention to be directed against the real enemies, France, or the Allied Powers in general; and the Nazi Party within Germany was also too weak to risk carrying its attack against the Weimar Republic to the point of compelling its Government to take vigorous action. . . . What was wanted was an enemy sufficiently concrete to be usable in the most vulgar propaganda addressed to the most ignorant sections of the populace, and sufficiently weak to give the Nazis a cheap victory, both psychological and physical. The Jews of Germany exactly supplied the need.[9]

To further fuel the growing anti-Semitic fervor, the *Protocols of the Elders of Zion* appeared in Germany in 1920. Originally published in Russia in 1903, the *Protocols* claimed to reveal the secret plans of the "international Jewish conspiracy" to take over the world. Although it was fictitious from beginning to end, the *Pro-*

tocols of the Elders of Zion became a best-seller in Germany as well as in many other countries where it appeared. (Today, it is still being sold all over the world, including by the Nation of Islam in the United States.)

The *Protocols* was proved to be a forgery in 1921, yet its anti-Semitic message confirmed Hitler's own racism and gave him more "evidence" that the Jews were a threat to the welfare of Germany.

Not many people outside of his party took Hitler and his fellow Nazis seriously. They considered him a harmless "raving maniac" because of his highly emotional speeches and self-aggrandizing claims. Yet, as economic conditions in Germany continued to deteriorate, more and more people came to listen to the man who promised them a better life and security if they joined his Nazi Party. In addition to his political organization, Hitler created a military wing of brownshirted storm troopers, Sturmabteilung (SA), who protected his meetings and harassed anyone who opposed him. With his inflammatory speeches and physical intimidation by his SA, Hitler was creating an atmosphere of hatred and fear that attracted those who felt alienated and hopeless about their lives. These people needed to find an outlet for their anger and frustration. Hitler's Nazi Party gave them a group to belong to and a cause to fight for.

Hitler claimed that he wanted to create a "good society" founded "on the consciousness of race, blood, and soil."[10] However, unlike a democratic society, where the political life of the people is only one aspect of their daily experiences, Hitler intended to control the social, cultural, and personal experiences of all Germans. He and his Nazi Party would determine what newspapers people could read, what books would be published (or burned), the art people could see in museums, and the clubs they could belong to. Hitler claimed he was making these choices and decisions in order to unify the German nation and make its Aryan citizens the greatest people on earth. By continually brainwashing the population with Nazi propaganda and physically threatening those who opposed him, Hitler eventually achieved control over all aspects of German life.

In 1923, as his followers continued to increase in number, Hitler tried unsuccessfully to overthrow the government. Although he was found guilty of high treason and sentenced to five years in prison, he served only nine months. During that time he dictated

Mein Kampf (My struggle) to Rudolph Hess, a close ally. *Mein Kampf* was supposed to be Hitler's autobiography. Instead, it turned into his explanation of why Germany lost World War I (the Jews) and his plan for how to regain Germany's former stature (get rid of the Jews). In his book, Hitler rambled from one subject to another, making outrageous claims without providing evidence or proof for his statements.

In the preface to *Mein Kampf* Hitler explained that he wrote his book "as it may serve to destroy the foul legends about my person dished up in the Jewish press." From that page on, the over-whelming theme in *Mein Kampf* was Hitler's intense hatred for the Jews. Jumping from one topic to another and writing in long, disorganized sentences, Hitler used images and language that combined the older Christian forms of anti-Semitism with the newer racist diatribes. He wrote:

> With satanic joy in his face, the black-haired Jewish youth lurks in wait for the unsuspecting girl whom he defiles with his blood, thus stealing her from her people. With every means he tries to destroy the racial foundations of the people he has set out to subjugate. . . . It was and it is Jews who bring the Negroes into the Rhineland, always with the same secret thought and clear aim of ruining the hated white race by the necessarily resulting bastardization, throwing it down from its cultural and political height, and himself rising to be its master.[11]

Often using words like "vampire," "toxins," and "plague" to describe the Jews, Hitler indirectly revealed his future plans in the final pages of his book: "If at the beginning of the War and during the War twelve or fifteen thousand of these Hebrew corrupters of the people *had been held under poison gas,* . . . the sacrifice of millions at the front would not have been in vain" (emphasis added).[12] Hitler made it very clear, for those who wished to take his words seriously, that there was nothing he would not do to rid his beloved Germany of the "satanic" Jew.

But Hitler's personal hatred of the Jews was not enough. Hitler understood that he needed to appeal to the emotions, not the minds, of the German people in rallying them behind his ambitions. In *Mein Kampf* he analyzed the methods and purposes of propaganda, proclaiming that "the whole art consists in doing this so skillfully that everyone will be convinced that the fact is real, the process necessary, the necessity correct, etc." He believed that the majority of people were of "the most limited intelligence" and therefore "all effective propaganda must be limited to a very few points and must harp on these in slogans."[13] In other words, while he insisted that the German people were superior to all others, he in fact believed that the vast majority of them were not very smart and were gullible enough to be controlled by slogans. Through the sheer force of his personality, through physical intimidation by his military forces, and by inundating the people with vicious anti-Semitic propaganda, Hitler set out to become the one and only Führer of Germany and eventually, he hoped, ruler of the entire world.

THE GREAT DEPRESSION

It wasn't until 1929 that Hitler's tyrannical ambitions had an opportunity to take root. The worldwide Great Depression that followed the New York stock market crash immediately affected the German economy. Factories and businesses were forced to close, unemployment increased dramatically, and once again people wanted someone other than themselves to blame for their troubles. Since the government of the Weimar Republic could not solve the nation's economic problems, a number of political parties reasserted themselves, including the Nazis, who pandered to those who wanted simple explanations and easy solutions.

Between 1928 and 1932 support for the Nazi Party grew dramatically. Nazi representation in the parliament grew from 12 seats in 1928 to 196 by 1932. Although this still was not a majority of the seats and represented only 33.1 percent of the vote, Adolf Hitler had created a following which the government in power believed could be useful in opposing the growing Communist movement. As a result, Hitler was appointed chancellor of Germany in 1933. The leaders who appointed him believed that Hitler would be more easily controlled once he was in office; once he too failed to resolve the economic problems of the nation, his potential power would be diminished, if not destroyed. They were disastrously wrong.

THE BEGINNINGS OF THE HOLOCAUST

Within eight weeks of becoming chancellor, Adolf Hilter made himself Führer, the sole ruler of the Third Reich of Germany. He had convinced the German people that in order to save the nation from being overthrown by Communists and Socialists they had to pass an Enabling Act giving him unlimited powers. By disbanding the existing government, he became a dictator who was free to make and break laws. He immediately ordered his storm troopers, both the SA and SS (the latter bodyguards for Hitler and his allies chosen from SA units who would become the notorious guards in concentration camps), to loot, burn, and wreck Communist and Socialist offices. People were assaulted and arrested without proof of wrongdoing, and the first concentration camp was set up in Dachau to contain those who "agitate and cause unrest."

At the same time that Hitler began eliminating those whom he considered a threat to his absolute power, he also began to reestablish the German economy and rebuild the country's military strength. He knew that he needed to point to real accomplishments to keep the trust and allegiance of the German people. Yet his overwhelming fixation continued to be his hatred of the Jews. From the very beginning of Hitler's dictatorship, Jews were beaten, taken into custody for questioning, and constantly intimidated by the SA and the Gestapo, the Nazi police. In addition, the first anti-Jewish decree was issued just two weeks after Hitler came to power. This decree provided for the dismissal of "non-Aryan" civil servants. Two weeks later, the Law Against the Overcrowding of German Schools and Institutions of Higher Learning established quotas for students of "non-Aryan descent." The quota was 1.5 percent! Soon, at the instigation of the government, Jewish businesses were boycotted and Jews were forced out of their professions.

THE NUREMBERG LAWS

By September 1935, the economic, physical, and psychological abuse against the Jews was intensified with the passage of the Nuremberg Laws. Jews were now "legally" a separate race and therefore not entitled to German citizenship and rights. In addition, the Law for the Protection of German Blood and German

Honor prohibited marriage and sexual relations between Jews and Germans. Through these racist laws and actions the Jews were increasingly impoverished and humiliated. Hitler had succeeded in cruelly differentiating the Jews from the rest of the population, and then he pointed to those differences as proof of the Jews' "natural" inferiority.

HITLER YOUTH

One of the most diabolical methods of indoctrination into Nazi ideology was the organization known as the Hitler Youth. Boys age six and up were required to belong to youth groups. The groups provided their youngest members with social activities and physical exercise, but increasingly also prepared their older members "to join the ranks of the fighters against the Jewish enemy."[14] Many boys initially joined the youth groups out of a desire to belong to a social club. However, as Hitler's power in Germany grew, he decided that the youth groups would be the key to his future success. The Hitler Youth would be systematically trained to obey their Führer and to do *anything* for the sake of Germany.

Racist ideology was the foundation of the Hitler Youth training. Every member was taught that as a Hitler Youth he was superior to those outside of the movement. Within the organization, however, a hierarchy existed that prepared young boys to acknowledge the superiority of those older and more experienced than themselves, as well as the inferiority of those younger. In the guise of brotherhood and adventure, Germany's young males were turned into obedient racists. As many as 200 times a day, a Hitler Youth would be expected to raise his right arm and say "Heil Hitler" out of respect to his Führer.

Constant identification with Nazi ideology shaped and distorted the minds of an entire generation of German youth. At the same time, superior physical strength and the ability to endure physical hardship were also critically important goals for Hitler Youth members. With terrifying foresight, Hitler was preparing a huge army of men who would follow all Nazi commands and would be willing to suffer any hardships in the name of their beloved country and leader.

German girls had a very different mission to accomplish. Their sole purpose was to breed German male offspring who would serve in the Nazi army. Unlike their brothers, German girls were not required, and sometimes not allowed, to take courses in the sciences, mathematics, or any other academic areas that would stimulate their intellect or ambition. Instead, females were required to develop their domestic skills. Girls were encouraged to marry at a young age. However, if a young female became pregnant out of wedlock, rather than being ostracized, she was supported by the state. Like their male counterparts, German girls were required to develop their physical stamina and physique, but only so that they could bear many healthy German children.

During Adolf Hitler's dictatorship, German boys and girls were brainwashed and poisoned psychologically. They were taught to be mistrustful of everyone, including their own parents and teachers, who could, according to Nazi propaganda, be enemies of the state. Young people were indoctrinated to believe that their allegiance was to their Führer and the nation, rather than to their families and friends.

In *How Democracy Failed*, former Hitler Youth members describe their experiences with the movement. One member's father had fought in World War I and had lost a leg in combat. Bitter about Germany's defeat, the father became an ardent Nazi and brought his young son with him to Nazi Party meetings. His son recalls:

> I thought he was a hero . . . and since most of my schoolmates ridiculed my father, I spent many evenings with him at meetings, listening to the speeches, singing the songs of the new Germany, where war heroes would be respected instead of despised, and waiting for the great day. . . . I used to take notes in class on teachers who didn't show proper respect for our country, because I felt that some day those notes would be useful in cleaning out the schools of traitors and cowards.

As an adult, this former Hitler Youth member now "wonders guiltily what may have happened to the men and women he denounced." However, "he still considers those early days in the Hitler Youth Movement as one of the high points of his life. 'Everybody thought I was important then,' he adds. 'Nobody considers me important now.' "[15]

German parents often reinforced Nazi policies and thereby made it easier for their children to accept injustices perpetrated against others. One German woman remembers:

> After Hitler came into power and I joined the girls' Hitler Youth Movement, I had a glorious time for a while. But my mother continued to look unhappy and worn. We were Catholics, and she spent more and more time in church. My father was furious with her for not joining the Nazi women's group in the neighborhood. Once, when she came home from Mass, he beat her. He told her in no uncertain terms that the priest in our parish was "a bad German" because he refused to obey party orders to report members of his congregation with Jewish ancestry to the local authorities. He ordered her to stop associating in any way with the Church. She obeyed.[16]

Hitler's indoctrination of the young people of Germany spread beyond the Hitler Youth groups and into every aspect of their lives. Textbooks were rewritten in order to present Germany's history in the most glorious and inspiring terms. Schools were required to remove other textbooks from their curricula, and libraries were required to remove certain titles from their shelves. Every kind of information was meant to convey the racial superiority of the German people and, conversely, the natural inferiority of all others, but especially the Jews.

At first, many lonely, alienated young boys and girls joined the Hitler Youth in order to feel important and to get the attention and sense of belonging they missed in their personal lives. Much like young people today who join gangs for camaraderie and status but end up in serious trouble or even dead, Hitler Youth members did not necessarily understand the full horror of what they were being trained to think and do. As Hitler's hunger for power escalated, all young people were required to join the movement. The Hitler Youth became accomplices to their Führer's diabolical ambitions.

KRISTALLNACHT

Many identify the horrifying beginnings of the Holocaust with the shocking events of Kristallnacht (night of broken glass). On November 9, 1938, a distraught Jewish student killed a Nazi diplomat in Paris. In retaliation, Hitler ordered "riots" to break out "spontaneously" throughout Germany and Austria. The sounds of breaking glass filled the night air. Synagogues, Jewish institutions, and over 7,000 Jewish businesses were looted, burned, and destroyed. Even though it was the Jews who were being attacked by the Nazis, Hitler ordered that 20,000 Jews be rounded up and sent to concentration camps. Jews were also held responsible for the damage done to their own property and were fined a billion marks, about $400 million.

By the time Kristallnacht was a reality, many thousands of Jews had already left Germany. In 1933, the year Hitler came to power, 37,000 Jews, among them Anne Frank and her family, fled to other European countries, Palestine, and the United States. Over the next six years, nearly 150,000 Jews out of 500,000 of the original Jewish population had left Germany. After Kristallnacht, another 150,000 Jews managed to escape from Germany before Hitler invaded Poland in 1939. Unfortunately, many of them did not move far enough away from Hitler's rabid ambitions. Using the excuse that the German people needed and deserved more *Lebensraum*, space in which to grow and flourish to their fullest capacities, Hitler declared war across Europe, invading one country after another and always targeting the Jew, who, Hitler claimed, "struggles for his domination over the nations. No nation can remove his hand from its throat except by the sword." With blind hatred, Hitler projected his own murderous aspirations onto every Jew in Europe, and in this way justified his "Final Solution to the Jewish Question."

JEWISH LIFE IN GERMANY

Anti-Semitism and overt violence against the Jews had been a part of German culture for hundreds of years. The Jews of Germany had not gained full civil and legal rights until late in the nineteenth century. Shortly after World War I Germany was once again inundated with anti-Semitic propaganda and then with the more dangerous anti-Semitic legislation that culminated in World War II and the Holocaust. Why did the Jews put up with these persecutions? Why didn't they leave Germany as soon as they heard Hitler's vicious speeches and saw the SA humiliating and attacking old Jewish men and destroying synagogues?

These seem to be simple questions that do not have simple answers. For one thing, life in other European countries was often

not any better for the Jews; thus, they did not have clear and obvious alternatives to German anti-Semitism. Over the course of
many centuries, some of the Jews who had settled in Germany had
intermarried or were assimilated enough to consider themselves
Germans rather than Jews. In addition, numbers of Jews had ben-
efited from the outstanding educational, scientific, and cultural institutions available in Germany. Well educated and active in their
professional and artistic pursuits, many of these Jews wrongly believed that they were a part of the fabric of Germany's life. They
were giants in a dazzling variety of fields: science (Albert Einstein);
psychology (Sigmund Freud, Erich Fromm); music (Jascha Heifitz,
Vladimir Horowitz, Artur Rubinstein); film (Billy Wilder, Ernst Lu-
bitsch); philosophy (Walter Benjamin). Most of all, the vast majority of Jews, as well as other citizens of the world, could not imagine
what was to happen.

Many Jews hoped that, as in the past, the humiliations and attacks would eventually subside. More important, most Jews had
neither the money nor the skills that would have made it possible
for them to leave their "homeland" and begin a new life somewhere else.

GERMANY TODAY

In 1995, on the fiftieth anniversary of the end of World War II,
there was much renewed attention given to the Holocaust, especially as it was being commemorated (or not) throughout Europe.
In particular, German citizens were scrutinized as to how they conveyed their all-to-recent history to their children and grandchildren. One German writer interviewed 300 young people and
discovered that although all of them knew about "the crime against
the Jews," the stories they were told still focused on the sufferings
of the Germans during World War II rather than on the "sufferings
inflicted by Germans on others."[17] Part of this historical "amnesia"
can be explained by the fact that in some cases the information
presented about World War II and the memorials dedicated to that
infamous period do not even mention the Jewish victims.

GERMAN YOUTH TODAY

Despite the sometimes distorted perspectives, some young Germans have participated in activities that have helped bring the hor-

rific events of the Nazi era closer to their own lives. Many make pilgrimages to Holocaust memorial sites, and some join organizations such as Action in the Sign of Atonement, which tries to make "history palpable" by having its members work on projects directly related to the history of the Holocaust. One such group spent weeks clearing and excavating an area around a former concentration camp. Working with Action Reconciliation Service for Peace, German youth atone "for the crimes of their elders" by "helping rebuild towns destroyed by the Nazis and . . . restoring lives through social service in Europe, Israel and the United States."[18]

Instead of serving in the military, young German volunteers came to New York City to work in a Jewish community. They helped elderly Jewish men and women with their daily chores, restored murals in a synagogue, and learned about the culture destroyed by the Nazis. As a result, young and old, German and Jew, discovered what they had in common beyond their devastating histories.

THE CATHOLIC CHURCH IN GERMANY

One of the most dramatic events of the fiftieth anniversary of the liberation of Auschwitz was the German Roman Catholic Church's admission that "Catholics share responsibility for the Nazi Holocaust." The German bishops asserted that "Christians did not carry out the required resistance to racist anti-Semitism." The statement included an admission that "there was much denial and guilt among Catholics. More than a few allowed themselves to be taken in by National Socialist ideology, and remained indifferent to crimes against Jewish life and property." The open declaration was welcomed as being long overdue and a significant "cry against forgetting, an appeal for reflection and remembrance."[19]

Ultimately, the history of the Holocaust in Germany will be transmitted to future generations by the young men and women whose own grandparents and great-grandparents were involved in the Nazi era. What the youth of today know about that grim period and how they understand their nation's past will greatly influence and shape the meaning of the Holocaust for those who are born in the years to come.

THE DOCUMENTS

Materials presented at the end of this chapter include anti-Jewish legislation implemented in Germany, excerpts from German speeches and publications on the role of women in Nazi Germany, *New York Times* accounts of Kristallnacht, excerpts of an interview with a Hitler Youth member, and an article on Neo-Nazis today.

NOTES

1. Ismar Elbogen, quoted in H. G. Adler, *The Jews in Germany: From the Enlightenment to National Socialism* (London: University of Notre Dame Press, 1969), 13.

2. Paul Johnson, *A History of the Jews* (New York: Harper and Row, 1987), 242.

3. Quoted in Robert S. Wistrich, *Antisemitism: The Longest Hatred* (New York: Pantheon Books, 1991), 39–41.

4. Johnson, *History of the Jews*, 242.

5. Lucy S. Dawidowicz, *A Holocaust Reader* (West Orange, N.J.: Behrman House, 1976), 27.

6. Ibid., 19.

7. Adler, *The Jews in Germany*, 23.

8. Heinrich von Treitschke, *A Word About Our Jewry: Readings in Modern Jewish History*, edited by Ellis Rivkin, trans. by Helen Lederer (Cincinnati: Hebrew Union College, Jewish Institute of Religion, 1958), 11.

9. James Parkes, *Antisemitism* (Chicago: Quadrangle Books, 1963), 87–88.

10. George L. Mosse, *Germans and Jews* (New York: Howard Fertig, 1970), xx.

11. Adolf Hitler, *Mein Kampf* (New York: Houghton Mifflin, 1943), 325.

12. Ibid., 679.

13. Ibid., 180–181.

14. Ellen Switzer, *How Democracy Failed* (New York: Atheneum, 1975), 48.

15. Ibid., 20–21.

16. Ibid., 70.

17. *New York Times*, December 3, 1995, 75.

18. *New York Times*, July 8, 1994, B3.

19. *New York Times*, January 27, 1995, A3.

ANTI-JEWISH LEGISLATION IN GERMANY

As soon as Hitler came to power in 1933, he began eliminating Jews from all positions of power and influence in the hope that they would leave Germany as their lives became increasingly difficult. The Enabling Act, passed on March 23, 1933, gave Hitler the power to issue legislation that soon deprived Jews of their civil rights. In the Law Against the Overcrowding of German Schools and Institutions of Higher Learning no mention is made of the Jews. Instead, Aryans are protected from overcrowding by severely limiting the number of non-Aryans accepted at German schools. This law was further spelled out in a "First Decree," which did allow for the inclusion of "*one* pupil of non-Aryan descent" under certain circumstances. It was this law and decree that convinced Otto Frank to leave Frankfurt, Germany, for the sake of his two young daughters, Margot and Anne.

FIRST DECREE FOR IMPLEMENTATION OF THE LAW AGAINST
THE OVERCROWDING OF GERMAN SCHOOLS, APRIL 25, 1933

Pursuant to § 6 of the Law Against the Overcrowding of German Schools and Institutions of Higher Learning of April 25, 1933 *(Reichsgesetzblatt I, p. 225)*, the following is decreed:

To § 1

(1) The law applies equally to public and private schools. To the extent that it is still necessary, the state government will determine to what particular schools and institutions of higher learning the law applies.

(2) The Reich Minister of the Interior may fix general numerical guidelines for limiting the number of pupils and students. . . .

To § 4

(8) The population ratio (§ 4, Paragraph 1) for use in new admissions is set at 1.5 per cent; the quota (§ 4, Paragraph 2) for use in reducing the number of pupils and students is set at a maximum of 5 per cent.

(9) Within university faculties the population ratio is to be maintained among new enrollments.

In each school the population ratio is to be maintained among new admissions for as long as the school is still attended by pupils of non-Aryan descent who remain there within the limits of the quota provided for in § 4, Paragraph 2.

Where the number of new admissions to a particular school is so small that under the population ratio no pupil of non-Aryan descent would be admitted, *one* pupil of non-Aryan descent may be admitted. However, in this case further admission of pupils of non-Aryan descent will be permissible only when the population ratio will not have been reached among the total of new admissions since the effective date of the law.

(10) When a pupil of non-Aryan descent who was newly admitted subsequent to the effective date of the law changes schools, he is to be counted in the population ratio at the school to which he transfers.

(11) Pupils of non-Aryan descent who have newly entered or will newly enter school at the beginning of the 1933 school year will in all cases count as not yet admitted. § 4, Paragraph 1, applies to them.

The same applies analogously to students who have been or will be enrolled for the first time in the 1933 summer semester.

Lucy S. Dawidowicz, *A Holocaust Reader* (West Orange, N.J.: Behrman House, 1976), 47–48.

RACIAL LAWS TO PROTECT GERMAN "BLOOD AND HONOR"

The Nuremberg Laws of 1935 declared that German citizenship was only granted to subjects of "German or kindred blood." These laws and decrees were based on the premise that German blood needed to be protected from the taint of non-Aryan pollution. The decrees revoked the political rights of Jewish citizens and forbade marriages between Germans and Jews. They further isolated and marginalized the already severely oppressed Jews of Germany.

FROM THE NUREMBERG LAWS: LAW FOR THE PROTECTION OF GERMAN BLOOD AND GERMAN HONOR, SEPTEMBER 15, 1935

Imbued with the insight that the purity of German blood is prerequisite for the continued existence of the German people and inspired by the inflexible will to ensure the existence of the German nation for all times, the Reichstag has unanimously adopted the following law, which is hereby promulgated:

§ 1 (1) Marriages between Jews and subjects of German or kindred blood are forbidden. Marriages nevertheless concluded are invalid, even if concluded abroad to circumvent this law.

(2) Only the State Attorney may initiate the annulment suit.

§ 2 Extramarital intercourse between Jews and subjects of German or kindred blood is forbidden.

§ 3 Jews must not employ in their households female subjects of German or kindred blood who are under 45 years old.

§ 4 (1) Jews are forbidden to fly the Reich and national flag and to display the Reich colors.

(2) They are, on the other hand, allowed to display the Jewish colors. The exercise of this right enjoys the protection of the state.

§ 5 (1) Whoever violates the prohibition in § 1 will be punished by penal servitude.

(2) A male who violates the prohibition in § 2 will be punished either by imprisonment or penal servitude.

(3) Whoever violates the provisions of §§ 3 or 4 will be punished by imprisonment up to one year and by a fine, or by either of these penalties.

§ 6 The Reich Minister of the Interior, in agreement with the Deputy of the Führer and the Reich Minister of Justice, will issue the legal and administrative orders required to implement and supplement this law.

§ 7 The law takes effect on the day following promulgation, except for § 3, which goes into force January 1, 1936.

Nuremberg, September 15, 1935
at the Reich Party Congress of Freedom
The Führer and Reich Chancellor   The Reich Minister of the Interior
The Reich Minister of Justice   The Deputy of the Führer

Lucy S. Dawidowicz, *A Holocaust Reader* (West Orange, N.J.: Behrman House, 1976), 47–48.

THE ROLE OF WOMEN IN NAZI GERMANY

Propaganda came in many forms during the Nazi era. Anti-Semitic propaganda reached out to the German public via films, billboards, textbooks, and public addresses, vilifying the Jews and encouraging the German people to discriminate against their neighbors. At the same time, the German people were encouraged to think of themselves as patriots who were expected to fulfill the goals of their Führer. While German men were barraged with messages about their inherent superiority to all other races, German women were told that their mission was to "be beautiful and bring children into the world." The following excerpts reflect the relentless propaganda inflicted on German women.

How would Anne Frank have responded to these messages? Write your own response to one or several of these pieces.

FROM GEORGE MOSSE, *NAZI CULTURE: INTELLECTUAL, CULTURAL AND SOCIAL LIFE IN THE THIRD REICH* (1966)

The Tasks of Women
Adolf Hitler

. . . So long as we possess a healthy manly race—and we National Socialists will attend to that—we will form no female mortar battalions and no female sharpshooter corps. For that is not equality of rights, but a diminution of the rights of woman. . . .

An unlimited range of work opportunities exists for women. For us the woman has always been man's most loyal comrade in work and in life. I am often told: You want to drive women out of the professions. Not at all. I wish only to create the broadest measure of possibility for her to co-found her own family and to be able to have children, because by so doing she most benefits our Volk! . . .

If today a female jurist accomplishes ever so much and next door there lives a mother with five, six, seven children, who are all healthy and well-brought-up, then I would like to say: From the standpoint of the eternal value of our people the woman who has given birth to children and raised them and who thereby has given back our people life for the future has accomplished *more* and does *more*!

From a speech to the National Socialist women's organization (Die Frauenschaft),
published in the *Völkischer Beobachter*, Sept. 13, 1936. (Wiener Library Clipping Collection.)

The so-called granting of equal rights to women, which Marxism demands, in reality does not grant equal rights but constitutes a deprivation of rights, since it draws the woman into an area in which she will necessarily be inferior. It places the woman in situations that cannot strengthen her position—vis-à-vis both man and society—but only weaken it. . . .

I would be ashamed to be a German man if in the event of a war even only one woman had to go to the front. The woman has her own battlefield. With every child that she brings into the world, she fights her battle for the nation. The man stands up for the *Volk*, exactly as the woman stands up for the *family*.

From a speech to the National Socialist Women's Congress, published in the
Völkischer Beobachter, Sept. 15, 1935. (Wiener Library Clipping Collection.)

• • •

The Female Bird
Joseph Goebbels

The mission of woman is to be beautiful and to bring children into the world. This is not at all as rude and unmodern as it sounds. The female bird pretties herself for her mate and hatches the eggs for him. In exchange, the mate takes care of gathering the food, and stands guard and wards off the enemy.

From Joseph Goebbels, *Michael: Ein deutsches Schicksal in Tagebuchblättern*
(Munich: Zentralverlag der NSDAP, Frz. Eher Nachf., 1929), p. 41. (Wiener
Library Clipping Collection.) (This extract has been taken from the 1934 edition.)

• • •

Faith and Beauty

Jutta Rüdiger, the Reich reporter of the Bund Deutscher Mädel, has on several occasions discussed the tasks of the BDM project "Faith and Beauty," such as at a convention of Hitler Youth leaders in Hammersbach on February 9 and in the Reich Youth Press Service.

According to her reports, the BDM program "Faith and Beauty" is not a radical departure for the BDM, but marks a logical step forward in the development of this girls' organization. Hence the usual uniform of the BDM will be maintained and participants in the program will be distinguished only by a special badge. It is planned to set up work communities for gymnastics, handicrafts, folklore, foreign affairs, games and music, health service, and the like. The groups meet weekly, and once a month the meetings take the form of evenings-at-home which are devoted to discussions of cultural life and the structuring and guidance of one's personal life.

From *Das Archiv: Nachschlagewerk für Politik, Wirtschaft, Kultur*, No. 47, Feb. 1938 (Berlin: Verlagsanstalt D. Stollberg, 1938), p. 1393.

• • •

Right Conduct

The district plant department of the NSBO [National Sozialistischer Betriebs Obman] in Unterfranken published a regulation in which it is stated that lately a great number of women had been accepted. This is a privilege of which women can be proud, and therefore it is also their duty to conduct themselves in a true National Socialist manner. It was therefore announced that *painted* and *powdered* women will be *forbidden* entry to all NSBO gatherings. Women who *smoke* in public—in hotels, in cafés, on the street, and so forth—will be *expelled* from the NSBO. Local officials are instructed to adopt similar rules.

From the *Frankfurter Zeitung*, Aug. 11, 1933. (Wiener Library Clipping Collection.)

• • •

The Honor Cross of the German Mother

"The prolific German mother is to be accorded the same place of honor in the German Volk community as the combat soldier, since she risks her body and her life for the people and the Fatherland as much as the combat soldier does in the roar and thunder of battle." With these words, Reich Physician Leader Dr. Wagner, head of the People's Health Section in the Reich leadership of the party, at the behest of the Führer, announced the creation of a Medal of Honor for prolific German mothers at the Party Day of Labor.

Three million German mothers, on the German Mother's Day in 1939, for the first time will be solemnly awarded the new badge of honor by the leaders of the party. These celebrations are to be held every year on Mother's Day and on the Awarding of Medals Day for prolific mothers.

The youth above all must be brought up with a reverence for the mothers of the people. Thus the honoring of German mothers with many children is not to be limited only to Mother's Day and to the Awarding of Medals Day. In the future the prolific mother will occupy the place that is due her in public life. *The young National Socialist will show his respect for her through the obligatory salute of all members of the youth formations of the party.* In addition, the wearers of the Honor Cross of the German Mother will henceforth enjoy all those privileges which are already possessed as a matter of course by meritorious racial comrades, disabled war veterans, and the martyrs of the National Socialist revolution—such privileges as honorary seats at party and government-sponsored gatherings, special treatment in government offices, and preferred seats assigned by conductors in rail coaches and trolley cars. Further, they are to be provided with old-age care and be given priority for acceptance in homes for the aged or in special sections of such homes already in existence.

For this honoring of the prolific mother and especially of the German aged mother by the Führer is not only an expression of thanks, but at the same time expresses the trust that the Führer, and with him the whole German people, has in all German mothers, that they will continue to help to pave the way for our people, and that they will make us a gift of that youth which, after perilous times, will crown the rise of our Volk. . . .

From the *Völkischer Beobachter*, Dec. 25, 1938. (Wiener Library Clipping Collection.)

• • •

Against the Political Woman
Engelbert Huber

There is no place for the political woman in the ideological world of National Socialism. . . .

The intellectual attitude of the movement on this score is *opposed to the political woman*. It refers the woman back to her nature-given sphere of the family and to her tasks as wife and mother. The postwar phenomenon of the political woman, who rarely cuts a good figure in parliamentary debates, signifies robbing woman of her dignity.

The German resurrection is a male event.

From Engelbert Huber, *Das ist Nationalsozialismus* (Stuttgart: Union Deutsche Verlagsgesellschaft, 1933), pp. 121–122.

KRISTALLNACHT

The *New York Times* reported on the "surge of revenge" taken against Jewish lives and property, including many synagogues, in response to the murder on November 9, 1938, of a German diplomat by a young Jewish student in Paris. Throughout Germany and Austria (which had been annexed by Germany in March 1938) Nazis looted and destroyed Jewish-owned businesses and attacked or arrested Jews who were out on the streets or in their shops during the rampage.

With literary precision, the news articles recounted the reactions of onlookers, the behavior of the Nazi storm troopers, and the fate of the Jews who were "sent to prisons or concentration camps." There is no mention of the fact that it was the Nazis who were behaving in a criminal manner and deserved to be imprisoned, rather than the Jewish victims.

On the following day, the German propaganda minister, Dr. Joseph Goebbels, insisted that the "spontaneous" outbreaks of terrorism were justified and were appropriate retaliation for an attack on a German citizen. Goebbels also asserted that "how Germany treats its Jews is her own business," and implied that German Jews would be further punished for the statements against Germany made by Jews abroad.

NAZIS SMASH, LOOT AND BURN JEWISH SHOPS AND TEMPLES
UNTIL GOEBBELS CALLS HALT

*All Vienna's Synagogues Attacked; Fires and Bombs Wreck
18 of 21*

*Jews Are Beaten, Furniture and Goods Flung
From Homes and Shops—15,000 Are
Jailed During Day—20 Are Suicides*

Vienna, Nov. 10—In a surge of revenge for the murder of a German diplomat in Paris by a young Polish Jew, all Vienna's twenty-one synagogues were attacked today and eighteen were wholly or partially destroyed by fires and bomb explosions.

Anti-Jewish activities under the direction of Storm Troopers and Nazi party members in uniform began early this morning. In the earlier stages Jews were attacked and beaten. Many Jews awaiting admittance to the British Consulate-General were arrested, and according to reliable reports others who stood in line before the United States Consulate were severely beaten and also arrested.

Apartments were raided and searched and gradually some 15,000 arrested Jews were assembled at police stations. Some were released during the day. Tonight arrests were continuing.

Many of those arrested were sent to concentration camps in buses. Mobs of raiders penetrated Jewish residences and shops, flinging furniture and merchandise from windows and destroying wantonly.

In their panic and misery about fifty Jews, men and women, were reported to have attempted suicide—about twenty succeeded.

Scores of bombs were placed in synagogues, blowing out windows and in many cases damaging walls. Floors that had been soaked with kerosene readily caught fire. . . .

At 9 A.M. the first fires broke out in the Hernaiser and Heitzinger synagogues. The Heitzinger synagogue, which was in Moorish style and was the largest and finest synagogue in Vienna, was gutted. . . .

Excesses in Many Cities

Berlin papers also mention many cities and towns in which anti-Jewish excesses occurred, including Potsdam, Stettin, Frankfort on the Main, Leipzig, Luebeck, Cologne, Nuremberg, Essen, Dusseldorf, Konstanz, Landsberg, Kottbus and Eberswalde. In most of them, it is reported, synagogues were raided and burned and shops were demolished. But in general the press follows the system of reporting only local excesses so as to disguise the national extent of the outbreak, the full spread of which probably never will be known.

On the other hand, the German press already warns the world if the day's events lead to another agitation campaign against Germany "the improvised and spontaneous outbreaks of today will be replaced with even more drastic authoritative action." No doubt is left that the contemplated "authoritative action" would have a retaliatory character.

Says the Angriff, Dr. Goebbel's organ:

"For every suffering, every crime and every injury that this criminal [the Jewish community] inflicts on a German anywhere, every individual Jew will be held responsible. All Judah wants is war with us and it can have this war according to its own moral law: "an eye for an eye and a tooth for a tooth.""

Possession of Weapons Barred

One of the first legal measures issued was an order by Heinrich Himmler, commander of all German police, forbidding Jews to possess any weapons whatever and imposing a penalty of twenty years confinement in a concentration camp upon every Jew found in possession of a weapon hereafter.

The dropping of all pretense in the outbreak is also illustrated by the fact that although shops and synagogues were wrecked or burned by so-called Rollkommandos, or wrecking crews, dressed in what the Nazis themselves call "Raeuberzivil," or "bandit mufti," consisting of leather coats or raincoats over uniform boots or trousers, these squads often performed their work in the presence and under the protection of uniformed Nazis or police.

The wrecking work was thoroughly organized, sometimes proceeding under the direct orders of a controlling person in the street at whose command the wreckers ceased, lined up and proceeded to another place. . . .

Crowds Mostly Silent

Generally the crowds were silent and the majority seemed gravely disturbed by the proceedings. Only members of the wrecking squads shouted occasionally, "Perish Jewry!" and "Kill the Jews!" and in one case a person in the crowd shouted, "Why not hang the owner in the window?"

In one case on the Kurfuerstendamm actual violence was observed by an American girl who saw one Jew with his face bandaged dragged from a shop, beaten and chased by a crowd while a second Jew was dragged from the same shop by a single man who beat him as the crowd looked on.

One Jewish shopkeeper, arriving at his wrecked store, exclaimed, "Terrible," and was arrested on the spot.

In some cases on the other hand crowds were observed making passages for Jews to leave their stores unmolested.

Some persons in the crowds—peculiarly enough, mostly women—expressed the view that it was only right that the Jews should suffer what the Germans suffered in 1918.

New York Times, November 11, 1938.

NAZIS DEFEND WAVE OF TERROR
BY OTTO D. TOLISCHUS

BERLIN, Nov. 11.—The National Socialist regime, through Dr. Joseph Goebbels, its Propaganda Minister, and other authorized spokesmen in declarations to the foreign press and in speeches to mass meetings, today openly sanctioned the wave of terrorism, destruction and incendiarism that swept over Germany yesterday. . . .

. . . it was asserted that the government had done everything to end the demonstrations as rapidly as possible, and it was announced that there would be further anti-Jewish laws for a comprehensive solution of the Jewish problem in a manner "that will equalize the status of the Jews in Germany in conformity with popular anti-Semitic sentiment."

No Word of Condemnation

But in all the declarations there was no word of condemnation or regret for the excesses themselves; on the contrary, in an article in the Voelkischer Beobachter Dr. Goebbels declared:

"We take the stand that the reaction of the German people to the cowardly murder in Paris must be explained by the nefarious baseness of the deed.

"In it the nation followed its healthy instincts, which told it that a representative of Germany abroad for the second time had been shot by a Jewish youngster and that if this misdeed were accepted silently and without reaction German diplomatic representatives would be put beyond the law." . . .

At the same time the National Socialist regime also moved today to silence all criticism abroad. It warned the foreign press that any "lies and exaggerations" would not only be ineffective but that the Jews in Germany might have to pay for them. . . .

. . . Dr. Goebbels further protested the statement that Jews had been hauled out of bed naked and put in concentration camps. He explained that the Jews had been arrested during the daytime and that they had not been naked because "in that case we should have had to furnish them with clothes."

Bids Jews Remain Silent

"If I were a Jew," said Dr. Goebbels, "I would remain silent. There is only one thing the Jews can do—shut up and say nothing further about Germany. I now receive innumerable letters from all kinds of foreigners complaining of the manner in which the press is misleading them about Germany."

Dr. Goebbels said it was contrary to National Socialist principles to let the people themselves solve their problems or let the people go their own way until everything got out of hand. For that reason, he said, the Jewish question would be solved by law. . . .

For the rest, Dr. Goebbels concluded in a warning tone, "the manner in which the Jews in Germany will be treated will depend entirely upon their good behavior and particularly that of the Jews abroad."

New York Times, November 12, 1938.

EDITORIAL: "NAZI DAY OF TERROR A THREAT TO ALL CIVILIZATION" BY ANNE O'HARE MCCORMICK

It is difficult to write calmly about what has happened in Germany. It is especially difficult for one who has watched the German people in the dark days of revolution and hunger they have endured since the war, who has seen close the hopelessness of the "little men" described in the novels written in monotone by Hans Fallada and has tried to understand what otherwise would be incomprehensible: how Hitler was able to create a mighty movement by stirring up the dregs of bitterness, envy and hate that rise from the bottom of any society in a period of defeat and despair. It is difficult because it is no longer a defeated people, and the suffering they inflict on others now that they are on top again passes all understanding and mocks all sympathy.

The darkest day Germany experienced in the whole post-war period was not so dark as Thursday. In all the humiliations experienced by a penalized nation, it has not been so humiliated as on that day of terror when organized gangs recruited from the ruling party pounded like an enemy army through the main streets of German cities and systematically sacked the shops, the homes and the altars of a helpless minority of German citizens. All the reporters on the ground agree as to the methodical character of the terror. They agree that in a day more property was destroyed than in the revolution of 1918. Glass is scarce and precious in Germany, yet the windows in nearly every Jewish store and restaurant throughout the country were smashed to atoms.

A Pitiable Exhibition

The German people were never more pitiable than when they stood by and watched this thing done. For the raiders who were let loose on the streets and given a day to sate the lowest instincts of cruelty and revenge were indeed an enemy army. No foreign invader could have done more harm. This is Germany in the hour of her greatest defeat, the best overcome by the worst. While many protested at the outrages, and millions must have been sickened and shamed by the crimes committed in their name, many others looked on stolidly or approvingly while the hunters hunted and the wreckers worked. There are stories of mothers who took their children to see the fun.

This highlights a tragedy more portentous than the tragedy of the Jews. It means that the millions who detest this brutality have lost the power to protest and that other millions have no desire to protest because they have been worked on by years of anti-Semitic propaganda. And this shows what the Nazi mentality plus the Nazi police power has done to an intelligent people.

It is quite true that the cruelty and violence exhibited in Germany are latent in every country. No nation is free of primitive passions and prejudices that can be exploited by unscrupulous or reckless leaders. We have all experienced outbreaks of the mob spirit and realized its savage force. The difference is that in most countries the fundamental aim and purpose of government is to keep this lurking beast under control. Civilization is a process of subduing the savage in man and teaching him to live by the rule of reason. In National Socialist Germany the mob spirit is deliberately cultivated, canalized and employed as an arm of government. As in Thursday's orgy of sadism, it can be turned on and off at will.

Terror May React

But suppose the time comes when those who lift the lid can't screw it down again? Terror as an instrument of policy is not a new weapon. Once, in Russia, at a time when there was a great round-up of class enemies and all the poor remnants of the submerged classes quaked, the writer asked a high Soviet official why a strong government found it necessary to use this method again and again. "Because when it was used against us in the old days it was effective," he answered. "If you cut a swath of terror through the population at regular intervals, you can keep the opposition down."

But the dosage of terror not only has to be repeated. It has to be increased, as Russia has demonstrated under two tyrannies, or it does not work. Therefore it is an invariable symptom of the weakness of the system in which it has to be used. A day of "punishment" for the Jews was permitted immediately after Hitler came to power to satisfy the violence he had aroused among his followers, and it is noteworthy that the raids made then did not compare in extent or intensity with the present pogrom. Does that mean that the dissatisfaction among the disciples demands more and more outlet? And what would happen if this savagery, whether cultivated or suppressed, breaks bounds and turns on the leaders themselves?

This isn't very probable at present, but Germany's Black Thursday suggests either that the scapegoat has to be publicly beaten for internal reasons or that a whole people have become callous to savagery. And this is a danger far greater than anti-Semitism on the rampage. It raises up in the heart of Europe, in a civilized country, a threat to the civilization of the world.

New York Times, November 12, 1938.

THE FAILURE OF GERMAN DEMOCRACY

The author of *How Democracy Failed*, Ellen Switzer, grew up in Germany during the years when the democratic Weimar Republic was disintegrating and Hitler was organizing the Nazi Party. As a young girl during those years, she was aware of the increasing numbers of uniformed men in brown and black shirts who carried flags decorated with swastikas and sang "aggressive-sounding songs." Like the Franks, Ellen Switzer's family left Germany when the warning signs became ominous. However, her family immigrated to the United States, crossing an entire ocean to get away from Hitler's horrifying "solution to the Jewish question."

Nearly twenty-five years after the end of the Holocaust, Switzer returned to Berlin in order to speak with Germans who had grown up during the early years of Hitler's rise to power. She interviewed hundreds of people about their memories of that period, asking them if and when they understood "that something had gone drastically wrong in their country."

Among the many Germans she interviewed, Switzer spoke with Joachim, a man who had lived in Frankfurt, the city in which Anne Frank's family had lived for several generations and from which they had fled in 1933.

Joachim's father had died when the boy was five, and his mother worked long hours as a secretary to the publisher of a Frankfurt newspaper. Lonely and vulnerable, Joachim joined the Hitler Youth Group. It provided him with the community and male companionship he craved, but it also indoctrinated him with Nazi ideology Joachim accepted as fact and which he was expected to accept on "faith."

FROM ELLEN SWITZER, *HOW DEMOCRACY FAILED* (1975)

Joachim also remembers the years before Hitler came to full power as exciting, vital and enormously satisfying. He had joined the Hitler Youth almost as soon as the first troop was formed in his neighborhood. Unlike Klaus, Rosel and Hedwig, he thought that he was deeply involved in politics. Actually, he realizes now, that he knew absolutely nothing about the political movement he had so enthusiastically joined and to which he planned to devote his life.

. . .

. . . His mother was appalled when he told her that he had decided to become a member of the group, but he refused to listen to her, and she was too tired to argue.

As part of the movement, he was exposed to many ideas that seemed perfectly logical to him at the time. He was interested in flying, but Germany was not allowed to have an air force. He wanted to build a life based on the legends of the flyers in World War I, especially Baron von Richthofen, the flying ace who had been killed in a dog fight after shooting down a record number of enemy planes, and Hermann Goering, another former flying ace, who was now one of the top leaders in the Nazi party.

As part of his Hitler Youth training, he learned to make model airplanes and was finally made a member of a glider group. He was given to understand that as soon as Hitler came into power, the Versailles treaty would be ignored and Germany would build a real air force. Then he would be able to put his glider training to good use. He would be several steps ahead of other young men who would be signing up for pilots' training.

He resented the lack of flying opportunities, and his resentment of the anti-air-force clause in the Versailles treaty extended to other aspects of that treaty (which he really didn't understand) and to the politicians who had agreed to sign it. He listened to leaders of his Youth Group, who seemed to have simple solutions to Germany's problems. In a well-run country, his mother would not have to work, he was told. She would be at home taking care of him, being a *mother*, which is what a good German woman was supposed to do. What's more, the paper for which she was working was an unpatriotic rag, which supported all the evil men who had lost the war for Germany. It was made clear to Joachim that his mother, unconsciously of course, was working for Germany's enemies. She should not be blamed for what she did, for she was being influenced by all the clever, treacherous liberals around her, and she, herself, was just not intelligent or perceptive enough to understand what was happening. Eventually, she would learn what Joachim already knew: that soon there would be a free, strong and aggressive Germany with its own army and air force, respected and feared in the world. Meanwhile, he could work hard to make this dream come true. One way he could help was to listen to her conversation carefully, to pick up clues from the stories she told about the newspaper and its editorial decisions that might be helpful to the movement.

Joachim tried to listen more carefully to her conversation. Actually, he seemed to pick up little except some office gossip. But his troop leaders paid attention to what he had to say and occasionally took notes on his reports.

He considered this a very minor part of his Youth Movement activities. The regular meetings gave him a feeling of belonging that he had not had before. He tried to quit school to become a regular party employee, but was encouraged to continue his education. He would need mathematics, geography and physics for his flying career, he was told. And besides, when Hitler came into power, it would be important to know which teachers were "reliable" and which were "unpatriotic." He should also report on the actions and words of his teachers. Did they praise the current German government? Did they seem to be interested in the Nazi movement? Did they show a special interest in boys who might seem to be intelligent, but who were also Jewish? Again, his reports usually contained very little. His teachers were probably as unpolitical as those in most other German schools. But whatever he said was listened to carefully, and the obvious interest he aroused in his leaders gave him a feeling of importance.

The night of the torch parade, celebrating Hitler's rise to power, was the highpoint of Joachim's life. He had never felt so happy and fulfilled.

Looking back on that night now, he is appalled at how little he really knew about the movement to which he had intended to devote his life. "We were told what we wanted to hear," he said. "We were assured that we were important. Nobody else told German adolescents that they were important . . . ever. Certainly our parents and teachers didn't. We were also assured that, once Hitler was in power, all the wrongs we saw about us would be fixed, and that we would be allowed to help create a marvelous new country. When I marched in that parade, I thought it was only the beginning. I had been privileged to be an important person in helping to create the Thousand Year Reich, the great new Germany that Hitler would bring forth out of the chaos and trouble around us. I didn't know how he would do this. Nobody had ever spelled out any kind of program for us. We were just told to have faith. I had faith, and I had never been so exhilarated in my whole life."

New York: Atheneum Books for Young Readers, 1975, pp. 71–74.

PORTRAIT OF A NEO-NAZI

Adolf Hitler reached his audiences through inflammatory public addresses held in large plazas where thousands of eager listeners gathered at one time. Through his claims of Aryan superiority and his insistence on the evil of the Jews, Hitler brainwashed many Germans into believing he would lead the nation to renewed greatness as soon as the Jews were eliminated from the fatherland.

Hitler's racist ideology culminated in the worst genocide in human history. Tragically, the racism did not vanish when millions of victims of Nazi anti-Semitism died. Instead, racists continue to flourish throughout the world, and now they have immediate access to each other through the Internet. What started out as a miraculous tool with which to connect people of all races, nationalities, and ages has also become a weapon with which to spread vicious propaganda against those who are not considered equal to "whites."

A young white supremacist, George Burdi, hopes to "build a global community of young neo-Nazi skinheads" by combining the powers of the Internet with the appeal of rock and roll. Like many of the troubled young Germans who joined the Hitler Youth Movement in order to belong to something beyond their own limited personal world, vulnerable teens are listening to the neo-Nazi music produced by Burdi's Resistance Records, and they are communicating with each other via the Internet.

Because of its history, Germany is particularly vigilant about the promulgation of neo-Nazi propaganda, and has forbidden access to some Internet sites which convey racist material. In contrast, such censorship is highly controversial in the United States, and as a result, white supremacists have far greater opportunities to spread their hate-filled messages across the anonymous spaces of the World Wide Web.

FROM STEPHAN TALTY, "THE METHOD OF A NEO-NAZI
MOGUL" (1996)

Most white supremacists are, by nature, nostalgic and would rather be living deep in the Aryan past. Not George Burdi. He is a racist from the future, and he is impatient for it to arrive.

At 25, Burdi is an archetype of the forward-looking neo-Nazi: he is taking an old idea (hard-core white supremacy), revitalizing it through a young art (rock-and-roll) and bringing it to mainstream America through a newly powerful network (the Internet). His tiny empire, Resistance Records Inc., includes a record label, a magazine, an Internet home page and a weekly electronic newsletter.

Burdi, a k a George Eric Hawthorne, is also the lead singer in a rock-and-roll band called Rahowa, short for Racial Holy War.

Remie666 is the on-line name of a 16-year-old Panorama City, Calif., fan of Burdi and Resistance Records. In an E-mail note, he describes himself as "straight AY"—Aryan Youth—and in a phone interview he says he uses the Internet to read Burdi's writings, to hear music samples and order CD's of white-power bands, to learn about new white-power novels and to E-mail other racist skinheads. "The Internet has quadrupled the number of white-power skins I'm in touch with," he says.

Another white-power devotee, a 27-year-old computer engineer in Dallas whose on-line name is Bootboy, has also seen the surge. "I have operated a P.O. box and a voice-mail system for four years now," he says. "And I have received more contacts, good ones, over the Internet in four months than I have in all four years. I get E-mail from other white-power skins from Sweden, Norway, Finland, Germany, Holland, Luxembourg."

This is one of the main goals of Burdi and other leaders in the new racist vanguard: to build a global community of young neo-Nazi skinheads. The majority of American skinheads are nonracist and nonviolent, embracing the same working-class pride and punkish style as their racist counterparts—who are responsible, says the Anti-Defamation League of B'nai B'rith, for 34 murders in the United States since 1990. The Southern Poverty Law Center estimates that there are at least 4,000 racist skinheads in the country, the hyperviolent edge of the movement that Burdi is trying to mobilize.

His ideology is hardly new. He holds the conviction that whites must reclaim their Nordic ferocity to protect their interests, that Jews control wide swaths of American life through a secret cabal and that the races are incompatible. "To put black men and women in American society," he says, "which is traditionally and essentially established on European traditions, and to say, 'Here you go, you're an equal, now compete,' is just as ridiculous as assuming that you could move white people to the Congo and have them effectively compete." Later, he elaborates via E-mail: "As I have said time and time again, the progeny of slaves cannot live in harmony with the progeny of slavemasters."

Wade Henderson, director of the Washington bureau of the N.A.A.C.P., says: "The information highway is the gateway to the future, which makes people like George Burdi particularly frightening. They are determined to transport the racial divides of today into the world of tomorrow."

The loudest opposition thus far to cyber-racists like Burdi has been voiced in Germany, where one on-line service last month barred its users from accessing the World Wide Web site of a Canadian white supremacist, Ernst Zundel, an early mentor of Burdi's. Meanwhile, Burdi, a Canadian who recently moved to Windsor, Ontario, just across the river from Detroit, has set out to reshape the racist landscape. "In the history of our country, there's been no one more effective in recruiting youth to the white-power movement," says Bernie Farber, national director of community relations for the Canadian Jewish Congress. When Burdi started out, Farber says, the average age of the movement went from 75 to 17.

Burdi is particularly bullish on the future of electronic racism. "We have big plans for the Internet," he says. "It's uncontrollable. It's beautiful, uncensored."

Rabbi Abraham Cooper of the Simon Wiesenthal Center in Los Angeles says that there are now some 75 hate groups on line. "The point is that all those groups have failed to ignite any significant interest in the mainstream," he says. "Now, suddenly, you have cheap, instantaneous communication through computers. Without the Internet, Burdi would be the equivalent of a one-watt light bulb." But with it, says Rabbi Cooper, "Burdi has discovered, Guess what, you can create your own Columbia House."

Already, Resistance Records has figured in two of the most notorious recent hate crimes in this country. The Pennsylvania skinhead brothers who killed their parents in February 1995 fled to the home of a Michigan friend they had met at a concert that Resistance promoted. And one of the soldiers at Fort Bragg in North Carolina who were arrested for murdering a black couple in December had a copy of Resistance magazine in his rented room.

Burdi is the editor of the quarterly magazine, a sort of neo-Nazi life style guide replete with movie reviews (five star movies—like "Pulp Fiction"—are "better than a cold beer on a hot Auschwitz afternoon!"), ads for Ku Klux Klan Kollectibles and a roundup of racialist news "suppressed by the mainstream press." The circulation, Burdi says, is 19,000 and growing with every issue. Mark Wilson, Burdi's partner and a co-founder of Resistance Records, says that they have a distributor or champion in "every white country in the world." Resistance's 12 bands sold about 50,000 CD's in the label's first 18 months of business—a minuscule figure by any measure but, taken with the sum of Resistance's offerings, concrete evidence of a new, coordinated marketplace for virulent ideas. It used to be that such ideas were spread via murky photocopies of obscure books and barely audible seventh-generation cassettes. Suddenly, the message, like the messenger, comes in a sleek new package.

• • •

. . . Burdi was an excellent student. After the school had a Black Pride Month, Burdi lobbied for equal time. "I said, 'How can we have a Black Pride Month and not a White Pride Month?' " he remembers. "And then there was an element of the population that started calling me a Nazi, and I really didn't understand the connection to what I was saying."

Perhaps the connection was strengthened when during history class, Burdi gave a report on the Holocaust-denial standard "Did Six Million Really Die?" He grew ever more fascinated with white separatism and began lifting weights obsessively, trying to build himself into another kind of Superman. His family was mystified by the change. In "Web of Hate," Andrew Burdi, George's brother, is said to have told a teacher that George had "gone off the deep end."

At the University of Guelph, some 50 miles west of Toronto, a fellow student handed Burdi a pamphlet about the Church of the Creator, an often violent, anti-Christian, white-supremacist group, now defunct, that had followers in dozens of countries, including the United States and South Africa. Immediately, Burdi's thinking jumped from the past to the future, and he became a Creator.

"The parts that appealed to me were the concept of a sound mind, a sound body, a sound society and a sound environment," he says. "In many ways I viewed myself as a racial ecologist. Basically what it says is that every race is primarily concerned with its own growth, its own development, protecting its own culture, having its own piece of land, the welfare of its own young people, so on and so forth." . . .

After a trip to the Church of the Creator's headquarters in the Blue Ridge Mountains, Burdi became a full-time proselytizer for white power. In 1990 he formed his rock band, and by 1992 he had become the Canadian representative of the church's leadership council. He also took up with Wolfgang Droege, leader of a white-supremacist umbrella group, Heritage Front, and he studied National Socialism with Ernst Zundel.

In May 1993 Burdi and several hundred other white-power skinheads were involved in a melee with antiracist protesters in Ottawa. Burdi was arrested for kicking a young woman named Alicia Reckzin; he was convicted of assault and served one month of a one-year sentence before being released on bail; an appeal is pending.

After his arrest, Burdi looked south. The lack of hate-speech laws in the United States and its roiling racial situation made it the natural destination for an ambitious young white supremacist. He and Mark Wilson, whom Burdi had met through the Church of the Creator, started Resistance Records in Detroit, along with a few other partners.

"I quickly learned that we didn't have to promote it at all," recalls Burdi, "because the demand was so strong. We started signing bands like one a month. It was going like crazy. Phone was ringing off the hook. Mailbox was full of mail every week."

The mail included lots of fan letters to Burdi's band. Concerts by Rahowa and other white-power groups have become vital bonding experiences for the racist faithful, drawing small but ardent crowds to clubs across the United States and Canada. Burdi, with his bare, sculpted torso and army-style pants and boots, is a commanding figure onstage, bellowing out songs like "Race Riot" in a deep, floorboards-shaking voice: "Tremble in fear, white man/The reaper's in the shadowland/Save your children, lock your door/You can't come out here no more." The teenagers in the mosh pit fling Nazi salutes into the air, and Burdi engages them in racist call-and-response chants.

White-power concerts sometimes give way to violence. The fight in Ottawa for which Burdi was jailed took place after a Rahowa performance; after an October 1994 concert in Racine, Wis., by six white-power groups, the lead singer for a Resistance band called Nordic Thunder was shot to death after a confrontation in a convenience store with a few black men, one of whom was arrested but not charged and was later released for lack of evidence.

In an editorial in Resistance magazine last spring, Burdi explained why music is so essential to his cause: "The reason that the so-called movement has been struggling over the years is because it has operated on a rational—not emotional—level. George Lincoln Rockwell was successful because he could stir people's emotions. . . . Adolf Hitler is considered one of the best orators in human history, by people that do not even understand German."

Like Burdi, Rabbi Cooper has seen rock-and-roll as the future of white power, and he is worried. "This is a seminal change in how to present racist ideology in a way that will reach middle America," he says. 'The idea of utilizing music is of special new concern to us because we can take a half-step back and think of all the wonderful things that have been achieved socially in terms of people in the music field. Music touches the soul, it leaps past the reason."

Most Resistance fans are white teen-agers, some as young as 11. They are often troubled—the eternal awkward youth. "The vast majority of our customers are disenfranchised young people," Burdi says. "More and more, these young people are coming to us and saying, 'They're teaching us in school that to be white is bad, that I should feel guilty for being white.' In many ways now, in tens of thousands of these young people, we have a captive audience."

White-power cliques are often the equivalent of Crips for white kids—the gang's ideology is secondary, at least in the beginning. "Sometimes they feel like an outcast and a loner," says Angela Lowry, an intelligence analyst for the Klanwatch project of the Southern Poverty Law Center. "And suddenly, they join a skinhead group and they belong." Once a teen-ager finds his way into a local clique, Resistance and other groups link him up with other white-power followers and give him the sense of belonging to an international and historical movement.

And Burdi, says Remie666, the teen-age skinhead, is probably going to be the main leader of white-power youth in the future. "He has a lot of power in his voice when he speaks," he says. "I think he's a very good influence. I see people listening to him more than anyone else."

Such enthusiasm is daunting to hate-group watchdogs. Rabbi Cooper has petitioned Internet providers to adopt a code of ethics that would outlaw hate speech on their services. "Just scrolling through the various racist sites on the Internet, a person can say, 'Look at how many groups there are—I'm not isolated,' " says Rabbi Cooper. "In schools, we're pushing our kids to look at that computer screen to do their homework, to do their research. That's the location where they're going to play their games and that's going to be the main area of engagement, the market-place of ideas."

Not that neo-Nazis go unchallenged on the Internet. Nonracist skin-heads in particular attack the Resistance site and other similar ones. They call the racists "boneheads" and consider Burdi a pathetic caricature, citing the time he wore a disguise when he appeared on Geraldo Rivera's talk show. Burdi recently posted a message on the popular news group "alt.skinhead" to advertise the latest Rahowa album, and the response was scathing. "Yay!!!" one person wrote back. "George 'I'm a moron' Burdi admits that all this WP-type [expletive]"—referring to white-power philosophy—"is just another form of cult . . . where they convince you they're the only people they can trust, and then they convince you to give them all your money, and then there are the little 'survivalist' camps."

Burdi himself is unperturbed by such responses. He has learned a les-son of direct mail marketing: 10 percent positive response is victory.

New York Times Magazine, February 25, 1996, pp. 40, 42–43.

TOPICS FOR WRITTEN OR ORAL EXPLORATION

1. Have you ever been a victim of prejudice? a perpetrator? bystander? rescuer? Write a story in which you recreate the situation you found yourself in and how it was resolved.

2. Have you ever not spoken up or not acted in a situation when you felt you should have? How did you feel? What did you do or not do? What do you wish you had done? Write a story in which you behave differently from the way you did in real life.

3. Identify prejudices in your community. What are the causes of these prejudices? What are the consequences?

4. Write down all incidents and examples of prejudice and discrimination that you see or hear around you for the next week. How do they affect the people involved? The people aware of it happening?

5. What steps can be or have been taken to combat prejudice in your community? Write a letter to your school or local paper recommending this action.

6. Find examples of prejudice and racism in newspaper articles and news magazines. What is the message being conveyed? Write a letter to the editor expressing your feelings about an article.

7. Many teens want to look and behave just like their friends. As a result of this desire to "fit in," teens are often stereotyped and misjudged. Make a list of the characteristics and behaviors of different groups in your school. What are the stereotypes associated with each group? Talk to members of these groups and write about the reality versus the stereotype.

8. Why do people need scapegoats? Find an example of a group in your community or a nation which serves as a scapegoat today.

9. Choose a period in European history and research specific anti-Semitic policies implemented during that time.

10. Research the Protestant Reformation and write about the way the Jews were treated by the "reformers."

11. Compare the development of Jewish culture in a European country which limited Jewish rights with that in a country which allowed Jews their civil rights.

12. Read France's Declaration of the Rights of Man and identify the ways in which it helped the Jews become full-fledged citizens.

13. What is propaganda? How is it different from advertising? Find examples of both in sources of information you refer to. Can entertain-

ment be used to spread propaganda? Find examples and develop a creative response to the propaganda—poster, video, song.

14. What were some of the methods the Nazis used to spread anti-Semitism in Germany? Find examples of propaganda directed specifically at young people.

15. Why did the Nazis issue anti-Jewish decrees gradually? What might have happened if all of the decrees had been instituted at one time? How did most Jewish people react? How did non-Jews react?

16. The nineteenth-century psychologist William James wrote: "When you have a choice to make and you don't make it, that in itself is a choice." Explain what he meant and give examples.

17. Write a research paper about the impact of the Great Depression on the people of the United States. How did Americans react to the Depression? How did it affect the U.S. government? Was it the same or different from what happened in Germany?

18. Imagine that you are a non-Jewish German teen watching the events of Kristallnacht. Write a diary entry describing what you see and how you feel.

19. Imagine that you are a Jewish teen observing the same events. Write a diary entry.

20. Imagine that you are an American teen reading about Kristallnacht in your morning newspaper. Write a diary entry. Compare it with the versions above. How are they the same? Different?

21. Read other news accounts of Kristallnacht. What is emphasized? Does the writer take a position?

22. Compare the editorial "Nazi Day of Terror a Threat to All Civilization" with one of the news articles about the event. How are they different?

23. Write your own editorial based on the information in the news articles.

24. Interview someone who remembers hearing or reading about Kristallnacht. Write their version of the events. Compare them to the news article as well as to the way Kristallnacht is described in a history text.

25. Does television affect the way we feel about what happens in other parts of the world? Do you think it would have made a difference if Kristallnacht and its aftermath had been televised on CNN? Find examples of recent events affected by television coverage.

26. Find examples of groups that appeal to people who feel left out of the mainstream of society. How do these groups find their members?

Write a report on one of these groups comparing and contrasting their techniques to the Hitler Youth Movement.

27. A number of organizations, including the Anti-Defamation League, monitor the activities of "hate" groups. Write a report on one of these counter-racist organizations.

28. Interview someone who once belonged to a gang or an organization they now consider dangerous or detrimental to themselves or society. Find out why they joined and what they gained from belonging to the group. Why did they leave? What have they learned?

29. Choose a recent incident of anti-Semitism in the United States. Write a report in which you describe the incident, its perpetrators, and the community's reaction to the anti-Semitic act. Were measures instituted to help prevent future acts of this kind?

30. Write a report on one form of racism in the United States. Who are the victims? How are they affected by discrimination? What is being done to resolve the problem? What can you do?

SUGGESTED READINGS

Anti-Semitism

Cohn, Norman. *Warrant for Genocide: The Myth of the Jewish World-Conspiracy and the "Protocols of the Elders of Zion."* Chico, Calif.: Scholars Press, 1981.

Parkes, James. *Antisemitism*. Chicago: Quadrangle Books, 1963.

Patterson, Charles. *Anti-Semitism: The Road to the Holocaust and Beyond*. New York: Walker and Co., 1988.

Wistrich, Robert S. *Antisemitism: The Longest Hatred*. New York: Pantheon Books, 1991.

History of the Jews and Anti-Semitism

Encyclopedia of Jewish History: Events and Eras of the Jewish People. New York: Facts on File Publications, 1986.

Facing History and Ourselves, National Foundation. *Resource Book: Facing History and Ourselves. Holocaust and Human Behavior*. Brookline, Mass.: 1994.

Goldberg, David J., and John D. Rayner. *The Jewish People: Their History and Their Religion*. New York: Viking Penguin, 1987.

Mosse, George L. *The Culture of Western Europe: The Nineteenth and Twentieth Centuries*. Chicago: Rand McNally, 1961.

Jews in Germany

Adler, H. G. *The Jews in Germany: From the Enlightenment to National Socialism*. London: University of Notre Dame Press, 1969.

Johnson, Paul. *A History of the Jews*. New York: Harper and Row, 1987.

Mosse, George L. *Germans and Jews*. New York: Howard Fertig, 1970.

Rühs, Friedrich. *The Claims of the Jews for Civil Rights in Germany*. Trans. by Helen Lederer. Cincinnati: Hebrew Union College, Jewish Institute of Religion, 1977.

von Treitschke, Heinrich. *A Word About Our Jewry: Readings in Modern Jewish History*. Edited by Ellis Rivkin. Trans. by Helen Lederer. Cincinnati: Hebrew Union College, Jewish Institute of Religion, 1958.

The Rise of Nazi Power

Browning, Christopher R. *Ordinary Men: Reserve Battalion 101 and the Final Solution in Poland*. New York: HarperCollins, 1992.

Dawidowicz, Lucy S. *A Holocaust Reader*. West Orange, N.J.: Behrman House, 1976.

Dolan, Edward F., Jr. *Adolf Hitler: A Portrait in Tyranny*. New York: Dodd, Mead, 1981.

Fischer, Klaus P. *Nazi Germany: A New History*. New York: Continuum, 1995.

Hitler, Adolf. *Mein Kampf*. Translated by Ralph Manheim. Boston: Houghton Mifflin, 1943.

Irving, David. *Hitler's War*. New York: Avon Books, 1990.

Koch, H. W. *The Hitler Youth: Origins and Development, 1922–1945*. New York: Stein and Day, 1976.

Koehn, Ilse. *Mischling, Second Degree: My Childhood in Nazi Germany*. New York: Puffin Books, 1990.

Mosse, George L. *Nazi Culture: Intellectual, Cultural and Social Life in the Third Reich*. New York: Grosset and Dunlap, 1966.

Owings, Alison. *Frauen: German Women Recall the Third Reich*. New Brunswick, N.J.: Rutgers University Press, 1993.

Shirer, William. *The Rise and Fall of Adolf Hitler*. New York: Random House, 1961.

Switzer, Ellen. *How Democracy Failed*. New York: Atheneum, 1975.

Germany Today

Elon, Amos. "The Jew Who Fought to Stay German." *New York Times Magazine*, March 24, 1996.

Hasselbach, Ingo, and Tom Reiss. "How Nazis Are Made." *New Yorker*, January 8, 1996. Pp. 36+.

Schneider Peter. "The Sins of the Grandfathers: How German Teen-agers

Confront the Holocaust, and How They Don't." *New York Times Magazine*, December 3, 1995.

Contemporary Novels About Germany and the Holocaust

Hegi, Ursula. *Stones from the River*. New York: Scribner Paperback Fiction, 1994.
Wolf, Christa. *Patterns of Childhood*. New York: Farrar, Straus and Giroux, 1984.

7

The Holocaust

CHRONOLOGY: GERMANY AND THE HOLOCAUST

November 11, 1918	World War I ends.
January 1923	National Socialist German Workers' Party (Nazi Party) holds its first rally.
Autumn 1925	Adolf Hitler's autobiography *Mein Kampf* is published.
1929	Worldwide economic depression begins.
January 30, 1933	Hitler is appointed chancellor of Germany.
March 23, 1933	Hitler declares himself Führer and the German parliament is dissolved.
Spring 1933	The Secret Police, the Gestapo, is created.
April 1933	Nazis proclaim boycotts against Jewish businesses and medical and legal practices. A "non-Aryan" law removes Jews from government and teaching positions.
July 1933	All political parties except for the Nazi Party are banned.
September 15, 1935	The Nuremberg Laws legalize anti-Semitic policies and deprive Jews of German citizenship.

1937	Jewish students are removed from German schools and universities. Jewish travel abroad is restricted.
1938	Anti-Jewish Decrees implemented: All Jews must carry identification marked with a "J"; Jews are "renamed" Israel and Sarah, not permitted to have German names; Jews may not head any businesses; Jewish doctors can no longer keep their medical licenses; Jews may not attend plays, movies, concerts; Jews must hand over their valuables, jewelry, securities.
March 12, 1938	Germany annexes Austria.
November 8–9, 1938	Kristallnacht. Pogrom in Germany and Austria initiated and supported by Nazi Party. Jewish-owned property and businesses looted and destroyed. Synagogues looted and destroyed.
March 15, 1939	Germany occupies Czechoslovakia.
September 1, 1939	Germany invades Poland. World War II begins. Polish Jews must wear yellow Stars of David on all outer clothing.
September 1939	Hitler implements program to kill the physically disabled, mentally handicapped, and institutionalized.
1940	Deportation of German Jews to concentration camps begins.
April and May 1940	Germany invades Denmark and Norway, the Netherlands, France, Belgium, and Luxembourg.
December 11, 1941	Germany declares war on the United States.
January 20, 1942	The Wannsee Conference is held. Implementation of the "Final Solution to the European Jewish Question" is begun.
1942	Auschwitz-Birkenau, Belzec, Sobibór, and Treblinka are fully operational death camps in Poland.
June 1943	All ghettos in Poland and the Soviet Union are "liquidated." Polish and Russian Jews are sent to death camps.

June 6, 1944	D Day. The Allies invade Western Europe.
January 1945	Soviet troops liberate Auschwitz death camp.
April 1945	American troops liberate Buchenwald death camp; British troops liberate Bergen-Belsen death camp.
April 30, 1945	Adolf Hitler commits suicide.
May 7, 1945	Germany surrenders. World War II ends in Europe.
November 1945	The Nuremberg Trials of Nazi war criminals begin in Nuremberg, Germany.

WORLD WAR II BEGINS

By 1939 Hitler believed that Germany was once again strong enough economically and militarily to reclaim its position as a world power with himself as its leader. He had peacefully annexed Austria in 1938, significantly increasing both his territories and available manpower. On September 1, 1939, his armies invaded Poland with the excuse that the German people deserved more *Lebensraum* (living space). With this invasion, World War II officially began. Eventually twenty-six nations led by Britain, the United States, and the Soviet Union would become allies against the Axis powers, Germany, Italy, and Japan.

Behind Hitler's seemingly nationalistic goal was his monomaniacal desire to rid Europe of all Jews. In every country he conquered, Adolf Hitler introduced his anti-Semitic policies and increasingly persecuted the Jewish populations. Often, citizens of the invaded countries were more than willing to assist the Germans in rounding up and slaughtering their Jewish neighbors. Ultimately, two out of every three Jews living in Europe during World War II were killed.

After decisively defeating the Polish army, Germany and the Soviet Union divided Poland based on a nonaggression pact they had signed shortly before the invasion. Twenty-two million Poles, among them three and a half million Jews who were to be targeted for death, were now a part of the German empire. The Polish population was terrorized, and political and religious leaders were executed. Hitler's goal was to make all Poles slave laborers for his expanded German empire.

GERMANY INVADES EUROPE

In April 1940 Germany invaded and captured Denmark and Norway, and in May 1940 Belgium and the Netherlands were conquered. On June 13, 1940, Paris fell to German troops, and France was soon divided between Germany and Italy, Hitler's ally. By June 1941 Germany had invaded the Soviet Union, and 3 million more Jews were at the mercy of Nazi aggression. Everywhere Nazi armies attacked, anti-Semitic propaganda was spread, and then increasingly harsh policies were enforced against the Jewish populations. Eventually, the Jews in many European cities were forced to move to ghettos, where they lived in poverty and desperation. Constantly in danger of being assaulted and killed by Nazi guards, those Jews who managed to survive the misery of the ghettos later became victims of the Nazi death camps.

THE WANNSEE CONFERENCE

Anti-Semitic policies had been disrupting and destroying Jewish lives in Germany and other parts of Europe even before the beginning of World War II; however, once war was officially declared, the Nazis actively rounded up and killed Jews by firing squads and in mobile gas vans. Yet these forms of extermination were not efficient enough nor on a large enough scale for the German Nazi leaders.

On January 20, 1942, German bureaucrats met at the Wannsee Conference to discuss and coordinate the implementation of "The Final Solution to the Jewish Question." There was neither debate nor consideration of other options for the fate of the Jews. Instead, those gathered for the meeting listened to a speech in which the "Jewish question" was reviewed. In less than an hour and a half, the extermination of the Jews became official Nazi policy. The "Final Solution" would be implemented by using the Jews for labor in the East. Then,

> In big labor gangs, with the sexes separated, Jews capable of work will be brought to these areas, employed in roadbuilding, in which

task a large part will undoubtedly disappear through natural diminution.

The remnant that may eventually remain, being undoubtedly the part most capable of resistance, will have to be appropriately dealt with, since it represents a natural selection and in the event of release is to be regarded as the germ cell of a new Jewish renewal. (Witness the experience of history.)

CONCENTRATION CAMPS

The infamous Nazi concentration camps had their origins well before the beginnings of World War II. Originally established to incarcerate political rivals and Communist Party members, the camps also became detention centers for anyone considered "asocial": tramps, beggars, criminals, and, later, homosexuals, Gypsies, and convicted prostitutes. As Hitler instituted plans for invading neighboring countries, and then as Nazi aggression escalated, new and larger concentration camps were established. Eventually, more than 9,000 camps existed throughout German-occupied Europe.

There were a number of different kinds of concentration camps. Labor camps, including Bergen-Belsen, were established to provide slave laborers for special war-related projects. Transit camps, like Westerbork in the Netherlands, held captured Jews and other prisoners until they could be transferred to other concentration camps. By 1942, six concentration camps had been established to serve as extermination centers where victims, the vast majority of them Jews, were gassed and then burned in crematoria. At Treblinka, Sobibór, Belzec, Chelmno, Majdanek, and Auschwitz-Birkenau, millions of innocent people were methodically sent to their deaths by Nazi SS officers.

THE DEATH CAMPS

All of the Nazi extermination centers were located on main railroad lines in Poland, far enough away from Germany so that the killings could not easily be observed or reported by German citizenry. As soon as a train arrived at a death camp, those victims who had succumbed in transit were removed from the train, and those who could not walk on their own were taken away, never to be seen again. Those who could still walk were sent to the first selection. Old people, young children, pregnant women, women with small children, and the infirm were sent to the left and immediate death. Those who could serve as slave laborers were sent to the right, reprieved from death for a while. They were branded with tattoos, their heads were shaved, and they were given prison uniforms which neither fit nor kept them warm. These selections, or "special actions," went on day after day, often more than once a day. Even when inmates escaped selection one day, they were repeatedly forced to face the same terrifying process as their strength and health deteriorated, and the likelihood of selection increased.

Charlotte Delbo, a French woman who was not Jewish, was sent to Auschwitz as a political prisoner because of her anti-German activity. Although political prisoners were not automatically selected for the gas chambers, they did suffer from the same extreme conditions as their Jewish counterparts, and eventually those who could no longer work were selected for extermination. Delbo describes the horrors of selection in her memoir *None of Us Will Return*:

> For days on end they had been hungry and thirsty above all. They had been cold, lying almost naked on boards without straws or blankets. Locked up with dying or crazy women, they awaited their turn to die or go mad. In the morning, they stepped outside. They were driven out by cudgel blows. Blows imparted to the dying and the insane. The living had to pull out into the yard those who died during the night, because the dead had to be counted also. The SS walked by. He enjoyed setting his dog on them. This was the howling heard at night. Then silence. The roll call was over. It was the daytime silence. The women still alive went back. The dead women remained in the snow. They had been stripped naked. Their clothes would be used for others.
>
> Every two or three days, trucks arrived to take the living to the gas chamber, the dead to the crematorium.[1]

Delbo conveys the victims' suffering in stark, terse language that forces us to confront what she calls the "inexplicable." In contrast, an SS captain in Auschwitz (a former university professor!) reveals in his diary what selection was like from the perpetrator's perspective:

9/2/42—Present for the first time at a "special action" at three o'clock in the morning. In comparison to this, Dante's inferno seems to me a comedy. . . .

9/5/42—This afternoon present at a special action from the women's KZ [concentration camp]. . . . here we are in the *anus mundi*. Toward 8:00 p.m. at another special action from Holland. . . .

9/6–7/42—Today we had an excellent lunch: tomato soup, half a chicken with potatoes and red cabbage, pudding and excellent vanilla ice cream. . . . Outside again at 8:00 p.m. for a special action.

9/9/42—Took part in a special action in the evening (four times). How many doubles do I have in this world?[2]

This SS captain describes his lunch in more detail than he describes the scene of death he "took part in." He wonders about his "doubles" without commenting on himself. Yet, it is clear from his references to Dante's *Inferno* and the *anus mundi* that he knows he is witnessing and participating in events that are incomparable in their horrors and have no parallels in human history.

JEWISH RESISTANCE AND RESCUE

Despite a long history of anti-Semitic attitudes and uprisings (pogroms) in which Jews were killed and their property destroyed, European Jews were utterly unprepared to combat the overwhelming brutality and magnitude of Nazi policy. As civilian citizens of villages, towns, and cities, they did not have an arsenal of weapons with which to defend themselves. Nor did they have experience in resisting and sabotaging Nazi orders. Most important, retaliation against Jewish resistance was swift, brutal, and always on a massive scale to discourage similar acts. In spite of these overwhelming limitations, however, there were significant numbers of Jewish men, women, and even children (see Yehuda Nir's memoir in Chapter 5) who actively resisted their oppressors and managed to save Jewish lives.

Resistance took a number of different forms. Jews forged documents and identification papers to help their people escape Nazi persecution. A number of Jews who had immigrated to Palestine before the war joined the British army and formed a Jewish Brigade. Among them was a young Hungarian woman, Hannah Senesh, who parachuted into occupied territory and spent months making her way to Hungary in an attempt to save Jews. Senesh was captured, tortured, tried, and executed as a traitor to Hungary.

Jews formed or joined resistance groups thoughout Europe. They rescued and protected their fellow Jews while hiding in forests and fighting the Nazis and collaborators. In many ghettos, including Warsaw and Vilna, underground resistance groups were led by young people who had been trained in Communist and Zionist movements before the war. Whatever weapons and explosives they could collect were used to fight their oppressors and free Jews. Sometimes in the midst of an uprising Jews were able to escape and hide out in nearby forests, while those who remained in the ghettos almost always either died there or were deported to concentration camps.

Even in the death camps, inmates occasionally killed guards and managed to blow up gas chambers and crematoria. In Auschwitz-Monowitz, the labor camp section of Auschwitz, four women working in a munitions factory smuggled out capsules of explosives and turned them over to Jewish underground members in the camp. One of the four crematoria was destroyed and a second one was damaged; however, the Germans were able to trace the explosives, and the women were hanged publicly. In the rare instances when concentration camp inmates were able to escape, once on the run they often found themselves at the mercy of the local inhabitants, many of whom were just as willing to kill them as give them food or shelter.

A more subtle form of resistance occurred whenever Jews did not succumb psychologically to the dehumanizing treatment inflicted on them by their captors. In ghettos and in concentration camps, as long as they remained alive, many Jews did whatever they could to protect the children. They continued to teach them about Jewish traditions and holidays; they sang songs and told stories, and they remained dedicated to providing whatever care they could while the children were alive.

THE UNITED STATES AND THE JEWS

Emma Lazarus, a Jewish poet, wrote the words inscribed on the base of the Statue of Liberty: "Give me your tired, your poor, your huddled masses yearning to breathe free." If she could have imagined the Holocaust she would have added, "and be sure to send me your victims of Nazi persecution." Regrettably, when it came to offering refuge to the many desperate Jews seeking asylum, the United States was less than enthusiastic and generous.

By 1939 the situation for Jews in Germany was clearly a matter of life or death. Those who still remained knew that time was quickly running out for any chance of escape. Only the intervention of other governments could offer any possibility of rescue. The United States was one such powerful nation with the resources to rescue many Jews. Unfortunately, as in other parts of the world, the Depression had left Americans fearful for their own economic well-being. They saw the Jewish immigrants as a threat to their jobs, and although 95 percent of Americans opposed the Nazi regime, only 9 percent approved of allowing more refugees into the country. Also, since anti-Semitism was already widespread in the United States, American Jews were afraid that additional pressure on behalf of Jewish immigrants would aggravate the situation further.

JEWISH CHILDREN NEED A REFUGE

As the situation in Germany became increasingly dangerous for the Jews, the Netherlands, Belgium, and Great Britain responded by welcoming thousands of German Jewish children into their still safe borders. Similarly, at the beginning of 1939, a proposal to admit 20,000 German children was presented to the White House and the U.S. Congress. The children would be temporarily adopted by American families, and their expenses would be paid by contributions from organizations and individuals. The response to this plan, to be coordinated by the American Friends Service Committee, a Quaker group, was immediate and overwhelming. Within days, 4,000 families of all faiths volunteered to care for the children, and hundreds of inquiries were made regarding the proposal. Yet precious weeks went by, and the proposal languished. President Roosevelt feared opposition from Congress in the form of even stricter immigration laws, and he did not wish to jeopardize other political priorities, including gaining approval of increased funds for defense.

There was also opposition to the plan from such organizations as American Women Against Communism, Society of Mayflower

Descendants, Sons of the American Revolution, and Daughters of the American Revolution. One spokeswoman who testified in support of a bill that would abolish all immigration to the United States for the next decade said:

> This nation will be helpless to guarantee to our children their rights, under the Constitution, to life, liberty, and the pursuit of happiness if this country is to become the dumping ground for the persecuted minorities of Europe. The refugees have a heritage of hate. They could never become loyal Americans.

She went on to describe the prospective young immigrants as "thousands of motherless, embittered, persecuted children of undesirable foreigners."[3]

Witnesses for and against the Wagner-Rogers legislation, as it was called, testified before a Congressional committee. People of all religious faiths argued for the moral necessity of rescuing the children. Others argued that rather than being an economic burden on the country, immigrants brought their talents to the United States, thereby creating new areas for development and economic growth. Finally, the Quakers prepared a booklet, *Refugee Facts*, which provided statistics to prove that despite immigration to the United States between 1932 and 1938 there had actually been a population decrease of 5,000. More important, in terms of passing the Wagner-Rogers bill, only 26 percent of the German quota had been filled during those six years, and therefore the United States could have legally admitted significant numbers of German refugees without passing additional legislation.

The final version of the Child Refugee Bill allowed visas to be given to 20,000 German children in place of, rather than in addition to, the German quota, thereby replacing 20,000 German adults with children. Senator Wagner was horrified by this amendment, pointing out that it would mean "needlessly cruel consequences for adults in Germany." In anguish, he withdrew the proposal. America was kept safe from the "motherless" Jewish children who could not defend themselves against the Nazi terror.

THE SS *ST. LOUIS*

One of the most infamous examples of the abandonment of the Jews occurred in the spring of 1939 when the SS *St. Louis*, a luxury liner, left Germany with 936 passengers, 930 of whom were Jewish. The refugees believed they had all necessary papers, visas, and payments to ensure their acceptance at their destination, Havana, Cuba. In fact, their landing certificates had been invalidated by the president of Cuba, but no one had notified the captain and passengers of the *St. Louis*. Completely unaware of the technical—but fatal—changes in their status, mothers and fathers, grandparents and small children luxuriated in their extraordinary good fortune. They were treated like cruise-ship guests by the captain of the *St. Louis* and his crew, and the enormously grateful refugees all believed that they had just barely escaped certain death at the hands of the Nazis.

Despite the intensive efforts of the American Jewish Distribution Committee (JDC), an organization involved in helping Jews emigrate from Europe, neither Cuba nor the United States would allow the refugees asylum after the situation became clear. Even those passengers who already had U.S. immigration numbers and were waiting their turn to enter the United States were not given special consideration. After several days of frustrating attempts at negotiating a "ransom," the *St. Louis* was forced to leave Cuba with most of its passengers still on board. As the ship began its somber journey back to Europe, it came so close to Miami, Florida, that its 907 remaining passengers could clearly see the lights of the U.S. city.

While people in the United States and around the world followed the shocking story of the *St. Louis* in their daily newspapers, no nation offered its passengers a safe haven. In one letter sent to a U.S. newspaper, Bishop James Cannon, Jr., wrote:

> And during the days when this horrible tragedy was being enacted right at our doors, our government in Washington made no effort to relieve the desperate situation of these people, but on the contrary gave orders that they be kept out of the country. . . . The failure to take any steps whatever to assist these distressed, persecuted Jews in their hour of extremity was one of the most disgraceful things which has happened in American history and leaves a stain and brand of shame upon the record of our nation.[4]

An editorial in the *New York Times* of June 8 decried the situation of the Jewish refugees and went on to say: "We can only hope that some hearts will soften somewhere and some refuge be found.

The cruise of the *St. Louis* cries to high heaven of man's inhumanity to man." Tragically, American hearts were not softened enough to offer even temporary safety to the men, women, and children who would face certain death if they were forced to return to Germany.

While the *St. Louis* slowly made its way back toward Europe, the Jewish Distribution Committee continued to implore European countries to open their doors to the 907 Jews. Through intensive and relentless negotiation, the JDC managed to find sanctuary for all of the *St. Louis* passengers in Belgium, Great Britain, France, and the Netherlands.

Tragically, with the outbreak of World War II in September 1939, many *St. Louis* refugees once again found themselves victims of Nazi anti-Semitism. Except for the 288 passengers who had been allowed to remain in Britain, the Jews of the *St. Louis* were doomed to the fate—extermination—they had so desperately tried to escape on their long voyage away from Hitler's Germany.

THE DOCUMENTS

This chapter includes excerpts from the minutes of the 1942 Wannsee Conference, articles from the *New York Times*, and a map showing the fate of millions of Jews during World War II.

NOTES

1. Charlotte Delbo, *Auschwitz and After*, translated by Rosette C. Lamont (New Haven: Yale University Press, 1995), 19.

2. Ernst Schnabel, *Anne Frank: A Portrait in Courage*, translated by Richard and Clara Winston (New York: Harcourt, Brace and World, 1958), 122–123.

3. Quoted in Arthur D. Morse, *While Six Million Died: A Chronicle of American Apathy* (New York: Random House, 1967), 260.

4. Quoted in ibid., 280.

"THE FINAL SOLUTION TO THE JEWISH QUESTION"

Hiding their genocidal design behind euphemism, whereby Jews who survived the harsh labor camps would be "treated accordingly," the fifteen participants of the Wannsee Conference (eight of whom held Ph.D. degrees) agreed to organize and administer the systematic killing of every remaining Jew in Europe.

FROM MINUTES OF THE WANNSEE CONFERENCE,
JANUARY 20, 1942

Secret Reich Business!

Protocol of Conference

I The following took part in the conference on the final solution of the Jewish question held on January 20, 1942, in Berlin, Am Grossen Wannsee No. 56–58:

Gauleiter Dr. Meyer and Reich Office Director Dr. Leibbrandt	Reich Ministry for the Occupied Eastern Territories
Secretary of State Dr. Stuckart	Reich Ministry of the Interior
Secretary of State Neumann	Plenipotentiary for the Four Year Plan
Secretary of State Dr. Freisler	Reich Ministry of Justice
Secretary of State Dr. Bühler	Office of the Governor General
Undersecretary of State Luther	Foreign Office
SS Oberführer Klopfer	Party Chancellery
Ministerial Director Kritzinger	Reich Chancellery
SS Gruppenführer Hofmann	Race and Settlement Main Office
SS Gruppenführer Müller	Reich Security Main Office
SS Obersturmbannführer Eichmann	

SS Oberführer Dr. Schöngrath, Commander of the Security Police and the SD in the General-gouvernement	Security Police and SD
SS Sturmbannführer Dr. Lange, Commander of the Security Police and the SD in the General District of Latvia, as representative of the Commander of the Security Police and the SD for the Reich Commissariat for the Ostland	Security Police and SD

II   At the beginning of the meeting the Chief of the Security Police and the SD, SS Obergruppenführer *Heydrich*, announced his appointment by the Reich Marshal, as Plenipotentiary for the Preparation of the Final Solution of the European Jewish Question, and pointed out that this conference had been called to clear up fundamental questions. The Reich Marshal's request to have a draft sent to him on the organizational, substantive, and economic concerns on the final solution of the European Jewish question necessitates prior joint consideration by all central agencies directly concerned with these questions, with a view to keeping policy lines parallel.

Primary responsibility for the handling of the final solution of the Jewish question, the speaker stated, is to lie centrally, regardless of geographic boundaries, with the Reichsführer SS and the Chief of the German Police (Chief of the Security Police and the SD).

The Chief of the Security Police and the SD then gave a brief review of the struggle conducted up to now against this enemy. The most important aspects are:

a. Forcing the Jews out of the various areas of life of the German people;
b. Forcing the Jews out of the living space of the German people.

In carrying out these efforts, acceleration of the emigration of the Jews from Reich territory, being the only possible provisional solution, was undertaken in intensified and systematic fashion.

By decree of the Reich Marshal, a Reich Central Office for Jewish Emigration was set up in January 1939, and its direction was entrusted to the Chief of the Security Police and the SD. In particular, its tasks were:
a. To take all measures toward *preparation* for intensified emigration of the Jews;

b. To *direct* the stream of emigration;
c. To expedite emigration *in individual cases.*

The objectives of these tasks was [*sic*] to cleanse the German living space of Jews in a legal way.

The disadvantages entailed by such a forcing of emigration were clear to all the authorities. But in the absence of other possible solutions, they had to be accepted for the time being.

In the ensuing period, the handling of emigration was not only a German problem, but also a problem with which the authorities of the countries of destination or immigration had to deal. Financial difficulties—such as increases decreed by the various foreign governments in the moneys which immigrants were required to have and in landing fees—as well as lack of steamship berths, continually intensified restrictions, or bans on immigration hampered the emigration efforts exceedingly. Despite these difficulties, a total of approximately 537,000 Jews was processed into emigration between the assumption of power and the date of October 31, 1941, consisting of the following:

Since January 30, 1933:	from the Altreich[1] approx. 360,000
Since March 15, 1938:	from the Ostmark[2] approx. 147,000
Since March 15, 1939:	from the Protectorate of Bohemia and Moravia approx. 30,000

Financing of the emigration was handled by the Jews or Jewish political organizations themselves. To avoid a situation where only the proletarianized Jews would remain behind, the principle was followed that well-to-do Jews had to finance the emigration of destitute Jews. To this end, a special assessment or emigration levy, staggered by property levels, was decreed, the proceeds being used to meet financial obligations in connection with the emigration of destitute Jews.

In addition to the funds raised in German marks, foreign currency was needed for the moneys which emigrants were required to have and for landing fees. To conserve the German supply of foreign currencies, Jewish financial institutions abroad were prompted by the Jewish organizations in this country to see to it that appropriate funds in foreign currencies were obtained. Through these foreign Jews, a total of approx-

1. *Altreich* was the Nazi term to designate Germany's boundaries prior to March 1938.
2. *Ostmark* was the Nazi term to designate Austria after the Anschluss [annexation of Austria].

imately $9,500,000 was made available by way of gifts up to October 30, 1941.

Since then, in view of the dangers of emigration during wartime and in view of the possibilities in the East, the Reichsführer SS and Chief of the German Police has forbidden the emigration of Jews.

III   Emigration has now been replaced by evacuation of the Jews to the East as a further possible solution, in accordance with previous authorization by the Führer.

However, these actions are to be regarded only as provisional options; even now practical experience is being gathered that is of major significance in view of the coming final solution of the Jewish question.

In connection with this final solution of the European Jewish question, approximately 11 million Jews may be presumed to be affected.[3] They are distributed among the individual countries as follows:

	Country	*Number*
A.	Altreich	131,800
	Ostmark	43,700
	Eastern Territories	420,000
	Generalgouvernement	2,284,000
	Bialystok	400,000
	Protectorate of Bohemia & Moravia	74,200
	Estonia—free of Jews	
	Latvia	3,500
	Lithuania	34,000
	Belgium	43,000
	Denmark	5,600
	France: Occupied territory	165,000
	Unoccupied territory	700,000
	Greece	69,600
	The Netherlands	160,800
	Norway	1,300
B.	Bulgaria	48,000
	England	330,000
	Finland	2,300

3. These statistics, the product of Eichmann's research, are far from correct. The size of the Jewish population of the U.S.S.R., for example, was grossly exaggerated.

Country	Number
Ireland	4,000
Italy, including Sardinia	58,000
Albania	200
Croatia	40,000
Portugal	3,000
Rumania, including Bessarabia	342,000
Sweden	8,000
Switzerland	18,000
Serbia	10,000
Slovakia	88,000
Spain	6,000
Turkey (European part)	55,500
Hungary	742,800
U.S.S.R.	5,000,000
Ukraine	2,994,684
White Russia, excluding Bialystok	446,484

TOTAL   over   11,000,000

However, the numbers of Jews given for the various foreign states reflect only those of Jewish faith, as definitions of Jews according to racial principles are still partly lacking there. The handling of the problem in the individual countries, especially in Hungary and Rumania, will meet with certain difficulties, on account of prevailing attitudes and ideas. To this day, for example, a Jew in Rumania can for money obtain appropriate documents officially confirming him to be of some foreign citizenship.

The influence of the Jews upon all areas in the U.S.S.R. is well known. About five million live in the European area, a scant quarter-million in the Asian territory.

The occupational breakdown of Jews residing in the European area of the U.S.S.R. was about as follows:

In agriculture	9.1%
Urban workers	14.8%
In commerce	20.0%

| Employed as government workers | 23.4% |
| In professions—medicine, the press, theater, etc. | 32.7%[4] |

Under appropriate direction, in the course of the final solution, the Jews are now to be suitably assigned to labor in the East. In big labor gangs, with the sexes separated, Jews capable of work will be brought to these areas, employed in roadbuilding, in which task a large part will undoubtedly disappear through natural diminution.

The remnant that may eventually remain, being undoubtedly the part most capable of resistance, will have to be appropriately dealt with, since it represents a natural selection and in the event of release is to be regarded as the germ cell of a new Jewish renewal. (Witness the experience of history.)

In the course of the practical implementation of the final solution, Europe is to be combed through from west to east. The Reich area, including the Protectorate of Bohemia and Moravia, will have to be handled in advance, if only because of the housing problem and other sociopolitical necessities.

The evacuated Jews will first be brought, group by group, into so-called transit ghettos, to be transported from there farther to the East.

An important prerequisite for the implementation of the evacuation as a whole, SS Obergruppenführer *Heydrich* explained further, is the exact determination of the category of persons that may be affected.

The intent is not to evacuate Jews over 65 years of age, but to assign them to a ghetto for the aged. Theresienstadt is under consideration.[5]

Along with these age groups (of the approximately 280,000[6] Jews who on October 31, 1941, were in the Altreich and the Ostmark, approximately 30 per cent are over 65 years old), Jews with serious wartime disabilities and Jews with war decorations (Iron Cross, First Class) will be taken into the Jewish old-age ghettos. With this efficient solution, the many interventions [requests for exceptions] will be eliminated at one stroke.

The beginning of each of the larger evacuation actions will depend largely on military developments. With regard to the handling of the final solution in the European areas occupied by us and under our influence, it was proposed that the appropriate specialists in the Foreign Office confer with the competent official of the Security Police and the SD.

---

4. Jewish occupational structure in the U.S.S.R. was actually quite different. About forty percent of the Soviet Jews were industrial workers and fewer than twenty percent were in the professions and government service.

5. Theresienstadt served a dual purpose. It was a ghetto for privileged categories of German Jews and at the same time a transit camp for assembling the Czech Jews prior to their deportation to Auschwitz.

6. Likely a typographical error in the original, this figure probably should read "180,000."

In Slovakia and Croatia the undertaking is no longer too difficult, as the most essential problems in this matter have already been brought to a solution there. In Rumania, likewise, the government has by now appointed a Commissioner for Jewish Affairs. For settling the problem in Hungary it will be necessary in the near future to impose upon the Hungarian Government an adviser in Jewish problems.

With regard to beginning preparations for the settling of the problem in Italy, SS Obergruppenführer *Heydrich* considers liaison with the Police Chief appropriate in these matters.

In occupied and unoccupied France, the roundup of the Jews for evacuation can in all probability take place without great difficulties.

On this point, Undersecretary of State *Luther* stated that thorough handling of this problem will occasion difficulties in a few countries, such as the Nordic states, and that it will therefore be advisable to postpone these countries for the time being. In consideration of the small number of Jews presumably affected there, this postponement does not constitute an appreciable curtailment in any case.

On the other hand, the Foreign Office sees no great difficulties with respect to the Southeast and West of Europe.

SS Gruppenführer *Hofmann* intends to have a specialist of the Race and Settlement Main Office sent along to Hungary for general orientation when the matter is taken in hand there by the Chief of the Security Police and the SD. It was decided that this specialist of the Race and Settlement Main Office, who is not to be active, should temporarily be assigned the official capacity of assistant to the Police Attaché.

IV   In the implementation of the final-solution program, the Nuremberg Laws are to form the basis, as it were; and in this context, a solution of the questions concerning mixed marriages and *Mischlinge* is a precondition for complete settlement of the problem.

From Lucy S. Dawidowicz, ed., *A Holocaust Reader* (West Orange, N.J.: Behrman House, 1976).

THE PLIGHT OF THE *ST. LOUIS*

The *St. Louis* was already heading back toward Germany when the following editorial appeared in the *New York Times*. The "cargo of despair" had not managed to soften the hearts of Cuban or American bureaucrats who could have issued temporary visas to the Jewish refugees seeking asylum, thereby saving their lives. Although this editorial is sympathetic toward the plight of the Jews, in general, the national press did not write in support of increasing the number of refugees allowed to enter the United States.

EDITORIAL: "REFUGEE SHIP" (1939)

The saddest ship afloat today, the Hamburg-American liner St. Louis, with 900 Jewish refugees aboard, is steaming back toward Germany after a tragic week of frustration at Havana and off the coast of Florida. She is steaming back despite an offer made to Havana yesterday to give a guarantee through the Chase National Bank of $500 apiece for every one of her passengers, men, women and children, who might land there. President Laredo Bru still has an opportunity to practice those humanitarian sentiments so eloquently expressed in his belated offer of asylum after the refugee ship had been driven from Havana Harbor. His cash terms have been met. But the St. Louis still keeps her course for Hamburg.

No plague ship ever received a sorrier welcome. Yet those aboard her had sailed with high hopes. About fifty of them, according to our Berlin dispatch, had consular visas. The others all had landing permits for which they had paid; they were unaware that these permits had been declared void in a decree dated May 5. Only a score of the hundreds were admitted. At Havana the St. Louis's decks became a stage for human misery. Relatives and friends clamored to get aboard but were held back. Weeping refugees clamoring to get ashore were halted at guarded gangways. For days the St. Louis lingered within the shadow of Morro Castle, but there was no relaxation of the new regulations. Every appeal was rejected. One man reached land. He was pulled from the water with slashed wrists and rushed to a hospital. A second suicide attempt led the captain to warn the authorities that a wave of self-destruction might follow. The forlorn refugees themselves organized a patrol committee. Yet out of Havana Harbor the St. Louis had to go, trailing pitiful cries of "Auf Wiedersehen." Off our shores she was attended by a helpful Coast Guard vessel alert to pick up any passengers who plunged overboard and thrust them back on the St. Louis again. The refugees could even see the shimmering towers of Miami rising from the sea, but for them they were only the battlements of another forbidden city.

It is useless now to discuss what might have been done. The case is disposed of. Germany, with all the hospitality of its concentration camps, will welcome these unfortunates home. Perhaps Cuba, as her spokesmen say, has already taken too many German refugees. Yet all these 900 asked was a temporary haven. Before they sailed virtually all of them had registered under the quota provisions of various nations, including our own. Time would have made them eligible to enter. But there seems to be no help for them now. The St. Louis will soon be home with her cargo of despair.

Her next trip is already scheduled. It will be a gay cruise for carefree tourists.

New York Times, June 8, 1939.

INFLUENCE OF WAR ON AMERICAN CITIZENS
(1942)

On Sunday, July 5, 1942, Anne Frank and her family were still living in their home in Amsterdam, and Anne was writing in her diary about her grades at school. On the afternoon of the fifth, Margot Frank received a notice to report for transport to a forced-labor camp outside of Holland. It was this notice that convinced Otto Frank that he and his family had to go into hiding immediately in order to save Margot's life. From that moment, all of their lives would change forever.

In the United States, the lives of American families were also changing as a result of World War II. Men were leaving their wives and children to go fight the Nazis across the ocean. Women were leaving their homes to replace men in factories and offices throughout the country. All kinds of food became less available, and many of the "necessities" of life became luxuries. The adjustments American citizens were making for the war effort in some ways paralleled the early changes in Anne Frank's domestic life, with less food and fewer material goods available. However, while some Americans may have found themselves inconvenienced by having less gasoline for their cars or by having "excursions to Winter resorts" restricted, the majority did not face the kind of abrupt and brutal disruption of their lives which the Franks and millions of other European victims of the war found themselves confronting.

"WAR WILL CHANGE LIFE OF AMERICAN FAMILIES"

Their Food, Their Clothes, Homes, and Amusements Will Not Be Same
W. J. Enright

Changes in our way of life are coming thick and fast and the factors that shape these changes are manifold. The best opinion is that the war will string out until 1944 and government agencies are working on that assumption. Hence the curtailment orders and other restrictions. . . .

The housewife has had her first taste of rationing and has got used to tearing off bits of paper in exchange for sugar. She knows that by the end of the year she will be going through a similar process for coffee and tea and cocoa. She has seen bananas gradually disappear from the fruit-stands and realizes that this tropical fruit may become a memory, except for isolated shipments. . . .

Drinks Curtailed

Both hard and soft drinks will be curtailed. While liquor stocks are still heavy and sufficient to care for normal needs, the conversion of distill-eries to the manufacture of alcohol for war purposes will practically stop the production of whiskey and gin. Beer can no longer be sold in tin cans and the bottled output is threatened by the restriction on caps, which usually contain tin. . . .

The clothing situation is seriously distorted by the curtailment of wool imports and the huge yardages of all types of cloths, from woolens to cottons, demanded by the armed forces. . . .

New Styles for Women

Women's apparel has undergone numerous restrictions of sweeping flares and other fashions calling for surplus material. Slacks are replacing the frilly dresses of yore, and when 500,000 women are in the female army, it will mean a great impetus to a mannish style of dressing.

Shoes will become a problem. The Army is commandeering practically all the top-grade sole leather and the soles on men's shoes will be thin-ner. Women's styles will have to be simplified, with colors both for men and women restricted to a few basic shades.

Wool for Blankets

. . . Sheets are no longer plentiful and must be repaired instead of going into discard. Replacement of all-wool rugs must be delayed for the duration because carpet wools are restricted and carpet looms are being converted to the manufacture of duck for the military forces. . . .

Even the American business office, that sanctum of routine and effi-ciency, is not unscathed. . . . By January rubber bands and clips, unless carefully husbanded, will have disappeared. . . .

Dark Streets

Perhaps the most marked change by January will have taken place on streets. Dimouts in Winter will be accentuated. The roar of traffic will die down as car after car is put to rest. Street cars and buses will be jammed. . . . For a while it looked as if bicycles [would] become a major means of locomotion, but now they are rationed carefully to defense workers only.

No longer will the business man in a hurry be able to phone a railroad station or plane terminal at the last moment and make a reservation to Chicago or the Pacific Coast. . . . Ski trains, excursions to Winter resorts will be but a memory, and people will have to renew their acquaintance with their own neighborhoods.

New York Times, July 5, 1942.

JEWISH VICTIMS OF THE HOLOCAUST

No one will ever know the exact number of Jewish men, women, and children slaughtered during the Holocaust. Although precise records were kept of the numbers of Jews deported to forced labor camps or killed in the gas chambers, thousands upon thousands of other victims—infants, small children, or those Jews who lived in remote villages that came under Nazi control throughout Europe—slipped through the Nazi accounting ledgers (see map on following page).

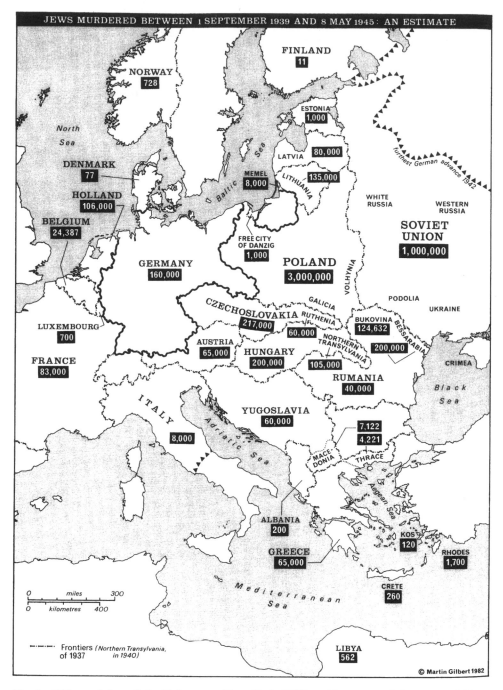

JEWS MURDERED BETWEEN 1 SEPTEMBER 1939 AND 8 MAY 1945: AN ESTIMATE

FINLAND
11

NORWAY
728

North
Sea

ESTONIA
1,000

LATVIA
80,000

MEMEL
8,000

LITHUANIA
135,000

DENMARK
77

HOLLAND
106,000

BELGIUM
24,387

Baltic Sea

WHITE
RUSSIA

WESTERN
RUSSIA

FREE CITY
OF DANZIG
1,000

GERMANY
160,000

POLAND
3,000,000

SOVIET
UNION
1,000,000

LUXEMBOURG
700

CZECHOSLOVAKIA
217,000

GALICIA

RUTHENIA
60,000

VOLHYNIA

PODOLIA

UKRAINE

BUKOVINA
124,632

BESSARABIA

AUSTRIA
65,000

NORTHERN
TRANSYLVANIA
105,000

200,000

FRANCE
83,000

HUNGARY
200,000

RUMANIA
40,000

CRIMEA

Black
Sea

ITALY

Adriatic Sea

YUGOSLAVIA
60,000

8,000

7,122

4,221

MACE-
DONIA

THRACE

Aegean Sea

ALBANIA
200

KOS
120

RHODES
1,700

GREECE
65,000

CRETE
260

Mediterranean
Sea

0   miles   300

0   kilometres   400

Frontiers (Northern Transylvania,
of 1937   in 1940)

LIBYA
562

© Martin Gilbert 1982

Martin Gilbert, *Atlas of the Holocaust* (New York: William Morrow and Co., Inc., 1988, 1993), p. 244.

TOPICS FOR WRITTEN OR ORAL EXPLORATION

1. Using the minutes of the Wannsee Conference, write a scene in which the participants at the conference discuss the "Final Solution."

2. What does the use of all of the numbers suggest about the attitude of the members of the conference toward the Jews? Find examples of language that distorts or hides the true meaning of their "solution."

3. What are the changes in American family life described in the July 5, 1942 news article? What reasons are given for the changes? Write a diary entry from the point of view of a teen living in the United States in July 1942. Describe the changes in your life caused by the war.

4. Write a report on the effects of the war on American life based on newspaper and magazine articles written between 1939 and 1945.

5. Find news articles that describe what was happening in Europe during that period. Report on the similarities and differences between the United States and Europe in terms of the lives of its civilian citizens.

6. Choose one of Anne's diary entries and look at an American newspaper from that date. What is the main focus of the front page articles? How much attention is given to the fate of the Jews?

7. Look at a current daily paper from your own community. How much coverage is given to the circumstances of people in other communities or countries? Does reading about them have an impact on your life? Look at a recent issue of a national news magazine. How is the situation in a wartorn country described? What is the focus of the material? Are the personal sacrifices of its victims communicated effectively?

8. Read editorials written during World War II. How are they different from news reports of the period? Do different newspapers take different positions?

9. Write an editorial about an issue in your own school or community. Pay careful attention to the language you use to make your point.

10. Interview a World War II veteran or a member of his/her family. Write a report using the information you have gathered, or write a series of letters or diary entries from the point of view of that person telling about what happened during the war.

11. Write a report about a famous Jew who escaped from Nazi Europe and came to America during World War II. Describe what efforts the person made to get to the United States and what his or her life has been like since that time.

12. Research events in a European country invaded by Germany. How did that nation respond to Nazi doctrines? How did people react to the persecution of their Jewish citizens?

13. In the past few years, other unfortunate "boat people," including Haitian and Liberian victims of war, have been reported by the media. What was the fate of these people? Did media coverage create public awareness that led to the rescue of these people? Do you think the passengers of the *St. Louis* would be treated differently today?

14. Watch a film about the Nazi period in Europe—for example, *Au Revoir les Enfants, Schindler's List, The Garden of the Finzi Continis, The Last Metro, Korscak*. Compare an aspect of the film with the movie version of *The Diary of Anne Frank*. What details about the war presented in the film help you understand what it was like? What do you learn about what it was like to be a Jew during this period in history?

SUGGESTED READINGS

History

Bauer, Yehuda, and Nili Keren. *A History of the Holocaust*. New York: Franklin Watts, 1982.

Berenbaum, Michael. *The World Must Know: A History of the Holocaust as Told in the United States Holocaust Museum*. Boston: Little, Brown, 1993.

Dawidowicz, Lucy. *A Holocaust Reader*. West Orange, N.J.: Behrman House, 1976.

———. *The War Against the Jews, 1933–1945*. New York: Bantam, 1986.

Eisenberg, Azriel. *The Lost Generations: Children in the Holocaust*. New York: Pilgrim Press, 1982.

———. *Witness to the Holocaust*. New York: Pilgrim Press, 1981.

Gilbert, Martin. *Auschwitz and the Allies*. New York: Holt, Rinehart and Winston, 1981.

———. *The Holocaust: A History of the Jews in Europe During the Second World War*. New York: Henry Holt, 1986.

———. *The Holocaust: The Jewish Tragedy*. London: William Collins Sons, 1986.

———. *Atlas of the Holocaust*. New York: Macmillan, 1982.

Goldhagen, Daniel Jonah. *Hitler's Willing Executioners: Ordinary Germans and the Holocaust*. New York: Alfred A. Knopf, 1996.

Gutman, Israel, ed. *Encyclopedia of the Holocaust*. New York: Macmillan, 1990.

Hilberg, Raul. *The Destruction of European Jews*. Chicago: Quadrangle Books, 1971.

————. *Perpetrators Victims Bystanders: The Jewish Catastrophe, 1933–1945*. New York: HarperCollins, 1992.

————, ed. *Documents of Destruction*. Chicago: Quadrangle Books, 1971.

Levin, Nora. *The Holocaust: The Destruction of European Jewry, 1933–1945*. New York: Schocken Books, 1968.

Marrus, Michael. *The Holocaust in History*. New York: New American Library/Dutton, 1989.

Meltzer, Milton. *Never to Forget: The Jews of the Holocaust*. New York: Dell, 1977.

Mosse, George L. *Toward the Final Solution*. New York: Howard Fertig, 1978.

Rogasky, Barbara. *Smoke and Ashes: The Story of the Holocaust*. New York: Holiday House, 1988.

Rossel, Seymour, *The Holocaust: The Fire that Raged*. New York: Franklin Watts, 1990.

Yahil, Leni. *The Holocaust: The Fate of European Jewry, 1932–1945*. New York: Oxford University Press, 1987.

America and the Holocaust

Lipstadt, Deborah. *Beyond Belief: The American Press and the Coming of the Holocaust*. New York: The Free Press, 1986.

Lookstein, Haskel. *Were We Our Brother's Keepers?* New York: Hartmore House, 1985.

Morse, Arthur D. *While Six Million Died: A Chronicle of American Apathy*. New York: Random House, 1967.

Wyman, David S. *The Abandonment of the Jews: America and the Holocaust, 1941–1945*. New York: Pantheon Books, 1984.

————. *Paper Walls: America and the Refugee Crisis, 1938–1941*. New York: Pantheon Books, 1986.

Fiction

Almagor, Gila. *Under the Domim Tree*. Translated by Hillel Schenker. New York: Simon and Schuster, 1995.

Appelfeld, Aharon. *Badenheim 1939*. New York: Washington Square Press, 1980.

————. *To the Land of the Cattails*. New York: Weidenfeld and Nicolson, 1986.

Demetz, Hana. *The House on Prague Street*. New York: St. Martin's Press, 1970.

Fink, Ida. *A Scrap of Time*. New York: Schocken Books, 1989.

Forman, James. *Ceremony of Innocence*. New York: Dell, 1970.

Fried, Erich. *Children and Fools*. New York: Serpent's Tail, 1994.

Friedman, Carl. *Nightfather*. Translated by Arnold and Erica Pomerans. New York: Persea Books, 1995.

Greene, Bette. *Morning Is a Long Time Coming*. New York: Archay Paperbacks, 1979.

————. *Summer of My German Soldier*. New York: Dial Books for Young Readers, 1973.

Hersey, John. *The Wall*. New York: Bantam Books, 1981.

Moskin, Marietta. *I Am Rosemarie*. New York: Dell, 1987.

Ozick, Cynthia. *The Shawl*. New York: Random House, 1990.

Schwartz-Bart, Andre. *The Last of the Just*. New York: Atheneum, 1973.

Wiesel, Elie. *The Gates of the Forest*. New York: Schocken Books, 1982.

Anthologies and Collections

Friedlander, Albert, ed. *Out of the Whirlwind*. New York: Schocken Books, 1989.

Glatstein, Jacob, ed. *Anthology of Holocaust Literature*. New York: Macmillan, 1973.

Hayes, Peter, ed. *Lessons and Legacies: The Meaning of the Holocaust in a Changing World*. Evanston, Ill.: Northwestern University Press, 1991.

Langer, Lawrence L., ed. *Art from the Ashes: A Holocaust Anthology*. New York: Oxford University Press, 1995.

Related Works

Miller, Judith. *One by One by One: Facing the Holocaust*. New York: Simon and Schuster, 1990.

Wiesenthal, Simon. *The Murderers Among Us*. New York: McGraw-Hill, 1973.

Biographies

Atkinson, Linda. *In Kindling Flame: The Story of Hannah Senesh, 1921–1944*. New York: William Morrow, 1992.

Scholl, Inge. *The White Rose: Munich, 1942–43*. Middletown, Conn.: Wesleyan University Press, 1983.

8

Other Holocaust Stories

GUSTAV RANIS

This chapter presents the accounts of two Holocaust survivors, Gustav Ranis and Anna Gelbman Rosner. Like Anne Frank, Gustav Ranis was born in Germany in 1929. Unlike the Franks, who immigrated to the Netherlands in 1933, Gustav's family remained in Germany, trusting that the increased expressions of anti-Semitism would subside as the nation regained its economic and political equilibrium.

Anna Gelbman Rosner was born in Czechoslovakia in 1924. Like Anne Frank, the young Anna was deported to Auschwitz with her family, including an older sister, Martha. Anna and Martha were later transferred to labor camps in Germany and spent their final months in captivity in Bergen-Belsen, the concentration camp where Margot and Anne Frank perished.

Although there are similarities between the stories of Gustav Ranis, Anna Gelbman Rosner, and Anne Frank, even more compelling are the many differences that can be attributed to decisions made or not made, risks taken or not taken, but most of all, the overwhelming circumstances they and their families could not control. As you read these other Holocaust stories consider the similarities and differences with Anne Frank's fate. Keep in mind that each and every Holocaust story is unique and valuable, a testimony to a history we must never forget.

The Holocaust stories are followed by my own reflections as the daughter of Holocaust survivors. Writing this book has enriched my own intellectual and emotional responses to the family stories I have heard all of my life.

The chapter concludes with three photographs from *The Auschwitz Album*. They are eloquent portraits of humanity brutalized and destroyed by the genocidal policies of Germany's Third Reich.

While the thirteen-year-old Anne Frank hid in a secret annex in Amsterdam, Gustav Ranis, a German Jewish boy, was celebrating his bar mitzvah in Havana, Cuba. The bar mitzvah is usually a joyous milestone in a thirteen-year-old Jewish male's life when he takes on the responsibilities of adulthood and dedicates himself to observing the laws and rituals of the Jewish religion.

Gustav's bar mitzvah was a bittersweet occasion, however. Having recently escaped from Nazi Germany with his mother, grandfather, and younger brother, Gustav was enormously relieved to find himself and his loved ones living as refugees in small quarters with other Jewish German émigrés. At the same time, Gustav already felt very old. The symbolic transition from boy to man had occurred in very real ways ever since Gustav was nine. The family had been separated from Gustav's father since Kristallnacht in November 1938, when the head of the family had been sent to a concentration camp. As a result, Gustav had become the "man" in the house.

It was he who had sustained his mother through the years of anxiety and terror as Nazi decrees increasingly limited every aspect of their lives. It was Gustav who had accompanied his mother on endless visits to Gestapo headquarters in attempts to accumulate all of the required papers that would allow them to join his father, who had managed to get a visa to immigrate to Great Britain and then, later, to the United States. Although Gustav did not know it at the time, his bar mitzvah, a celebration of his future life as a Jew, was in marked contrast to the fate of other Jewish boys and girls who were being killed at that very moment in concentration camps all over Eastern Europe.

FROM AN INTERVIEW WITH GUSTAV RANIS, NEW HAVEN, CONN. (SPRING 1996)

I was born in Darmstadt, Germany in October 1929. My father was a prominent lawyer in the city, and my family enjoyed a comfortable upper middle-class life. Although we were assimilated Jews, my father, Max, was president of the local Reform synagogue (a branch of Judaism established in Germany that modernized many of the ancient Jewish traditions and laws). Above all else, my father considered himself a German patriot. He had fought as a German in World War I and was enormously proud of the many medals he had received for his courageous service to the fatherland. As this highly educated and well-read man watched Hitler's rise to power and then his implementation of anti-Semitic legislation, he insisted that what was happening was a "phase" not very different from earlier anti-Semitic episodes in German history. He believed that once Hitler got the German economy back to its former strength, the Jews would no longer be so vigorously scapegoated and harassed.

So my family stayed in Darmstadt, even after the Nuremberg Laws were issued in 1935. I was required to go to a Jewish school and was separated from the German friends I had played with and had considered exactly like myself. Going to a Jewish school was not a great hardship for me at six years old because my Jewish teachers were well qualified and kind; however, going to and from school became an exercise in terror. Almost every day, some Jewish children were accosted by Hitler Youth, boys in uniform who taunted and beat them up because they were "dirty Jews." In one particularly terrifying encounter, I was tied to a tree and had knives thrown at me by a gang of Hitler Youth. What made these continual attacks particularly distressing was the fact that we could not turn to the German police or other German authorities for protection. Anyone in a German uniform represented the state, and the German state was not at the service of its Jewish citizens no matter how innocent or vulnerable we were.

It was only inside my own home that I felt safe, but that sense of security came to an end on Kristallnacht. On November 10, 1938, my father was awakened with the news that his synagogue was on fire. He rushed over to the burning building hoping to salvage the religious objects and do what he could to put out the fire. Everywhere the sound of breaking glass filled the night air. Not only was the synagogue burning, Jewish store windows were being smashed, and there was a free-for-all of destruction aimed at Jewish businesses and homes.

Two hours after he had left the house, my father returned in the company of two Gestapos who gave him a half-hour to pack his belongings before he would be taken into "protective custody." What he was being protected from was never explained, but we were supposed to believe that the German Nazi police were protecting this Jewish citizen from German mobs.

My father spent several months in Buchenwald, a German concentration camp. When he briefly returned to our family he was no longer the confident, authoritarian patriarch he had once been. He did not describe what he had seen at Buchenwald, but he made it clear from his silence and his broken spirit that he realized his support of Germany's nationalism had been a terrible mistake. It was clear that we had to get out of Germany immediately in order to survive.

Having a relative in another country, and especially in the United States, was one of the few ways German Jews could get visas to leave the country. However, the U.S. quota for German and Austrian Jews was 28,000 and after Kristallnacht about 250,000 Jews were trying to emigrate to the United States. My father had been released from Buchenwald because we were able to get him a British visa through relatives in the U.S. In March 1939, my father left for England, convinced that the only hope for his family was his own escape from increasing Nazi persecution.

When World War II broke out six months later, the rest of our family was trapped in Germany. Daily life now became even more difficult because Jews suffered not only from the anti-Semitic prohibitions and regulations, we also began to feel the effects of living in a country that was at war. Rations for Jews were more limited than rations for "Aryans," and the number of restrictions escalated. One decree required Jews to bring in all their gold and silver articles to Gestapo headquarters. I helped my mother carry our precious family heirlooms and religious artifacts, and understood that we were not only losing objects which had meaningful connections to our heritage, we were also losing valuable financial assets, gold and silver that could have been sold if we became desperate for money.

Punishments for what should have been considered "humane" behavior were also severe and unpredictable. My mother was jailed for two months after she gave bread to her brother-in-law who was shoveling snow in a forced labor detail. He, like my father, had been picked up during the Kristallnacht roundup, but because my uncle had "talked back" to Nazi officials, he was not released from captivity. By making life increasingly onerous for the Jews, the Nazis had planned to force them to leave Germany. Unfortunately, far too many Jews remained trapped in Germany by circumstances they could not control, and by 1940, the Germans instituted a state by state "clean-up" of those Jews who still remained in the country. This meant deporting Jews to concentration camps which in almost all cases meant eventual, if not immediate, death.

By the time my father got to the United States and was able to send for our family in 1940, the U.S. would not let us come into the country. Despite some national debate and attempts at increasing refugee emigration into the United States, fewer and fewer Jews were able to enter the U.S. as all the while the situation in Germany became increasingly critical. Then our other escape route, the Trans-Siberian Railway, was closed off when Germany attacked the Soviet Union. As time was quickly running out, my father managed to collect enough money from relatives in the U.S. to buy us visas to Cuba. Profiting from the misery of desperate Jews, Cuba was "selling" visas at great cost. Nevertheless, unlike many other countries which simply refused to accept Jews under any circumstances, Cuba did make it possible for those Jews who could afford it to escape certain death.

With legitimate visas in hand we thought we were finally on our way to freedom, but once again, Nazi policy hindered our plans. Just as we were about to leave Germany, a new law was instituted which required all Jewish women between 18 and 45 to report for labor camp. My mother fell into this category. Suddenly, my brother and I had to face the possibility of leaving our mother behind to suffer enormous hardship alone. We did not know that the "labor" camps were often really concentration camps where inmates were routinely worked to death or killed in gas chambers, but we decided that if our mother were forced to report for German labor camp, we would remain in Germany. Our only chance of leaving Germany together was the fact that we had had all of the papers necessary to leave the country before the new law had been passed. We hoped we would not have to comply retroactively with this latest "death sentence."

My mother and I sat in Gestapo headquarters in Berlin for ten excruciatingly long days waiting to hear the verdict. I knew that our lives were at the mercy of German officials who were "following orders." I also knew that other parts of Germany had already been "cleaned of its Jews" and that it was only a short time before the Jews of Berlin would also meet that fate. Just as I had tried to make myself inconspicuous going from my Jewish school to my home in fear of the Hitler Youth, I sat beside my mother, afraid to look at the Gestapo, afraid to answer their questions, afraid I would not be allowed to leave.

Finally, our papers were deemed in order, and we could escape from Germany. Relief turned to despair once more, however, when we were stopped at the train station and told that because we had not followed orders, (we had taken a taxi to the train when we had been told many days before not to) our tickets were withdrawn. I was horrified that the official who was following these Nazi orders was a Jew! Once again, my family had to wait while anonymous forces arbitrarily played with our lives. I could see that this ordeal had broken my mother. It was up to me to get us to safety.

In October 1941, my grandfather, mother, brother and I made our way by train through occupied France and Spain and finally reached Havana, Cuba, by boat in November 1941. Despite the enormous hardships and anxieties, we were extremely fortunate. Had my family not had relatives in the United States who could get my father a precious visa to leave Germany, had my father not been able to collect enough money to buy his family visas to Cuba, had the Gestapo decided not to make an exception when we had finally gotten all of our papers in order, and had the Jewish official at the Berlin train station not returned our tickets to us, we most surely would have found ourselves in a German concentration camp. Like six million other Jews from all over Europe, we would have died of disease or starvation or exhaustion, or most likely, been "gassed" and incinerated in a crematorium designed to eliminate all Jews.

Life in America

The Ranis family was reunited in February 1943 in Danbury, Connecticut. By then, the United States was deeply involved in fighting the war in Europe. Radio reports and newspaper accounts of battles and invasions monopolized all my thoughts. My father and I followed the progress of the war, constantly aware of the fact that we had had no news of beloved relatives left behind. My young cousins and aunts and uncles had not escaped from Berlin, and while we tried to believe that our family members had been relocated to labor camps, and therefore could not send or receive mail, we also began to hear reports of concentration camps where Jews were being exterminated in gas chambers. Still, since the reports were buried deep within the pages of *The New York Times* and the reported atrocities did not get constant coverage, my parents, like many other readers, tried to convince themselves that the unthinkable "news" could not be true, could not possibly be happening in a "civilized" world.

Ten months after the family was reunited in America, my father died of a heart attack at the age of forty-nine. Once again, I found myself responsible for the welfare of my increasingly fragile mother, my aged grandfather, and my younger brother.

While attending public school full-time, I also worked at a number of jobs after school as well as on weekends. By the time I graduated from Danbury High School, I was fluent in English and was selected valedictorian of my class.

The college selection process was totally unfamiliar to me, so I turned for guidance to a rabbi in the community. He suggested a number of outstanding universities, but also told me about a new school, Brandeis University, founded in 1948 by Jewish leaders and educators. Fortunately, I was accepted at all of the colleges I applied to, but was delighted to accept a full scholarship to attend Brandeis. Four years later, I found myself serving as valedictorian for the very first graduating class of the soon to be world-class university.

After Brandeis, I went on to get a doctorate in economics from Yale University and have since served as economic adviser to leaders around the world, the United Nations, and Presidents of the United States. Presently, I am the Frank Altschul Professor of International Economics at Yale University, and Director of the Yale Center for International and Area Studies.

Returning to Germany

I have returned to Germany a number of times since the end of the war. Recently, my wife Rachel, a sociologist, and I spent a year living in Berlin, Germany, where I, along with other international scholars, had been invited to join a "think tank." While at the Institute, we lived in a suburb of Berlin and only five blocks from the railroad station which had been used to transport Berlin's Jews to concentration camps in the East. This station had been especially chosen by the Nazis because it was situated outside of the city. As a result, most Berliners would not see the procession of defenseless Jewish men, women and children walking past the elegant German houses. Only those who watched from behind their delicate lace curtains could see the bewildered Jews being herded onto trains to be sent to their destruction.

In recent years, a large concrete memorial to the Jews has been erected at the train station. On its base are words engraved into the material in such a way that they almost disappear. Thus, a viewer can easily avoid reading the message inscribed, and can avoid knowing for certain what occurred at this bland suburban train station. Whether it was intentional or not, this barely visible reminder of the Holocaust is a metaphor for the way in which the citizens of Berlin could escape from seeing the Jews rounded-up and deported.

In contrast, the city of Berlin has a number of permanent reminders of this infamous period in German history. Throughout the main shopping area of the city individual flags announce each of the Nuremberg Laws instituted against the Jews in 1935, and in front of one of Berlin's major department stores are permanently displayed the names of the concentration camps to which the Jews and many other "undesirables" were sent to their deaths.

Also, the citizens of Berlin have invited the German Jewish men and women who survived the Holocaust to write about themselves and to tell about their lives since they left Germany. The many contributions to public and private life chronicled in these pages remind the Germans and the rest of the world how much talent and potential was destroyed as a result of the genocide of the Jews.

ANNA GELBMAN ROSNER

Anna Gelbman Rosner is a Holocaust survivor who was born in a small Czechoslovakian city in 1924. Until she was fourteen, Anna considered herself "the luckiest girl in the world." Then the Hungarian army invaded her country, and everything Anna had known and loved about her life changed overnight.

FROM AN INTERVIEW WITH ANNA GELBMAN ROSNER,
AVENTURA, FLA. (SPRING 1996)

I adored my gentle, loving parents, Joseph and Rachel, and enjoyed the company of an older sister, Martha, and two younger brothers, Béla and Lazar. My family lived in Berehovo, Czechoslovakia (*Beregszaz* in Hungarian). We owned a candy store which was located just a few streets away from our home and around the corner from my maternal grandparents whom I visited often.

Berehovo was an exceptionally lovely city with a crystal clear stream running alongside its main thoroughfare and a large plaza where families strolled on Saturday afternoons. My friends and I would "hang out" there, showing off our best clothes and stopping for ice cream and sodas at the cafés. At the center of the plaza was the main synagogue, the heart of the Jewish community's religious and social activities.

The highlight of my childhood was the annual summer vacations I spent with my father's parents on their small farm. Every June I would travel alone by train through the beautiful Carpathian landscape, past forests and vineyards, until I arrived at my grandparents' home. For several carefree weeks I fed the goats and chickens, drank fresh milk still warm from the cow, and ate my grandmother's extraordinary breads and cakes. I felt thoroughly admired and spoiled by this beloved couple, and all year long I looked forward to these visits.

Life in Czechoslovakia in 1938 was secure and comfortable for the Jewish population living in Berehovo. In our small city of 25,000, Jews and gentiles lived and worked side by side. I played with the gentile children who lived next door, often running back and forth between our houses. Although my parents were Orthodox Jews, they were on very friendly terms with the owner of the non-kosher butcher shop located next to our candy store.

I did not have any sense of anti-Semitism in my school nor in my social life. I loved school and especially public speaking. I was also very popular and had many friends who were attracted to my sense of humor and my enthusiasm for adventure.

Nazi Invasion

The emotional and physical security of my first fourteen years of life came to an abrupt end when the Hungarian army arrived in Berehovo in the spring of 1938. Before World War I, this region of Czechoslovakia had been a part of the Austro-Hungarian Empire. In 1918, the Empire was dissolved and the region became a part of Czechoslovakia. When Hitler split up the Czechoslovak Republic in 1938, he gave this portion of the country back to Hungary, hoping to gain Hungary's cooperation in his quest to conquer all of Europe.

Without much coercion from Germany, the fascist Hungarian invaders began implementing anti-Semitic policies, and the Jews of Berehovo felt the first stings of discrimination and deprivation. Those Jews who could not prove that they had lived in the region for one hundred or more years were immediately deported to the Ukraine where they were either harshly treated by the native Ukrainians or soon deported to concentration camps and eventual death. As a result, some of our friends suddenly disappeared, and we were left with the terrifying knowledge that anything could happen to those of us who remained. For those Jews like my family who had documents to prove that we had lived in Berehovo for more than a century, fear replaced freedom, anti-Semitism replaced friendship.

I saw old Jewish men humiliated in the streets by Hungarian soldiers, and a short while later I witnessed the people of our own community joining in on the attacks, pulling at the white beards and even hitting and kicking men who had been respected and esteemed only weeks before. One night, my mother and I dressed ourselves in long dark dresses, covered our heads with large kerchiefs to hide our faces, and cautiously made our way to my grandparents' house. Having already seen so much physical abuse aimed at elderly Jews, we were worried sick about the safety of my mother's mother and father. At the same time, we were terrified of being stopped on our way by Hungarian soldiers. I will never forget the feeling of my mother's hand gripping mine as we kept our eyes on the ground and made our way around the corner to my grandparents' home.

Nazi policy quickly transformed life for the Jews in Berehovo. Our candy store was closed in 1939, and my father had to set up a tiny shoe repair shop in the shed next to our home. Our once economically secure family was now less and less able to maintain its comfortable way of life.

In 1939, Nazi policy forbade Jews from entering the *gymnasium*, the equivalent of high school. As an outstanding student who loved learning, I was deeply disappointed. I wanted more than anything to get a good education, and now, all I had was my middle school diploma. A Christian friend tried to intervene on my behalf with school authorities, but the anti-Semitic orders were not waived.

Instead of continuing my education, I became an important source of badly needed income for my family. For long hours every day, and often into the early hours of the next morning, I would spin angora, long rabbit hairs, into yarn. My small, nimble fingers created especially fine yarn which the family was able to sell at a good price. Many nights my mother would sit up with me, keeping me awake by telling stories and singing songs. She sometimes cried out of pity for me, yet we needed the money too much and there were few ways for Jews to make a living. Sometimes I would sneak off and work odd jobs for gentile storekeepers to bring in additional money. I knew my parents would be heartbroken if they found out that their daughter had to work at menial jobs, so I kept my work a secret.

Since there was little information available about what was going on outside our community, the Jews of Berehovo tried to endure the best that we could. By 1940 there was little chance of escaping to a European country that was not under Nazi domination, and the opportunities to leave for America were almost impossible since the United States did not "open its arms" to Hitler's refugees. My brother Béla decided he would not wait passively until he was taken away to labor camp. With false papers which claimed that he was a gentile, my seventeen-year-old brother made his way to Budapest, Hungary, where he hid out for the entire war. With the help of a gentile family, and especially with the courageous efforts of their ten-year-old daughter, Béla was able to save a number of other Jews, including a young woman, Klara, who became his wife after the war.

Unlike Béla, I chose to stay at home with my family. I could not imagine life without my parents and siblings, and when I was offered false papers, I refused to consider leaving. Everything I knew and loved about my life was disappearing, yet I wanted to remain close to what was still left of my precious childhood.

In 1942, my father was taken to labor camp. Now I was nearly the sole support of my shrinking family. My sister, Martha, who had married in 1941, remained behind with her infant son when her husband was also taken for forced labor. With the men gone, anxieties escalated, but still, no one could imagine what was yet to come. Every day was a matter of getting by until the next and hoping that life would eventually return to how it had been before the Nazi invasion.

In 1944, the Nazis brought the Jewish men back from the labor camps to be with their families. With diabolical insight into family dynamics, they understood that the women and children would be far less willing to leave Berehovo if we did not have our fathers and husbands with us, in fear that we would never be reunited. Once the men returned, families were placated into believing that whatever would befall us, at least we were together.

In 1944, at the very end of the eight days of Passover, the holiday which commemorates the Jewish exodus from Egypt where the Jews were slaves, ghettos for 300,000 Jews were created in the region which included Berehovo. For four weeks all the Jews of Berehovo and outlying areas, 10,000 in all, were held in a brick factory, a ghetto from which we would all be transported to Auschwitz.

I remember two Hungarian soldiers with rifles on their shoulders appeared at our home one morning and ordered us to pack a few essentials and be ready to go to the ghetto in a matter of minutes. We grabbed some clothes and a few household items. As if in a nightmare, everything we had ever known and loved ended forever. I heard the front door of my house slammed shut by one of the soldiers. Then he locked the door, and we never saw that house again.

Young and old, healthy and sick, the Jews of Berehovo waited for the unknown. All too soon, my parents, grandparents, sister, little brother, baby nephew and I were shoved into a freight car headed for Auschwitz. As unbelievable as it may seem, during the three days in transit, I watched in horror as my forty-four-year-old father's black hair and beard turned pure white.

Auschwitz and Bergen-Belsen

As soon as we were released from the suffocating cattle cars, my father and little brother were sent off in a different direction from the rest of the family. I watched as my father, holding Lazar's hand, was pushed along to move more quickly. No one knew where they were going or why we were being separated. No one knew they were being marched to their deaths. We were too stunned to think about what was happening to us. We simply followed orders and hoped we would be given something to eat and drink.

Martha holding her baby, our mother, and I waited for instructions. A Jewish inmate in a striped uniform walked past us and whispered to Martha, "Give the baby to an older woman." Immediately, Fishele was being pulled from my sister's arms. Our mother had overheard the inmate's fatal message and had wrenched her grandson from her eldest daughter's protective clasp. My mother stood holding the exhausted child close to her chest as Dr. Mengele, the SS doctor, surveyed the latest shipment of Jews. Martha and I were "waved" to the right and spared immediate death. Our forty-two-year-old mother and her eighteen-month-old grandson were sent to the left, into the gas chambers of Auschwitz.

For seven agonizing weeks, Martha and I sat hunched together on a bunk we shared with eleven other women. There was never enough room to stretch out on the wood plank, and there was nothing to do but wait for the next roll call. We quickly learned that the daily selections could always mean death. When we dared to ask a woman SS guard what had happened to our parents, she pointed to the black smoke pouring out of the huge crematoria chimneys and said, "You see that smoke? That's where they are."

We decided that no matter what happened, Martha and I would stay together at all times. We realized that the Nazi guards tried to separate family members out of a vicious desire to prevent even the slightest source of comfort or support for their helpless inmates. However, since Martha was registered under her married name, neither of us revealed our kinship, and we were able to remain with each other throughout the entire ordeal.

Seven weeks after arriving in Auschwitz, we were transferred to Hamburg, Germany, where we did hard labor throughout the fall and brutally cold winter. Wearing nothing but a short-sleeved dress and wooden clogs, I shoveled snow and dug ditches for bunkers. The cruelty of the guards made the physical hardships even more devastating. If we didn't pay attention to what we were doing, the guards would beat us. If we tried to sneak away for a sip of water, they would shoot us. Although I was skinny, malnourished, and exhausted, I kept telling myself that I would not let Hitler win. My hatred for the Nazi murderers fueled my determination to remain alive, but there were also inexplicable occurrences which felt like some higher power was protecting me.

On one occasion, Martha, five other young women, and I were working in a wooded area when bombs began to fall. The guards ordered us to lie down where we were and warned that anyone moving from the spot would be shot. We all threw ourselves onto the ground and beneath the protection of a large tree. Suddenly, I had a "feeling." Despite the warning that we would be shot if we moved, I grabbed Martha's hand and told her to run. Within less than a minute, the bombed tree covered the remaining women, killing all five.

A few weeks later, while working in Eidelstadt, I was once again rescued by a combination of circumstances and by what I eventually came to call God. When it happened, I didn't think about it that way, but now

I know it was God. Despite our efforts to remain with each other at all times, Martha and I were assigned to different trolley cars on our way back from a labor detail. As our trolley moved through the town, a bomb-damaged building collapsed on two of the three trolley cars, burying us in rubble. I was in one of those cars. Martha was in the trolley car which had not been damaged. She ran from her car, calling for me, digging through the piles of twisted metal and brick, and finally managing to pull me from the wreckage.

Trucks arrived to take the dead and badly injured women directly to the crematoria. The piercing pain in my back made it nearly impossible for me to walk upright, but Martha supported my weight and made me walk to the truck which would take us back to our barracks. Thirty-two out of one hundred women were killed by the collapsed building. Many more were also put to death because they could no longer work. I went back to manual labor the next morning with five broken ribs. The one time we had been unwillingly separated from each other was the one time being separated meant saving my life.

From Hamburg, Germany, Martha and I were transferred to Bergen-Belsen in March, 1945. Everywhere I looked, I saw "mountains" of corpses waiting to be removed. That unimaginably grim and painful assignment would become my job. Barely skin and bones myself, I had to drag dead bodies, pulling them by their arms or legs, to a huge pit. I tried not to look into the faces of the victims, afraid that I might recognize an aunt or cousin or schoolmate, even though they didn't really look human anymore, but just in case.

In those last few weeks before liberation there was no system of food distribution in Bergen-Belsen. Looking back on that grim time, I cannot remember ever being given food, the way I can remember black bread or potatoes being distributed in Auschwitz. I do, however, remember occasionally finding a beet or potato still clutched in the hands of a dead victim. Although I was desperately ashamed to be "stealing" from the dead, I sometimes managed to recover the precious root and share it with Martha.

Many years after liberation I came across Anne Frank's *The Diary of a Young Girl*, a book my daughter was reading for a school assignment. On the back cover of the book was a description of Anne Frank and the words *Auschwitz* and *Bergen-Belsen*. I read that Anne Frank and her sister had died in Bergen-Belsen some time in March, 1945, and I thought to myself, "I wonder if their bodies lay in those huge piles I was forced to dispose of?" Even though I tried not to look at the faces, I could often tell when I was holding the fragile wrist or leg of a young girl. I held far too many.

Liberation

On a Saturday morning, April 15, 1945, Martha, several other women and I were sitting in the sun talking about *cholent*, a traditional Sabbath dish made of beans and barley and beef. Suddenly we heard screaming, yelling, music, automobiles. The British troops had arrived to liberate our pathetic horde of barely living survivors. We had had no idea that the war was nearly over. We certainly had not expected this wildly exuberant entrance with all kinds of "delicacies" being thrown to us from armored vehicles. Ravenous women ran to grab chocolates, sardines, salamis. Tragically, countless inmates were too weak to digest what they had been so ecstatic to receive, and they died within hours.

My sister and I were still alive, but starved and depleted by a year of extreme physical and emotional suffering. First Martha, and then I came down with the typhus which had ravaged Bergen-Belsen. Fortunately, we were nursed back to health in a British Red Cross infirmary. At one point during my illness, I became delirious with a high fever and cried because the blanket which covered me was unbearably rough. In my delirium, I kept calling out for an onion. By the time I was once again aware of my surroundings, a young soldier had brought me a soft sheet and an onion waited by my bedside. Only a few weeks before the roughest blanket, or even a shriveled root, would have been a luxury in Bergen-Belsen.

Within a few weeks, Martha and I were strong enough to make our way back to Berehovo to see who and what remained of our former lives. First, however, we went to Budapest where we hoped to be reunited with our brother Béla. Every day in hundreds of cities, towns, and villages, Jewish survivors either made their way back to their old homes or waited for trains returning with concentration camp survivors. For weeks, Béla, and Martha's husband, Victor, whose fate we did not know, met every train coming into Budapest, desperately searching each face for a beloved family member. Finally, one day, Martha and I got off one of those trains. Our reunion was a mixture of extreme relief, joy, and grief. We brought news of others who had been gassed, burned, shot, beaten, starved, tortured. We heard news of those who had been caught while in hiding, killed while resisting, or died while rescuing others.

We did not know if there was a "home" to go back to. Most Jews who returned to their towns and villages found that their possessions had been confiscated by the Nazis, or often, by gentile neighbors. For example, when I returned to Berehovo, I saw my mother's beautiful Sabbath tablecloth on the table of a gentile woman who pretended she did not know me and did not admit that she was not the original owner of the handmade white lace cloth. One day, walking in Berehovo, I saw a woman wearing a suit made from the fabric my mother had been saving to make into a dress for herself to wear on my wedding day. Memories like these never become less painful. Everything we had ever known and loved had been taken away from us, and we returned to a world which was completely alien. We belonged nowhere.

When I returned to Berehovo, I moved in with an aunt and uncle who had also survived the concentration camps. Soon I was welcoming back other survivors, among them, Sigmund Rosner, a tall handsome young man who had managed to outwit his German and Russian captors. He had moved from labor camp to labor camp, working at any job which would provide food and an opportunity to stay alive. Sigmund proposed to me within weeks of our reunion and when I announced my engagement to my aunt and uncle they were happy that I now would have a partner with whom to begin my new future.

In November 1945, less than seven months after I had been liberated from Bergen-Belsen, Sigmund and I were married in my uncle's living room with several of our siblings as witnesses. Still, it was the loneliest day of my life. Our parents, grandparents, and two young brothers were not there to share our *simcha*, our celebration. Ghosts haunted every corner of Berehovo. We returning Jews had no way of recreating the lives we had known before the war, nor did our gentile neighbors offer to return the houses and valuables which had once belonged to us. Also, after the war, the Russians had occupied Czechoslovakia. We decided to get out before we were trapped once again in a dangerous political situation.

A New Life in America

The next three-and-a-half years of our lives were spent trying to get to the United States. Sigmund and I escaped to Germany and spent two years in a Displaced Persons' Camp while we collected all the papers and forms required to emigrate to America. The process was difficult and frustrating. No one made it easy, and regulations were constantly being changed. Finally, in May 1949, Irving (Sigmund's Americanized name), our two-year-old daughter, Hedda, and I arrived by ship to New York Harbor. Ellis Island and the Statue of Liberty greeted us as did elated aunts and uncles, my father's siblings who had emigrated to the U.S. years before World War II. With their financial support and loving attention, our young family struggled through the first years in America as refugees. Irving began working as a carpenter for my uncle for one dollar an hour. We had a second daughter, Ellen, and I cared for our children with all the passionate concern of a mother who has everything invested in her daughters' well-being.

Fortunately, Martha, her husband, and their young daughter had also awaited us in America. For the next five decades, we moved together from neighborhood to neighborhood in Brooklyn, each move a step up the American ladder of success. Eventually, we built houses next door to each other where we raised our four daughters. Throughout the years, Martha and I continued to be devoted to each other, linked by the indestructable chain of our memories, both exquisitely sweet and incomparably bitter.

A DAUGHTER'S RESPONSE

Friday, April 14, 1995

My parents, Anna and Irving Rosner, sit at our Passover seder table surrounded by their family: two daughters, two sons-in-law, four grandchildren, and the fiancée of their eldest grandchild. It has been an exceptionally lively and emotional seder for all of us because it is the first Passover in the house we have just finished building, the first time in several years that we have all been together for a seder, and the first at which Jeffrey (named Joseph in Hebrew, in memory of my mother's father) and Stephanie have been engaged. There is more singing and laughter than usual. At one point, Sara gets up and does a dance with her grandfather. Rachel (named after my mother's mother) and Emily keep time with a tambourine and spoons. Passover, the story of the Jews' enslavement and liberation from Egypt, is always a bittersweet occasion for the family because the Haggadah we read also refers to the other enslavement, the Holocaust. Additional sections in the Haggadah describe the anguish of Holocaust victims. We read these passages out of respect to the dead and also the living, our parents, but it is an awkward spot in the evening, dredging up the same complicated feelings we have had whenever the Holocaust is mentioned.

As the long, celebratory evening is about to conclude, Sara asks if anyone wants to say anything before we leave the table. No one expects a response, so my mother surprises us when she begins to speak with great composure: "This is a very special night for me. Fifty years ago tonight, on a Friday night just like this, I was still in Bergen-Belsen. I thought I wouldn't live. I didn't know that the very next day we would be liberated, and that fifty years from that night I would be sitting here with my family, with all of you, celebrating Pesach. Could I have imagined this?" She reaches out her arms to her children, grandchildren, and devoted husband and says softly, "Could I have imagined this?"

It is a stunning moment. What can any of us possibly say? None of us has ever known the simple fact that our vivacious, elegant mother and grandmother had been liberated on April 15, the day we only thought of as Income Tax Deadline. We should have known. We could have known had we asked or read our history texts carefully; but we were ignorant in the way that we have mostly been for decades. No matter how many times my mother talked about her experiences in the "camps" I could not remember which camp she was sent to first or from which camp she had been liberated. No matter how many times she talked about her family, I had never asked her the name of her little brother who had died in Auschwitz or how old my grandmother had been when she walked into the gas chamber with her baby grandson. By not having the details I was keeping my little "uncle" and "old" grandmother (42!) at a distance—mythic, and, somehow, not real.

As a young child, I was afraid to ask questions because they might make my mother too sad. My questions might remind her of something which would stir up images and terrors I would not know how to respond to. So I listened politely when my mother talked about spinning angora or eating only black bread, but I never asked for more details. I never asked for "stories" about her life before the war either. Those too seemed loaded with enormous sadness because they were cut short by devastating circumstances and without hope of any restoration. There *was* no old neighborhood to go back to. There was no sign in Berehovo of the tranquillity and love my mother had known there as a young girl. Listening to my mother's stories also meant that I would be forced to confront not only her grief, but also the huge disparity between my mother's lost life and my own good fortunes. Better not to talk about it, unless my mother wanted to tell.

At the same time, I have always been aware as the "child" of Holocaust survivors that other people thought of us (survivors and their offspring) as having emotional or psychological characteristics which made us different from everyone else. Didn't the traumas of our mothers and fathers affect the way we saw the world? Weren't we paranoid, terrified, damaged as a result of our parents' experiences?

While the Holocaust and its survivors seemed to hold a place of awe in the imaginations and hearts of many others, for me the possibility of irrevocable loss and irremediable memory was a fact of life. My mother never explained the meaning of her narratives to me. She did not try to teach me lessons with her tales; however, from the time I was old enough to listen to my mother's stories, I knew that good and loving people can find themselves facing brutal, terrifying circumstances they cannot control. I knew that mothers and fathers can disappear and that babies can be killed for no reason. But, I also knew that despite those atrocities, survivors could and would get married again, have babies again, and would love those children with tenderness and joy. These were the amazing truths I inherited from my mother's life.

Although her memories of Auschwitz and Bergen-Belsen are still vivid and terrible, and though they visit her often and unexpectedly, her life continues to be filled with the pleasures of the living—walks with my father around a lovely marina early in the morning; lunch with friends, many of them Holocaust survivors as well; lectures and meetings at the synagogue; a nap by the pool. And always, without end, the absolute devotion to her family, her children and grandchildren who have been blessed with both the heavy burden of her sorrows and the countless gestures of her love.

EPILOGUE

The striking similarities between Anne Frank's and my mother's histories in Auschwitz and Bergen-Belsen are what have inspired me to work on this book. By writing about Anne Frank I will now never forget that both Anne and my mother were in Auschwitz and *then* Bergen-Belsen. I will never forget that my mother arrived in Bergen-Belsen in March 1945, the month Anne Frank died there, and that my mother and her sister, but not Anne and her sister, were liberated on April 15, 1945.

Both Anne Frank and my mother, Anna, suffered the terrors of standing in line for selections, the humiliations of having their beautiful dark hair shaved from their heads, and the miseries of starvation, extreme cold, and disease. Both Anne and Anna "lost" their mothers in Auschwitz, but both were fortunate enough to have older sisters to share their ordeals with, one small shred of family to cling to in the horrific darkness.

In celebrating my mother's life since the Holocaust I more deeply mourn Anne Frank's death in that conflagration; for surely the Anne Frank we have come to love through her diary would have become a remarkable woman and a magnificent writer. There is no question that had she survived, the critical mind and deep sensitivity Anne reveals in her writings would have matured into a creative talent expressed not only in her art, but also in the way in which she lived her precious life.

THE AUSCHWITZ ALBUM

Lili Jacob, a young woman from a small town only twenty-five miles from Berehovo, was among the Hungarian Jews transported from the Berehovo brick factory ghetto to Auschwitz-Birkenau in May 1944. For some unknown reason, the men, women, and children from that particular transport were photographed by an SS guard who waited by the boxcars as the doors were unlocked and the stunned, exhausted prisoners fell to the ground. With shocking objectivity, the anonymous photographer created a pictorial narrative of the journey from boxcars to crematoria, focusing on the moment-to-moment events that culminated in the destruction of the innocents captured in his lens.

No other photographic evidence has been discovered that documents that fate of the more than 1 million Jews who had already arrived in Auschwitz. This SS photographer took his assignment seriously, shooting photos from many angles and thoroughly documenting the grim events in Auschwitz-Birkenau, including the "selection" of infants, children, pregnant women, and those who were considered too old to work as "slaves."

On the day of her liberation from another concentration camp, Lili Jacob found these photographs. Astonishingly, when she looked carefully at the faces of the men and women in the photos, she recognized them as being from her own community; she even found photographs of her family members among the nearly two hundred pictures. *The Auschwitz Album*, as it came to be called, traveled with Lili on her difficult journey back from the concentration camp universe to a new life in the United States. Reproductions of some of these photographs have been included in museums and Holocaust exhibits around the world, including Yad Vashem in Jerusalem and the Polish museum created at Birkenau.

The photographs that follow document just three of the countless moments in Auschwitz when Jewish victims of Germany's genocidal policy were still alive and probably did not yet know their fate. The first photo, taken in front of a transport boxcar, captures the stoic calm of the women and children who have already been separated from the male members of their family. Children over the age of six were required to wear a yellow star.

The second photograph provides a panoramic view of the "selection" process. Men and women have already been separated, and now the Nazi SS in uniform points to either the left (gas chamber) or right (barracks) as each line of prisoners comes before him. The men in striped uniforms in the lower left corner of the photo were "slaves" who worked for the Nazis. Often, they were able to whisper messages to arriving prisoners. (For example, see the account of Anna Gelbman Rosner, above. Her sister was told by one of the "slaves" to give her baby to an older woman.) In this second photo we can see a woman walking away from the line with a baby in her arms. Her covered head is a sign that she was a married Orthodox Jewish woman. She and the baby were probably being sent to their deaths.

The final photograph of an old woman and three small children is particularly poignant. Their anonymity reminds us that this small, bent figure and the three carefully swaddled children were only four of millions of helpless innocent human beings slaughtered because of a racist ideology. Since we know the fates of the youngest and oldest in Auschwitz, we must assume that their moments of survival were numbered.

FROM *THE AUSCHWITZ ALBUM: A BOOK BASED UPON AN ALBUM DISCOVERED BY A CONCENTRATION CAMP SURVIVOR, LILI MEIER*, WITH TEXT BY PETER HELLMAN (NEW YORK: RANDOM HOUSE, 1981)

TOPICS FOR WRITTEN OR ORAL EXPLORATION

1. Interview someone who was born in 1929. Compare what was happening in that person's life to the life Anne Frank led during the years she was hiding in the secret annex; during the time Anne was in Auschwitz and Bergen-Belsen.

2. Interview someone who was a teenager during World War II. Ask your subject to describe what he or she knew about the war, about the Jews, about the concentration camps. Where did most of his or her information come from?

3. Interview a survivor of the Holocaust. Use a video camera or tape recorder, if possible, in addition to taking notes. Write the survivor's story, focusing on both the similarities and differences with Anne Frank's story.

   Facing History and Ourselves has an audiovisual resources guide that provides an extensive list of films, videotapes, and filmstrips available for classroom use. Testimonies of Holocaust survivors are included in this catalogue and can be used instead of interviews. (Facing History and Ourselves Audio-Visual Resources, 16 Hurd Road, Brookline, MA 02146.)

4. Read other memoirs and diaries that describe life during the Holocaust period. Write a narrative of the subject's experiences, comparing and contrasting them to Anne Frank's story.

5. Find local newspaper articles from 1938 to 1945. How was the news about Kristallnacht reported? How much newspaper coverage did the persecution of the Jews receive? On which page or section of the paper was it reported? What does this suggest? Were there reports about the concentration camps? Were there other news items that took precedence over coverage of the atrocities?

6. Look at editorials and letters to the editor in a local newspaper from 1938 to 1945. Was the plight of the Jews a topic of concern? Was there debate over U.S. involvement in saving Jews?

7. Immigrating to a new country, no matter what the reasons, is always a difficult and challenging transition. Interview a person who left his or her country and write a narrative explaining why that person came to America and what kind of life he or she left behind. How has this person's life been changed by the move? What obstacles did he or she have to overcome to get to the United States? What obstacles did your subject face when he or she arrived?

8. Make a photo album or pictorial collage of an experience or event you consider significant. Write a narrative to go with it that explains why you selected the particular photos and what you wanted to communicate.

Appendix

Anne Frank's Legacy

Anne Frank dreamed of seeing her writing in print someday. She dreamed of going to Paris, and perhaps even to Hollywood. Her ambitions were not all that unusual for a bright, enthusiastic adolescent who believed that her future depended upon her own will and talent. Since she was blessed with both, we can easily believe that Anne's life could have been all that she imagined.

Yet, not even Anne Frank could have hoped to achieve the enormous impact and reknown that have grown out of her remarkable diary and tragic history. Her name has come to represent all that was best—courage, hope, love—and all that was worst—betrayal, suffering, death—about that infamous period in history. In addition to the several editions of her diary, and the plays, films, and books written about her, there are also the Anne Frank Foundation in Basel, Switzerland, the Anne Frank House in Amsterdam, and Anne Frank Centers in New York City, Great Britain, and Berlin that are dedicated to providing educational programs that fight against "violence, anti-Semitism, hate crimes, and discrimination."

The Anne Frank House, located at 263 Prinsengracht, is now a museum. Hundreds of thousands of visitors from all over the world visit Anne's secret annex every year. Visitors see the movie-star pinups on the wall over Anne's bed and can easily imagine the energetic young girl confined to the silence and anxiety of hiding.

In 1985 the Anne Frank House created a traveling exhibit, "Anne Frank in the World: 1929–1945," which has been seen in hundreds of cities and towns in Europe, North and South America, and Asia. Communities that present the exhibit participate in creating their own educational and cultural programs focusing on the dangers of prejudice and intolerance and emphasizing the importance of actively combatting discrimination. In Boise, Idaho, for example, an Anne Frank quilt, titled "Always Remember," was created in honor of the exhibition. In Birmingham, Alabama, a commemorative Anne Frank Tulip Garden was planted as "an annual reminder of the life and legacy of the young diarist."

The Anne Frank Center USA's exhibit, "The Anne Frank Story," travels across the country and includes photographs of Anne and her family, text from the diary, and educational materials for teachers. The exhibit focuses on the theme of individual responsibility and is designed for middle-grade students. A follow-up exhibit, "Learning from the Past," will focus on current issues of intolerance and discrimination in the United States. All those associated with Anne Frank Centers are dedicated to providing the public, and especially young people, with the information and tools necessary to fight all forms of discrimination.

HOLLYWOOD AND THE WORLD WIDE WEB

Although Anne Frank aspired to have her words read by a large audience, she certainly would have been overwhelmed by the notion that in 1996 she would have her own World Wide Web Site where people from all over the world could learn about her life, read excerpts from her diary, and find out about the activities of the Anne Frank Centers. In addition, Anne has made it to Hollywood. A feature-length documentary, *Anne Frank: A Life Remembered*, won an Academy Award in 1996. The documentary not only contains interviews with Miep Gies and several people who knew Anne Frank, but also includes a very brief glimpse of the twelve-year-old Anne as she leans out of an apartment window to watch a bride and groom below.

Everything we have imagined about this dark-haired girl, her playfulness and sweet romanticism, is confirmed by the stunning images. Anne turns her head from side to side, tosses her hair, and laughs with pleasure. In seeing the "real" Anne Frank before our eyes, we understand that the icon we have all created pales in comparison to this vivacious young girl who delighted in life and who did not survive to enjoy her own wedding day.

TOPICS FOR WRITTEN OR ORAL EXPLORATION

1. Contact an Anne Frank Center and get information on its educational programs. Report to the class on your findings and/or arrange for a program in your school or community.
2. Visit an "Anne Frank in the World" exhibit. Write about your response to the exhibit. What was most disturbing? surprising? interesting?
3. Find the Web page for the Anne Frank Center. Report on what you find there to your class.
4. Would Anne Frank still keep a diary if she were alive today? Write a diary entry for Anne Frank in 1996.

SUGGESTED READINGS

Anne Frank in the World, 1929–1945. Amsterdam: Uitgeverij Bert Bakker, 1985.
Shawn, Karen. *The End of Innocence: Anne Frank and the Holocaust*. New York: Braun Center for Holocaust Studies, 1994.

Glossary

Allies   the United States, Great Britain, France, and Russia. They fought against the Axis forces—Germany, Italy, and Japan—in World War II.

annihilation   complete destruction.

Anti-Semitism   prejudice and discrimination against Jews, including hateful attitudes and acts.

Aryan   Nazi term for the blond and blue-eyed "superior" German race. This category has no biological or racial validity.

assimilation   to absorb into a culture.

atrocity   a savagely brutal or cruel act.

boycott   an economic sanction. Used against all Jewish shopkeepers by the Nazis in April 1933.

collaborate   to cooperate with an enemy force during a war.

concentration camps   sites in Germany and Poland where Jews and other "undesirables" were confined. Usually refers to the death camps that were designed for mass murder.

crematories   ovens in which dead bodies were burned to ash.

deportation   removal of Jews from Nazi Germany and Nazi-occupied countries to concentration camps.

discriminate   to make distinctions on the basis of class or category without regard to individual merit; to show preference or prejudice.

fascism   a system of government in which authority is centralized under a dictator. Characterized by use of stringent socioeconomic controls, suppression of the opposition through terror and censorship, and typically a policy of belligerent nationalism and racism.

genocide   the planned killing of an entire racial or cultural group of people.

Gestapo   abbreviation for German Secret State Police. Established by the Nazis to stamp out all opposition to Hitler's regime.

ghetto   section of a city where Jews were forced to live after the Nazis occupied an Eastern European country.

Holocaust   the annihilation of 6 million Jews by the Nazis during World War II.

Jew   a person whose religion is Judaism.

Kapos   prisoners of concentration camps who supervised other prisoners in exchange for privileges from the Nazis.

Kristallnacht   Crystal Night, "Night of Broken Glass," November 9–10, 1938. Rampage of violence in Germany and Austria against the Jews, their synagogues, and their businesses.

Nazi   an acronym for Nazionalsozialische Partie—National Socialist German Workers' Party. This fascist organization implemented Hitler's plan to annihilate the Jews.

NSB   name for the Dutch National Socialist Movement, a Nazi party.

Nuremberg Laws   laws implemented in 1935 in Germany which repealed the Jews' German citizenry and forbade marriages between Jews and non-Jews.

pogrom   an anti-Jewish riot.

propaganda   the spreading of ideas and information to further one's own cause.

refugee   a person who flees for safety, especially to another country.

round-up   the unannounced gathering up of Jews, often for transport to concentration camps.

selection   process by which Jewish inmates of concentration camps were sent to their deaths in the gas chambers or designated for slave labor.

synagogue   the house of worship of a Jewish congregation.

Third Reich   the German government under Nazi control between 1939 and 1945.

Index

About the Author

HEDDA ROSNER KOPF teaches in the English Department at Quinnipiac College in Hamden, Connecticut. She is also a scholar/facilitator for public library book discussions in libraries throughout the state and lectures extensively on women writers.